D1365266

TechVenture

New Rules on Value and Profit from Silicon Valley

TechVenture

New Rules on Value and Profit from Silicon Valley

Mohan Sawhney
Ranjay Gulati
Anthony Paoni
The Kellogg TechVenture Team

WILEY

John Wiley & Sons, Inc.
New York • Chichester • Weinheim • Brisbane • Singapore • Toronto

Published by John Wiley & Sons, Inc.

Published simultaneously in Canada.

This publication is designed to provide accurate and authoritative information
in regard to the subject matter covered. It is sold with the understanding that
the publisher is not engaged in rendering professional services. If professional
advice or other expert assistance is required, the services of a competent
professional person should be sought.

Library of Congress Cataloging-in-Publication Data:

ISBN 0-471-41424-7

Printed in the United States of America.

10 9 8 7 6 5 4 3 2 1

Contents

The Kellogg TechVenture Team

Chapter 1
Mohan Sawhney
Deval Parikh

Chapter 2
Eduard Baijs
Sandeep Gupta
Daniel Jaglom
Daniel Szlapak

Chapter 3
Robert Grossi
James Lange
Deborah Rebell
Lisa Stern

Chapter 4
Evan Auyang
Craig Cartwright
Yi Gao
Jean-Noel Poirier

Michael Riskind
Serge Vidal

Chapter 5
Kelly Cornelis
Dana Hagendorf
Jon Horvath
Thomas Weaver

Chapter 6
Josh Daitch
Rahul Kamath
Rahul Kapoor
Andrew Nemiccolo
Jagdeep Sahni
Sandeep Varma

Chapter 7
Scott Barkley
Mike Biddlecom
James Dietrich

Cory Fischer
Robb Hoenick
A. Teaque Lenahan
Chris Millner
Stephen Moon
John Roman
Andrew Young

Chapter 8
Matt Demaray
Scott Frasure
David Nelson
David Pacchini
John Perkins

Chapter 9
Pierre LeComte
Steve Sherman
Benoit Vialle

Chapter 10
Dominic Engels
Jeremy Liou
Clay McDaniel
Brian Novelline
Tyler Vaughey
Todd Wincup

Chapter 11
Richard Bruch
Rob Leonard
Ryan McKinney
Brian Sprafka

Chapter 12
Mohan Sawhney
Deval Parikh

Foreword

During the 1990s, in a few geographic clusters of economic activity in the United States, several factors combined to produce some of the most dramatic economic growth the world has ever known. Combine an innovative set of information technologies, a financial infrastructure that funnels large amounts of venture capital to entrepreneurs, a critical mass of intelligent and well-educated workers, and an economy that can absorb a high level of technological products, and you have magic. This book is about how those factors came together in the recent past, and their potential for continuing to produce growth and wealth in the future.

TechVenture is a groundbreaking book in terms of both process and content. It admirably breaks many of the rules and crosses many traditional boundaries that govern how professors produce books about business. Perhaps most remarkably, these professors have let their students do much of the writing and research. The academics themselves only selected and edited the MBA-student papers that serve as the core of the book. Because of the judgment the professors exercised as editors (and perhaps the large amount of candidate research from which they chose), the quality of the analysis and writing is consistently high. Not only do students learn better through this approach, but we readers benefit as well. The students' work is clear and insightful, and has equally high levels of both rigor and relevance. This combination—the relevance in particular—is not often encountered in the research efforts of business school professors. Consistent with that focus on relevance, the book involves actual field research and contacts with technology companies; there is plenty of practice and no more theory than necessary. Every chapter is illustrated with a rich lode of examples.

Another departure from common practice is that the book crosses functional boundaries within the university. Its perspective on technology venturing incorporates ideas from finance, marketing, and technology management. It even ventures outside the business school, combining business and engineering insights. Anyone who has received an MBA will know just how rare it is to find these alternative views combined into an integrated and holistic analysis.

TechVenture was also produced with admirable speed. It is well timed as one of the first detailed postings from the new high-tech frontier. Since the fundamental values of Silicon Valley and other high-tech regions changed in the year 2000, we have had no guide to how the goal of profitability has changed the companies and the dynamics of their success. This book still incorporates some of the earlier broad enthusiasm for technology companies, but introduces substantial material on the new responsibility for fiscal results.

In terms of content, the book is similarly boundary-spanning. It addresses not only computer and software technologies—those at the heart of Silicon Valley—but also telecommunications and biotechnology. Certainly some of the same growth factors drive all these industries, and it makes for interesting comparisons to look across them. The book's authors also occasionally draw on more traditional firms as examples, providing an interesting contrast to the smaller high-tech firms on which it is primarily focused.

A key content target is the evolving set of new organizational structures that fall outside of any traditional category. The networks or *keiretsu* of technology firms it describes are neither stand-alone nor fully aligned organizations. Incubators, which are described in detail in one chapter, combine aspects of venture capital, consulting, and business service providers. Even some of the venture capital firms described in the book have taken on roles that include staffing and infrastructure provision.

Throughout, the content emphasis is on the new and emerging approach. In asset analysis, the focus is on intellectual capital valuation and management. In financial analysis, traditional discounted cash flows and multiples analysis are eschewed in favor of real options and wave models. The ideas in the book are at the cutting edge of many different content domains.

Many of the early descriptions of the nineties' technology boom were just as incautiously optimistic as were technology investors. They gave us little knowledge of the factors that lead to success or failure in a tech-centric economy. In today's environment, where the phrases "Valley tech firm" or "VC-funded startup" are no longer unambiguously positive, it is extremely useful to have a set of guidelines for what works and what does not. The chapters in this book do not shrink from failure; some even focus on tech-firm success as the result of *missing* key failure factors. But the book content also avoids an overly pessimistic view. For once we have an objective appraisal of this hype-ridden subject.

I believe there is no better guide available for the student considering whether to make a career in an entrepreneurial technology startup, for an investor attempting to understand the new realities of high-tech, or even for the manager already charged with making one of these firms a success. I hope that succeeding generations of Kellogg students and their professors give us similarly insightful pictures of the technology sector as it continues to change in the future.

Thomas H. Davenport
Director, Accenture Institute for Strategic Change
Distinguished Scholar in Residence, Babson College
Visiting Professor, Tuck School of Business, Dartmouth College

Acknowledgments

At Kellogg, the "team" is a central theme of the learning experience and the TechVenture course is no exception. Many people deserve our thanks for their support in the planning and execution of the TechVenture experience. We are greatly indebted to Rob Wolcott for his superb feedback and suggestions to student teams during the evolution of the papers. Dean Jacobs was a key supporter of TechVenture, and on behalf of the students and faculty we sincerely thank him for his encouragement. We offer deep thanks to the Dean's Technology Fund, created by the Kellogg Alumni Advisory Board, for funding this project and for enthusiastic support of our efforts. We wish to thank the following people for their part in making TechVenture a successful learning experience: Dipak Jain, Associate Dean for Academic Affairs; and Roxanne Hori, Director of Career Management Center.

Our deepest thanks to the TechVenture Student Leaders who worked tirelessly to make this course a unique learning experience. Zeene Chang and her academic team spent many sleepless nights to make this anthology happen. The other Student Leaders who logged untold hours are: Mike McLaughlin, Tim Dang, Azhar Ghani, James Kim, Holly Staid, Shad Weaver, and Christine Wu. This is truly your work and your vision in action.

Finally, we would like to thank Jeanne Glasser and the entire John Wiley & Sons team, who were instrumental in bringing this book to fruition.

Introduction

We live in a world where technology is transforming the business landscape. As an example, the explosive growth of the Internet as a vehicle for business innovation is an outcome of advances in enabling technologies such as networking, software, and semiconductors. These technologies have created dramatic new possibilities for reinventing the way firms develop new offerings, go to market, connect with customers, collaborate with their suppliers, and share knowledge. As a result, we are witnessing an unprecedented level of business innovation across a wide range of industries. Industry boundaries have been blurred to the extent that the very concept of an industry has been somewhat devalued and made irrelevant. In today's business environment, managers can be truly effective only if they have a firm understanding of the technologies that are affecting their organizations and the trends that are reshaping their businesses and their markets.

Technology is the enabler of change. E-business and e-commerce are the outcomes. To truly appreciate new possibilities, managers must understand both. At the Kellogg School, we have not been isolated from the technologies that affect the business world and we have been faced with the problems of responding to businesses' changing needs. In 1998, students posed a challenge to us. They wanted us to help them understand the rapidly evolving landscape of enabling technologies, as well as the impact these technologies were having on business strategy and organizations. The result of this challenge was a new course called "Kellogg TechVenture." Kellogg faculty and students collaborated on a new course to study the intersection of technology, marketing, and entrepreneurship. The purpose of the TechVenture course is to provide students with a solid understanding of the technologies and the co-evolving business trends that are driving the evolution of e-business. Now in its third year, the course is one of the most sought-after at Kellogg. "Kellogg TechVenture" is one of the reasons that the Kellogg School was rated by *Business Week*, in its 2000 business-school rankings, as having the most innovative curriculum.

The TechVenture course is unique in many ways. First, TechVenture is a transfunctional course. A team of faculty that cut across faculty-functional boundaries teach the course (Mohan Sawhney from Marketing, Ranjay Gulati from Management of Organizations, Anthony Paoni from E-Commerce and Technology, and James Conley from Mechanical Engineering). The topics covered in the course transcend functional areas—mirroring the reality that e-business cuts across functional borders. We worked together to define course topics in ways that drew upon our individual strengths, yet were truly transfunctional in their implications.

Second, TechVenture blends theory with action learning. For 10 weeks, we expose students to the theoretical concepts, technologies, and trends they need to understand the landscape of e-commerce. The lectures are custom-tailored by the professors for the class and, as a result, highlight the latest trends and issues arising in this new era of technological change. At the conclusion of the course, students and faculty spend a week in Silicon Valley, meeting a broad cross-section of companies and witnessing what they have learned in action. The research in this book benefited from first-hand visits to 87 companies spanning a broad range of the Silicon Valley ecosystem. Learning in the field complements theory in the classroom and amplifies the learning experience.

Third, TechVenture is a collaborative effort with students. The faculty members play the role of coaches and mentors, presenting the theoretical models and best practices in lectures and then guiding students in their exploration of specific knowledge domains. Students are responsible for many aspects of the course: the design, the administration, and the Silicon Valley field research. Empowering students is a hallmark of the Kellogg culture, and the TechVenture course is a wonderful example. In developing this course, we have treated students as peers and co-developers of knowledge.

Fourth, TechVenture is a fluid and adaptive course. Although its purpose remains constant, the course topics evolve in response to the evolution of technology and e-commerce. Every year, we strive to survey the topics and issues that are most important and most relevant. This adaptive design is essential, given the pace of change in the knowledge domain.

■ ABOUT THIS BOOK

As the faculty designing the TechVenture course, we were faced with a difficult challenge: How do you survey a landscape that is unpredictable and changes so rapidly? How could we keep pace with such a vast and dynamic knowledge domain? The answer is obvious, in hindsight. We capitalized on a simple, yet powerful insight: *Students do not merely consume knowledge, they co-create knowledge.* We realized that the collective energies of the students, with guidance from the faculty, could be a powerful engine for knowledge creation. This book is the result of the collaborative knowledge creation effort and serves as testimony to the power of teamwork.

This book originated in 60 research topics that we identified as interesting, important, and underresearched within the domain of technology and e-commerce, and we broadly defined each topic for the students. Student teams chose from these topics, and their mission was to develop a comprehensive and insightful white paper on each topic that surveyed, distilled, and synthesized the most current thinking on the topic. The white papers were also designed to highlight what the future might hold for each specific knowledge domain, and to create conceptual and analytical frameworks that would advance the domain. During the term, the teams met with the faculty several times to refine their ideas and flesh out their thinking. The papers were turned in at the end of the quarter, and we provided each team with written feedback and suggestions for improving its paper. During the field trip to Silicon Valley, the students conducted interviews that helped test their hypotheses and generated first-hand case study examples for their papers. They then incorporated these ideas, along with our feedback, into a revised version of the paper. These final versions were carefully edited, and a subset of the papers was selected for inclusion in this book.

As faculty guiding these projects, we were astounded by the quality of the output. We felt that we needed to share our work more widely, for two reasons. First, given that much of the research contained in the book represents some of the most forward thinking on each topic, it seemed a significant and timely endeavor to create a single volume that presents the myriad of enabling technologies that are revolutionizing the economy. There was a wealth of ideas, concepts, and frameworks that would tremendously benefit managers, entrepreneurs, and investors. Second, few articles and volumes attempt to tackle the subject of emerging technologies in a systematic or comprehensive way. The quality of the papers created by our students is such that gathering those papers together in one volume creates a powerful portrayal of the state of technological advancement at the millennium. Thus, when Jeanne Glasser from John Wiley & Sons asked us about doing a book on the financial infrastructure and business models in Silicon Valley, we knew what we had to do. Based on this raw material, we worked with Jeanne to weave the individual ideas into a rich tapestry that would portray the most cutting-edge thinking on the various themes that are emerging.

The result is this book, which combines a broad overview of the manner in which enabling technologies can affect a spectrum of industries with specific analyses, hypotheses, and predictions about a range of technology trends. The book ties the various student-generated thoughts into a coherent body that tackles recent market developments, such as the shift from "get big fast" to "get profitable fast" and new, innovative business models. The result is exactly what has been missing: an analytical look at how technology has changed the way in which business is created, organized, financed, and sustained.

This book is intended for not only entrepreneurs and investors, but also for managers in larger companies, particularly in bricks-and-mortar organizations that are slowly but steadily making their way into the Internet space. Put another way, this book is not designed just for those in the know, who confront enabling technologies and their effects on a daily basis, but also for those managers in larger organizations who have not yet dealt with new technologies and their effects but will have to do so in the next few years.

■ THE ORGANIZATION OF THIS BOOK

The structure of this book evolved through a process of understanding and distilling the major themes running through the diverse topics of the course. We believe that technology should be seen as an enabler that affects strategy, sector, and business models. We wanted to focus on how technology has created ways of developing new types of businesses and then to examine how these models can be structured to generate sustained profits. We also wanted to examine the financial infrastructure that supports and propagates growth into new areas. We wanted to show how emergent trends and technologies can disrupt certain sectors and force changes in business models and perspectives on financial measurement. In line with this thinking, we organized this book into four conceptual parts: the financial infrastructure and business enablers that allow new ventures to grow and prosper; the strategic implications for profitability in the new economy; the emerging business models that are made possible by new technologies; and key e-business and technology trends. The ultimate goal of the book is to provide the most forceful evidence of how critical changes in technology have affected and will continue to supplant traditional methods of looking at business growth, development, and profitability. The specific descriptions of each part follow.

➤ Financial Infrastructure and Business Enablers

Without a durable, but flexible, financial infrastructure that rewards profitable innovation, new business models and potential profits from those models will not exist. To see the full effect of enabling technologies in a business development sense, it is critical to take a step back and examine how new technology has altered the role of business enablers that make technological innovation a reality. Technology has profoundly changed the mechanisms that enable new business development. The speed of change and the need to aggressively enter new markets, against both other startups and established incumbents, have forced a reevaluation of how business development organizations operate. Incubators and venture capital (VC) firms have been buoyed by a tremendous growth in the availability of capital, even with the recent market corrections. Nevertheless, as funding becomes more of a commodity for successful entrepreneurs, business-enabling forms must develop new methods of differentiating themselves from the competition and attracting the best and brightest ideas. To accomplish this feat, incubators and VC companies have tried to position themselves as having the most complete package of business experience and networking capabilities. Business enablers have used technology to harness the power of networking and information management.

The first chapter, "Where Value Lives in a Networked World," introduces the concept of network intelligence, describing it as the key for executives and entrepreneurs who must decipher the phenomena shaping the business world. In a networked world, the location and mobility of information directly influence the way companies organize their people, market their products, manage their information, and work with their partners. In this chapter, the authors explain why the network is the economy; it serves as an important introduction to the methods, strategies, and applications described throughout the book.

The second chapter in this section examines technology incubators that focus on developing young, immature business ideas into successful companies. Technology incubators combine industry expertise, network connections, common but necessary services, and a significant amount of business development coaching to help new companies. "Inside Technology Incubators" focuses on fleshing out the value proposition of incubators and describing the market forces and participants, as the number of incubators increases exponentially and places more pressure on competitor venture capitalists.

The third chapter, "The Startup Graveyard," distills 10 important lessons from nascent companies that have succeeded and those that have failed in the e-commerce marketplace.

➤ Strategic Implications for Profitability

The key question one should ask, given the plethora of new business models, is how these models can be effectively harnessed to create sustained wealth over time. After all, profitability and sustainability have become the new mantras, because the honeymoon and land grab of e-commerce are over. The Internet has altered the traditional flow of money and the way in which companies are valued. The promise of future wealth lured investors to stake claims in young technology-based companies that had not even turned profitable. The rapid increase of technology-enabled companies that acquired enormous valuations even before making a profit has forced a reevaluation of how a company's worth should be assessed. Using traditional metrics for valuation, it is hard to understand the astounding market capitalizations of unprofitable, new economyeconomy startups like Amazon.com. Internet companies must be valued in new ways that take into account the critical importance of culture and the acquisition of knowledgeable and talented individuals. Companies fight tooth and nail for access to employees with experience, but the question remains of how these employees are to be valued. In addition, the Internet presents unique opportunities that profoundly change the ways in which money is transferred from consumers to businesses and between businesses.

Chapters 4 and 5 address these issues by carefully assessing the ways in which companies have dealt with the strategic issue of profitability. Each chapter provides an analytical framework that elucidates the strategic issue created by the rise of the Internet.

Chapter 4, "Valuation Techniques for Internet Firms" describes the inappropriateness of traditional methods for new economy companies and analyzes different tools presently used to value companies both before and after an initial public offering (IPO). It describes in detail two relatively recent measures of valuation: real options theory and the use of wave theory to quantify momentum. The chapter also offers a preliminary valuation methodology prepared by the authors.

Chapter 5, "New Economy Metrics," examines how to measure intellectual capital when evaluating a company's worth, and assesses different methodologies used for the accounting of intangible assets such as intellectual worth. It evaluates the use of various metrics for measuring intellectual capital at the firm and operating levels and offers case studies of eBay, Pfizer, and Merrill Lynch.

➤ Emerging Business Models

The chapters in this section show how emerging business models create: new opportunities for increased access to information, more efficient and effective value creation through strategic use of information, and opportunities for innovation that can fundamentally change the way a company does business. Chapters 6 through 8 focus on the specifics of different technological innovations, how to sustain these innovations, and the implications for all parties involved in the product cycle.

Chapter 6, "Wireless E-Business," dives into the emerging field of m-commerce and identifies three killer apps for the evolving new economy. Each of these applications has customer sensitivity at the core of its business model, which leads right into our next chapter, "Customer Competencies: Data Mining and Customer Relationship Management." Chapter 7 explores how companies can harness information about past actions and customer preferences to assist in making more knowledgeable marketing and strategic decisions.

Chapter 8 focuses on how the Internet is revolutionizing the way in which money is exchanged between parties, by examining new technologies such as e-payment and digital currency. "Electronic Payment Systems" outlines the inherent paradox of the payment space: despite the rapid development of technology and e-commerce, payment systems are sorely lacking. It identifies the new hot spots in the value transfer space, pinpointing how three contributors to the paradox—path dependencies, network externalities, and infrastructure—affect each.

➤ E-Business and Technology Trends Worth Watching

Another way to assess the evolution of technology and e-commerce is to look beyond general trends that affect the entire business landscape and instead to focus in depth on specific industries and sectors to uncover the exciting developments within them. The final set of chapters aims to study the themes shaping the evolution of specific sectors. These chapters are "vertical" in scope. They dive deep into a sector and survey the players, the plays, and the evolving shape of competition within the sector. Each chapter also looks at the likely future within the sector and the potential for a breakdown of sector boundaries that can no longer be easily delineated. Admittedly, the choice of sectors is biased toward those that have perhaps been affected the most by recent technological developments.

Just as new technology is affecting the supply chain for businesses, disruptive technology is affecting the manner of product delivery for consumers. Chapter 9, "The Music Controversy" explores how new audio technologies, like MP3, are changing the music industry. It describes the technology required to make digital music a reality, and how that technological capability changes the value proposition for the music industry. It lays out the competitive landscape, describing the various retail Web sites, content aggregators, and online sharing communities that threaten traditional record labels. Lastly, the authors hypothesize about the future of electronic music over the next decade.

Chapter 10 analyzes the battle between cable and DSL providers and the race for broadband capability. "The Battle for the Last Mile" surveys the technological, regulatory, and economic issues surrounding broadband. It provides a global perspective and features case studies about blockbuster mergers affecting the industry, such as AOL–Time Warner and SBC–Sterling Software. It also makes some observations about the future.

Chapter 11 discusses the future of the genomic field and the potential effect on the pharmaceutical industry. "Commercializing Genomics" provides an overview of developments in the field of genomics, widely held to be the next big revolution after e-commerce. The chapter analyzes the process by which genomics companies can turn their research into profitable products and the potential ramifications for pharmaceutical competitors. It also delves into the myriad of public policy issues, such as ethical and intellectual property concerns, that result from genomics research.

Our final chapter, "Net Economy Boundaries," encourages readers to view boundaries as learning tools that will help make clear the evolution of business and technology trends. With this context in place, readers are free to create innovative approaches to extending the lines of business boundaries. We hope that the ideas and information provided in this book will help readers devise innovative ways of shaping their business and industry for the future.

Chapter

Where Value Lives in a Networked World

■ INTRODUCTION

In recent years, it seems as though the only constant in business has been upheaval. Sweeping changes have transformed every level of business, from the way industries are structured to how companies interact with customers and carry out day-to-day operations. In response, many business thinkers have proclaimed an era of radical uncertainty. Business has become so complex, they say, that trying to predict what lies ahead is futile. The best you can do is become as flexible as possible and hope that you will be able to ride out the waves of disruption.

There is some validity to that view. The business world has become much more complicated, and the ability to adapt and respond has become as important as the ability to anticipate and act. Our view, though, is that these changes are not simply random, disconnected events. We believe that these upheavals share a common root, and that root lies in the nature of intelligence in networks. The digitization of information, combined with advances in computing and communications, has fundamentally changed the workings of all networks, human as well as

1

technological. This change in the very nature of information has had and will continue to have profound consequences for the way work is done and how value is created throughout the economy. Network intelligence is the key for executives and entrepreneurs who must decipher many of the phenomena shaping the future of business.

Network intelligence has immediate and very concrete real-world implications. In a highly connected world, the location and mobility of network intelligence directly influences the way companies organize their people, market their products, manage their information, and work with their partners. "The network is the computer," Sun Microsystems has famously proclaimed. We would go even further to say that the network is the economy. The future of many technology companies, from Dell Computer to AT&T to hordes of Internet startups, hinges on their ability to recognize and adapt to shifts in network intelligence. Even if your company is not directly involved in the high-technology business, it will not be immune to the impact of shifts in network intelligence.

■ INTELLIGENCE IN THE NETWORK

The intelligence of a network is its functionality—its ability to distribute, store, assemble, or modify information (see Table 1.1). A simple, analog network is considered "dumb"; it is just a pipe that transports information without enhancing it. A complex, digital network, like the Internet, is "smart"; it can improve the utility of information in many different ways. That is crucially important for a simple reason: In an information economy, improving the utility of information is synonymous with creating economic value. Where intelligence resides, so too does value.

As network technologies have advanced in recent years, both the location and the mobility of network intelligence have changed dramatically (see Figure 1.1). By understanding the patterns underlying those changes, valuable insight can be gained into the way economic value is shifting across industries and among companies. This insight will enable you to act while others merely react.

➤ The Decoupling of Intelligence

In the absence of a network, intelligence can be applied only where it lives. If different kinds of intelligence are needed to perform some task,

Table 1.1 Aspects of intelligence in networks.

Activity	Definition	Physical Analog
Configuring	Arranging information in a particular way to respond to a need	Configurator software
Dispatching	Moving information from its source to its appropriate destination	Router
Storing	Collecting information in a way that can be easily and speedily accessed when needed	Database
Processing	Converting raw information into useful outcomes	Microprocessor
Interacting	Facilitating the exchange of information among sources and objects	Keyboard
Coordinating	Harmonizing activities performed by multiple entities to reach a common goal	Operating system
Learning	Using experience to improve the ability to act	Expert system
Sensing	Detecting and interpreting signals in the environment	Antenna

they all have to be bundled together in the same place. Consider a personal computer that is not connected to a network. It has to contain all of the intelligence needed to process, store, and display information for a wide variety of user tasks—but *front-end intelligence*, needed to interact with users, is very different from *back-end intelligence*, needed to process and store information. The user wants a computer that is easy to use, portable, flexible, and personalized. Under the hood, the machine has to be powerful, reliable, and easy to maintain. The bundling of these two very different types of intelligence necessitates compromises in design.

When a personal computer is connected to a high-speed network,

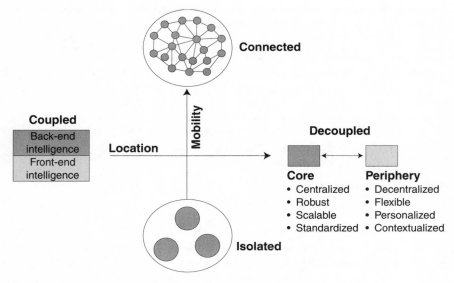

Figure 1.1   The two patterns of intelligence migration.

different types of intelligence are no longer co-located. Front-end intelligence can be decoupled from back-end intelligence. Instead of having to be replicated on every individual PC, the back-end intelligence can be consolidated in powerful, efficient, and reliable network servers. The front-end intelligence, freed from basic processing functions, can be customized to particular users and tasks. The PC morphs from a single jack-of-all-trades-master-of-none machine into an array of small, specialized electronic tools.

In more general terms, modern high-speed networks push back-end intelligence and front-end intelligence in two different directions, toward opposite ends of the network. Back-end intelligence becomes embedded in a shared infrastructure at the core of the network, while front-end intelligence fragments into many different forms at the periphery of the network, where the users are. Because value follows intelligence, the two ends of the network become the major source of potential profits. The middle of the network gets hollowed out; it becomes a dumb conduit, with little potential for value creation. As value diverges, so do companies and competition. Organizations that once incorporated diverse units, focused on both back-end processing and front-end customer management, split apart into separate infrastructure and customer-relationship management businesses, each with very different capabilities and strategies.[1] (See the sidebar on "Value Trends.")

Value Trends

In a network world, where everyone and everything is connected, economic value behaves very differently than in the traditional world. Here are four high-level value trends that all companies should be conscious of as they position themselves to succeed in the digital economy.

Value at the ends. Most economic value will be created at the ends of networks. At the core, which is the end most distant from users, generic, scale-intensive functions will consolidate. At the periphery, the end closest to users, highly customized connections with customers will be made. This trend pertains not only to technological networks like the Internet, but also to networks of companies engaged in shared tasks and even to the human networks that exist within companies.

Value in common infrastructure. Elements of infrastructure that once were distributed among different machines, organizational units, and companies will be brought together and operated as utilities. Shared infrastructure will take the form not only of basic computing and data-storage functions, but also of common business functions, such as order processing, warehousing and distribution, and even manufacturing and customer service.

Value in modularity. Devices, software, organizational capabilities, and business processes will increasingly be restructured as well-defined, self-contained modules that can be quickly and seamlessly connected with other modules. Value will lie in creating modules that can be plugged into as many different value chains as possible. Companies and individuals will want to distribute their capabilities as broadly as possible, rather than protecting them as proprietary assets.

Value in orchestration. As modularization takes hold, the ability to coordinate the assembly and disassembly of modules will become the most valuable business skill. Much of the competition in the business world will center on gaining and maintaining the orchestration of separate pieces.

➤ The Mobilization of Intelligence

In a connected world, intelligence becomes fluid and modular, floating freely like molecules in the ether, coalescing into temporary bundles whenever and wherever necessary to solve problems. Consider SETI@home, a project launched by the University of California at Berkeley to search for extraterrestrial life. Radio signals received by the world's biggest telescope dish—the 1,000-foot Arecibo Observatory in Puerto Rico—are carved into 330-kilobyte "work units" and distributed over the Internet to personal computers located around the world. Individual computer owners donate their spare computing cycles (their processing intelligence) to the project by allowing their computers to analyze data in the background or when idle. Within a year of its launch in May 1999, more than 2 million people in 226 countries had provided about 280,000 years of computer time to the effort. SETI@home has a total computing power of about 12 teraflops, making it four times as powerful as the world's fastest supercomputer. This network makes it possible to pool the intelligence that resides in millions of computers across the globe into an ad hoc system with massive computing capability.

The mobilization of intelligence has profound implications for the organization as well. Connected by networks, different companies can easily combine their capabilities and resources into temporary and flexible alliances to capitalize on specific market opportunities. As such "plug-and-play" enterprises become common, value shifts from entities that own intelligence to those that orchestrate the flow and combination of intelligence. Companies such as Cisco and Hewlett-Packard have evolved into intelligent hubs that coordinate interactions among a network of channel partners, suppliers, and customers. By connecting the business processes of manufacturing service providers (such as Solectron and Flextronics) to the business processes of channel partners and customers, Cisco and HP are able to coordinate the flow of information between their business networks. As a result, they are able to extract the spectrum of value created by the network.

Just as the decoupling of intelligence requires a reliable, high-speed network, the mobilization of intelligence requires a common language. Without the existence of universal protocols for information exchange, individual pieces of intelligence could not collaborate or be communicated. For instance, the mobilization of intelligence among devices requires device-to-device communication protocols such as Bluetooth and Jini. The mobilization of intelligence from the Internet to wireless devices requires protocols like the Wireless Application Protocol (WAP), and the organization of plug-and-play business networks requires the widespread adoption of protocols for describing products and processes, such as Extensible Markup Language (XML). The development of these and other network standards will play a large role in determining the future shape of business.

■ RESHAPING INDUSTRIES

Two patterns of intelligence migration are changing the competitive landscapes of a number of very large industries (see Table 1.2). The most dramatic effects, not surprisingly, are being felt in network-based businesses like telecommunications. When traditional telephone companies built their analog systems, they had to bundle many different kinds of intelligence (for processing, transport, and user functionality) into the middle of their networks. The wires had to be smart because the user device was dumb—a simple rotary phone. The emergence of digital networks based on the Internet Protocol (IP) has turned old networks into huge, expensive burdens. Now that intelligence can be embedded in servers, software, and intelligent devices located at the core and the periphery of the network, the middle of the network can and should be dumb. All that is needed is a fast and reliable pipe with a little bit of routing intelligence.

This shift poses a grave threat to service providers like AT&T, who rely on voice and data transport for the bulk of their revenues. As transport becomes a commodity, rates for long-distance telephony are plummeting, and startups like Dialpad and Go2Call are taking advantage of the market opportunity by offering PC-to-phone long-distance service for free over the Internet. The real value in telecommunications is shifting to the ends of the network. At the core, infrastructure providers such as Sun, Cisco, Nortel, and Lucent are earning big profits. At the periphery, companies such as Yahoo!, Infospace, Phone.com, and America Online are extracting value by controlling the user interface and managing customer relationships. Service providers in the emerging broadband and wireless arenas are finding it difficult to make money just by selling access to the Internet. They will have to provide value-added infrastructure services—for example, hosting, systems integra-

Table 1.2 Intelligence migration patterns in different domains.

Domain	Intelligence migration patterns	Strategic implications
Telecommunications	Intelligence is migrating to the edges and the core of the network. The network can be dumb because endpoints are smart.	Long-haul information transport will become a commodity. Value will migrate to differentiated services and end-user solutions.
Computing	Device intelligence is getting separated from infrastructure intelligence. Computing is becoming a utility.	Functionality will migrate from desktops and corporate servers to infrastructure companies. Storage, e-mail, and computing power will become services delivered over the network.
Information appliances	Devices can collaborate and federate on an *ad hoc* basis to solve problems. Devices can borrow intelligence from other devices.	Single-use information appliances will proliferate. New service revenue streams will emerge from products like automobile and household appliances as they get connected to the network.

Enterprise software	Software is becoming a service that is delivered over the network through application service providers (ASPs) or business service providers (BSPs).	Pricing models will change from upfront licenses to "pay as you go." Software applications will become services that are rented over a network.
Organization design	Skills and resources can be located anywhere and assembled on an as-needed basis, from within the firm or from external providers.	Organizations will evolve into front-back designs with a "core" (shared-services back end) and an "edge" (customer- and partner-facing front end). Firms will create internal markets for skills and services. Organization structures will become more fluid.
Higher education	Learners can be located anywhere. Content can be separated from delivery. Knowledge objects can be assembled by end users on an as-needed basis.	Universities will have to shift from providing "just-in-time" knowledge. Classroom learning will be supplemented with technology-enabled distributed learning.
National security	Threats are distributed, not centralized. CIA and military need to cope with threats from diverse locations and unknown enemies.	"Central" intelligence must be decentralized and dispersed. Military should be reorganized into decentralized autonomous units at the "edges" that are linked to the "core" through a command-and-control information backbone.

tion, and network maintenance—or find a way to earn commissions on the transactions that flow through their pipes.

The computing business is going through a similar transformation. The functionality that once was built into computers or sold as software packages can now be delivered over the Internet. Corporations and consumers will soon be freed from having to own their own computing hardware and applications. Already, consumers can use Yahoo!'s servers to store their e-mail messages, calendars, address books, digital photographs, digital wallets, faxes, and data files; businesses can now purchase, on an as-needed basis, the applications required for customer service, human resource management, accounting, and payroll from outside service providers.

Obviously, this trend has profound implications for traditional hardware and software companies. They will have to transform themselves from product companies into service providers, or they will have to shift their focus from selling primarily to end users to selling to the big infrastructure providers (such as Yahoo! and Exodus) if they are going to go where the value is. Dell Computer is taking both paths, in a major effort to reinvent itself. In February 2000, Dell announced a series of initiatives, called "Dell E Works," aimed at broadening its revenue base beyond traditional hardware. It now offers its enterprise systems and storage products over the Internet through its Dell Hosting Service, and it is expanding into services like e-consulting and Web hosting. Its customer base is also growing to include Internet service providers (ISPs) and hosting companies that provide computing as a utility. As part of this effort, it is moving beyond its reliance on the Windows operating system by embracing Linux, an operating system better suited to running the robust servers owned by the computing utilities. These new initiatives are already paying off. In the quarter ended July 28, 2000, Dell's "beyond the box" revenues increased 40 percent over the year-earlier period, making up 16 percent of the company's net revenues.

■ RESHAPING COMPANIES

The impact of intelligence migration is being felt within companies as well as across industries. The shrinking of middle management in many organizations is another result of the "hollowing out the middle," as intelligence gets pushed from the core (in this case, top management) to the periphery (front-line employees). Before there were robust digital networks and easy-to-use collaboration tools like e-mail, groupware, and Intranets, it was difficult to communicate information throughout a large business organization. A lot of middle managers were needed to package and distribute information; they provided communications intelligence between top management and front-line employees. Now that people are connected electronically, however, the distribution of information and intelligence is seamless. As a result, the information-transport function that middle managers performed has become superfluous. Just as the telecom network can have dumb pipes with intelligent ends, an organization can have a dumb information network that allows senior managers to communicate directly with front-line employees. Leadership and strategy get centralized at the top management level, while the ability to act and make decisions is pushed out to the fringes of the organization. The challenge for the remaining middle managers is to redefine their roles as coordinators, facilitators, organizers, and mentors providing new kinds of intelligence.

The mobilization of intelligence is also changing the way organizations work. Rather than being centralized in discrete units, a company's organizational capabilities are becoming more distributed and more modular. Using the power of the Internet, geographically dispersed individuals and teams can connect as needed. The interaction of distributed units is mediated, moment by moment, by the network, rather than by a large, expensive, and slow-moving managerial staff. In fact, it may now make more sense to talk about the "distributed capabilities" instead of the "core capabilities" of the corporation. (See the sidebar "Beyond Business.")

Beyond Business

The migration of network intelligence does not only affect business. It is also changing the way we think about public sector activities, such as government, national security, and education. Governments, for example, will be challenged to use electronic networks in general, and the Internet in particular, to deliver information and functions to citizens in much more

(continued)

diverse and personalized ways. The monolithic government bureaucracy will shatter, and new forms of distributed government will emerge. Interestingly, some of the most creative governmental applications of the Internet can be seen in developing nations. One example is the Indian state of Andhra Pradesh, with a population of 70 million. Under the leadership of its cyber-savvy chief minister, Chandrababu Naidu, it is rolling out an "e-government" system that will enable citizens to pay taxes and fees, apply for licenses and permits, and participate in municipal meetings through their home computers or through public kiosks.

The defense establishment will also need to radically reshape itself to adapt to the digital world, where threats to national security tend to be distributed among far-flung terrorist "modules" rather than centralized in powerful states. Centralized intelligence will have to be decentralized and dispersed. (Perhaps the CIA will be replaced by the DIA, the Distributed Intelligence Agency.) The military itself will have to be reorganized to emphasize relatively small autonomous units at the "edges" connected through a network to a central "core" of coordination and command.

Some of the most radical changes will take place in education. Students will no longer be forced to come together in centralized institutions to take general courses. Using the intelligence of the Internet, they can remotely access modules of education and training content, assembling courses of instruction that respond to their immediate and particular needs. Universities will begin to shift from providing generalized "just-in-case" knowledge to providing customizable "just-in-time" knowledge.

The same kind of flexible collaboration is also occurring among companies. We see it in the sharing of basic pieces of the business infrastructure. For example, direct competitors are sharing supply-chain platforms by forming consortia such as Covisint (in the automobile industry), Envera (in the chemicals industry), and Transora (in the packaged goods industry). More profoundly, the ability to combine capabilities existing among many different companies is enabling complex virtual enterprises to be formed on the fly. A whole new class of software, created by companies like Bowstreet, G5 Technologies, and Hewlett-Packard's E-speak unit, is emerging that will form the glue binding such plug-and-play organizations together. By coding business processes in common protocols, such as XML, this software enables different companies' processes to be easily connected or disconnected as circumstances warrant.

When companies understand how the patterns of intelligence migration are reshaping business, they are often able to use the Internet in a much more powerful way. Avon is a good case in point. Its first response to the Internet, back in 1997, was to launch a site for selling cosmetics directly to customers. The site failed to generate much business, accounting for only 2 percent of the company's sales in 1999. More importantly, it felt like a threat to the company's most valuable asset: its half-million-member independent sales force.

Now Avon is rethinking its Internet strategy, planning to create a site that provides "personal portals" for each of its sales representatives. The reps will use the site to place and track orders, get current information on products, and analyze the buying patterns of their customers—it will, in effect, become the shared "back office" for their individual businesses. Here again, we see infrastructure intelligence migrating to the core (to Avon), and customer intelligence being pushed to where it can be applied with the highest degree of customization (at the periphery, with the reps). Consolidating the infrastructure provides an important benefit to Avon. One of the company's biggest problems is high turnover among sales reps. The reps, who often work part-time, tend to drift in and out of the workforce, and when they leave, they take their customer relationships with them. Now, for the first time, Avon will have centralized information about all its end customers. This information will outlive the tenures of the individual representatives and can easily be transferred to new reps.

■ PROFITING FROM INTELLIGENCE MIGRATION

In addition to changing the way existing businesses operate, the decoupling and mobilization of network intelligence are opening attractive new business opportunities. Forward-thinking companies are beginning to use four strategies to capitalize on the migration patterns (see Figure 1.2).

Aggregation	Pool dedicated infrastructure intelligence spread across multiple enterprises into shared infrastructure intelligence that can be delivered over the network as a utility or service.	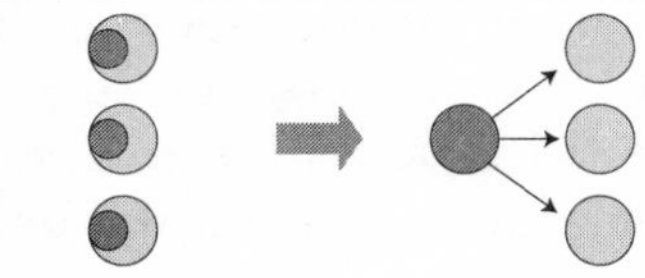
Arbitrage	Change the location of intelligence by sourcing inputs or resources on an as-needed basis from a geography or entity with lower costs.	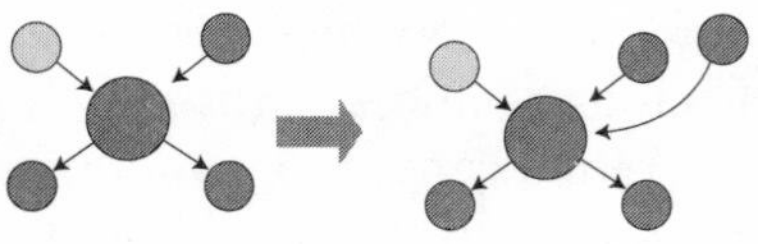
Rewiring	Connect islands of intelligence by creating a common information backbone to connect multiple entities that need to pool their intelligence to collaborate on a business process.	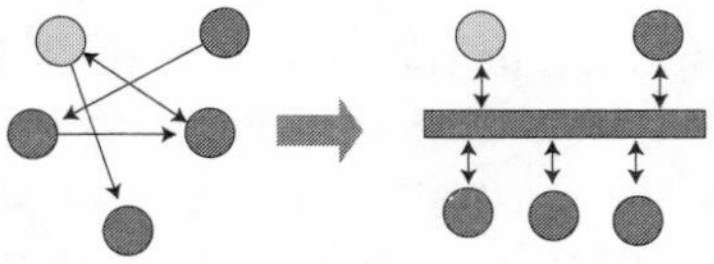
Reassembly	Dynamically assemble pieces of intelligence from diverse sources into a seamless solution that solves a complete problem for the end user.	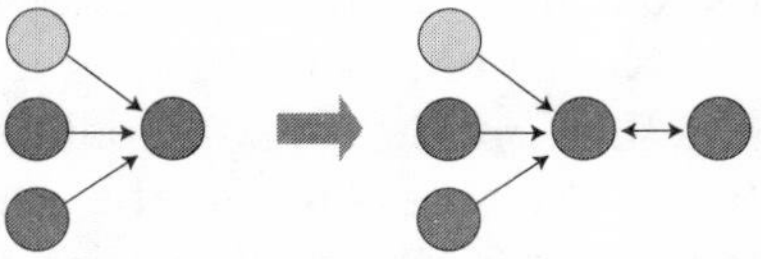

Figure 1.2 Four strategies for profiting from intelligence migration.

➤ Aggregation

As intelligence decouples, companies have the opportunity to combine formerly isolated pools of dedicated infrastructure intelligence into a large pool of shared infrastructure that can be provided over a network. Loudcloud, based in Sunnyvale, California, is an example of an emerging new breed of utility that employs the aggregation strategy. Loudcloud offers "instant" infrastructure to e-businesses by converting the various aspects of intelligence required to operate a Web site into a suite of services, which it calls Smart Cloud. Each aspect of intelligence is offered as a distinct service, including a Database Cloud (storage), an Application Server Cloud (processing), a Mail Cloud (dispatch), a Staging Cloud (testing), and an eServices Cloud (applications). The Smart Cloud services are coordinated by Opsware, an operating environment that automates tasks such as capacity scaling, configuration, service provisioning, and software updating.

Nike used Loudcloud's services to accommodate a dramatic increase in the traffic on its site during the 2000 Olympic Games in Australia. Opsware enabled Nike to scale up its computing needs on a temporary, just-in-time basis, allowing it to avoid the complexity and expense of expanding its capacity permanently. As Nike's traffic increased, it received more server and storage capacity; when the traffic died down after the Games, Opsware decommissioned the added computers. Loudcloud billed Nike just like a utility, on the amount of services actually used.

➤ Arbitrage

Because intelligence can be located anywhere on a network, there are often opportunities for moving particular types of intelligence to new regions or countries where the cost of maintaining the intelligence is lower. Such an arbitrage strategy is particularly useful for people-intensive services that can be delivered over a network, because labor costs tend to vary dramatically across geographies. One company that employs the arbitrage strategy is PeopleSupport, Inc. PeopleSupport operates a large center in Manila for providing live, online help services to the customers of its clients in the United States. By transporting the intelligence of a distant support staff over the Internet, the company is able to exploit the difference in labor costs between the Philippines and the United States to its advantage. The arbitrage strategy can also be used for other people-intensive services, such as medical transcription, software development, market research, transaction processing, and even management consulting. Areas like India, Eastern Europe, and Latin America provide rich pools of low-cost human resources that can be accessed over a network.

➤ Rewiring

The mobilization of intelligence opens the potential for creating intelligent information chains to connect a diverse set of entities that must collaborate to accomplish a task. In essence, this strategy involves creating an information network that everyone connects to and establishing an information exchange standard that allows the entities to communicate. Consider how the startup firm eTrak is rewiring the information chain for the towing of illegally parked vehicles. The towing process involves a complex sequence of interactions among the police officer at the towing site, the dispatcher in the police station, the towing company, and the towing company's drivers. Traditionally, the police officer radios the dispatcher in the police station, who then contacts various tow companies by phone. The tow companies in turn radio their drivers to locate a suitable truck in the area. Once a truck is located, confirmation is passed from the towing company to the dispatcher and back to the officer. This complex and inefficient process takes a lot of time, during which the officer is forced to remain near the vehicle.

eTrak sets up an information network that connects law enforcement agencies to towing companies. Police officers arrive on the scene and initiate a tow request through a radio link or a mobile display terminal connected to a computer. The tow information is sent to the eTrak system, which uses a database to automatically select the best towing company based on availability and proximity. The company receives the tow information through an eTrak terminal in its office, and it communicates with the driver via radio, computer, or pager. The eTrak system has allowed law enforcement agencies to cut response time from 30 minutes to 10 minutes, enabling them to handle twice as many tows without increasing their staff.

➤ **Reassembly**

Another new kind of intermediary can create value by aggregating, reorganizing, and configuring disparate pieces of intelligence into coherent, personalized packages for customers. One example of such a reassembler is Yodlee, a startup that has developed technology to consolidate and summarize information from multiple online sources on one Web site. Users get one-click access to a diverse set of personal information, including bank balances, travel reservations, investments, e-mail, shopping, bills, and calendars, and they can access it from a personal computer, handheld device, or Web-enabled telephone. The Yodlee platform also allows the different pieces of intelligence to communicate with each other, by securely and intelligently transmitting personal information across multiple accounts, services, platforms, and devices. For example, weather data transmitted to a Web-enabled phone could initiate an automatic phone call to inquire about a travel reservation.

■ WHAT MANAGERS NEED TO DO

The migration of intelligence raises various challenges for different companies, but your company can prepare itself by undertaking a straightforward analysis. First, define what "intelligence" is for your business. List the different types of intelligence that exist in your organization, using Table 1.1 as a guide. Think about intelligence that resides in objects, such as software applications, databases, and computer systems, as well as the intelligence in the skills and knowledge of your people. Next, ask yourself where intelligence currently lives in your organization. Is it organized by geography, by line of business, or by customer type? Then ask yourself where intelligence *should* live—assuming you could connect all your customers, employees, business processes, and trading partners in a seamless network with infinite bandwidth. Is the current location of intelligence the best location?

Think about the decoupling pattern. Are you making compromises by bundling intelligence that is best centralized with intelligence that is best decentralized? Conceptualize your organization as a network with a core (the back end) and a periphery (the front end). At the back end, can you centralize processes that are shared across different business units to create an internal "utility company?" Can you convert dedicated infrastructure into shared infrastructure by pushing some business processes beyond the walls of the organization to external utility companies? At the front end, can you get closer to your customers and partners by pushing intelligence nearer to them? Can you allow your customers, your sales force, and your channel partners to access and process intelligence directly, so that they can configure and personalize it themselves?

Think about the mobilization pattern. Are there opportunities to connect, combine, and configure isolated pools of intelligence in creative ways? Rethink your business in terms of the sequences of activities that your customers are trying to accomplish. Think about gaps in the information flows needed to support those sequences. Are you currently doing things in time-consuming, manual ways that could be automated if the right information were available? Think about opportunities to rewire your information chains by creating a single network for all your partners. And think about how you might aggregate and reassemble pieces of intelligence from different sources in ways that will save your customers time and effort.

By understanding the implications of intelligence migration for your own company, you will be better able to chart a clear-headed strategy in a time of apparent turmoil. Strategy has always been about finding the right position in a chain of value-creating activities—a position that gives you, rather than your competitors, control over the flow of profits. That has not changed. What *has* changed is the nature of the value chain itself, in that increasingly, it takes the form of a network.

■ NOTE

This chapter is adapted, with kind permission, from Mohan Sawhney and Deval Parikh, "Where Value Lives in a Networked World," *Harvard Business Review* (January 2001).

1.   John Hagel and Marc Singer, "Unbundling the Corporation," *Harvard Business Review* (May-June 1999).

■ REFERENCES

Hagel, John, and Marc Singer. "Unbundling the Corporation." *Harvard Business Review* (May-June 1999).

Sawhney, Mohan, and Deval Parikh. "Where Value Lives in a Networked World." *Harvard Business Review* (January 2001)

Chapter

Inside Technology Incubators

■ INTRODUCTION

Business incubators are a terrific way for young companies, especially those in the technology sector, to get off the ground. Incubators nurture these startups by providing management expertise, financial support, and access to critical resources. Whereas the traditional definition of an incubator focused on four key services (space, shared equipment and services, management advice, and access to capital), today the term is loosely defined and widely used. Companies that provide capital and a few limited services, as well as those that provide a full array of value-added services, all fall under the "incubator" umbrella, and the boundaries between traditional incubators, venture capitalists, and match makers have become increasingly blurred.

Although the recent turmoil in the public markets has revealed substantial limitations and challenges faced by many new incubator operating models, it is important to examine the real value provided by each model, and understand what could be an enduring aspect of new venture development and what incubator strategies might fail to persist over the long term. Like the companies they build, incubators must ultimately offer substantial, sustainable business value to justify their existence in the marketplace.

This chapter will help readers understand the value provided by incubators and how they might properly be matched with startups. The chapter also looks at the globalization of incubators, explores the emergence of new incubator business models, and suggests which incubator models will be sustainable in the future.

■ HISTORY AND EVOLUTION

Although the idea of an incubator has only recently been popularized, the approach originated in the 1960s, when universities created centers to leverage academic knowledge and laboratory equipment. The incubators, commonly known as *industrial parks*, were usually state-owned and were intended to facilitate the commercialization of ideas within the universities, as well as to offer outsiders access to university-based resources. These industrial parks leveraged the existing technological infrastructures of universities and made use of the rich human capital available.

In the 1970s and 1980s, incubators were created to promote economic development, primarily sponsored by government entities and philanthropic organizations. The development of the Internet in the 1990s gave rise to a new model of incubator. Internet visionaries were often young entrepreneurs with little or no business experience. To make matters worse, the amazingly rapid growth of the Internet led to intense competition and the first-mover advantage meant that speed to market was crucial. This competitive environment gave rise to incubators whose role was to provide the entrepreneur with the services and business expertise needed to maximize speed to market. As the influence of the Internet became undeniably clear, particularly in the last few years, we witnessed an explosion in the number of incubators. We also saw the incubator model evolve from a physical one, where incubees shared office space, to a virtual one, where firms are housed outside the incubator but still use its resources.

Additionally, although incubators traditionally took on companies in the product development stage, modern-day incubators are getting involved at an earlier stage and are often offering more services, as described in Figure 2.1.

The newest approach to emerge is the *keiretsu* model, in which the incubator has a controlling interest in a number of companies and creates synergies to maximize value. We expect that the next type of incu-

Process of Business Creation

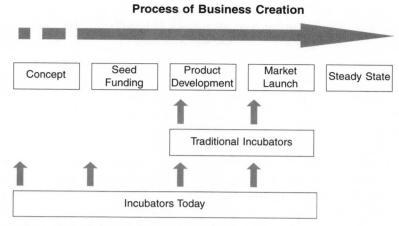

Figure 2.1   The process of business incubation.

bator to evolve will be the global incubator, under which a network of local incubators will cooperate to leverage ideas and expertise and make use of local competitive advantages.

In 1980, only 12 business incubation programs operated in North America, but that number increased to nearly 900 in 2001, according to the National Business Incubators Association (NBIA). Of these, 40 percent are technology-focused. Statistics reveal that incubees have enjoyed a relatively high rate of success. According to a recent NBIA report, 87 percent of all firms that graduated from their incubators are still in business.

➤ **Rapid Emergence of Incubators . . . and the Shakeout**

The explosion of new Internet-related companies (these include Web, infrastructure, and appliance businesses) has heightened the importance of differentiation and speed to market. To provide entrepreneurs with both of these important elements, several private, for-profit business incubators have emerged that focus on hatching technology companies. The primary driver for the proliferation of incubators and the evolution of traditional venture capitalists (VCs) is the emergence of the network economy. Kevin Kelly, executive editor of *Wired*, characterized this networked economy as "a grand scheme to augment, amplify, enhance, and extend the relationships and communications between all beings and all objects." We can readily see the results of the networked economy in increased initial public offering (IPO) activity, particularly as it relates to the technology sector, and the rise in venture capital investments. In 1999, venture capitalists invested $19 billion in Internet companies alone, and close to another $30 billion in other technology sectors combined. This investment grew an unprecedented 151 percent over the next year.

Since the crash in the public markets, many incubators have experienced substantial pressure, and in some cases the shakeout threatens their continued existence. Divine interVentures, an ambitious, well-connected, and well-funded incubator, saw its IPO postponed repeatedly, and its share price lose a substantial portion of its value following the offering. Established incubators like idealab! and Garage.com have since cancelled their planned IPOs, in hopes of finding more receptive markets in the future. Even long-time public high-flyers such as Internet Capital Group and CMGI have witnessed a precipitous drop in their market values over the past six months.

■ WHY INCUBATORS?

So, in the midst of this uncertainty, what value do incubators offer new firms, and how and when should startups choose to seek their assistance? When is it more efficient and more effective to let the incubator provide the services and lose the freedom to buy services on the free market? What are the advantages of using an incubator over the free market?

The transaction cost theory helps explain the value of incubators, because it compares the value of insourcing with that of outsourcing products or services. The theory states that a firm should seek the option that minimizes costs and maximizes value. Remember that for the startup, the costs are not always monetary. Costs may also involve a limited choice of services offered to incubees and a reduction of corporate independence.

In the transaction theory, nonmonetary transaction costs are taken into consideration and must be quantified by the individual entrepreneur. It is important to understand that there is no simple way to convert the nonmonetary costs into monetary values; the exchange rate depends on the specific startup, the industry in which it operates, and its management team.

The following section looks at the incremental costs and benefits of the incubator over the nonincubator alternative. These costs and benefits are then used as part of a framework for deciding whether being part of an incubator is right for your firm.

➤ Cost Analysis

Monetary Costs

Monetary costs are defined as the monetary discount under which equity is transferred relative to its current market value. It can be understood using the following formula (Equation 1):

Cost = Capital raised by selling × shares to provider of capital only minus Capital raised by selling × shares to incubator

Equation 1

Note that we use "shares" as a proxy to describe value that is transferred to the incubator (in actuality this may include shares, options, convertible loans, etc.).

Nonmonetary Costs

To relate *nonmonetary costs* to the expanded transaction theory, each startup needs to evaluate these costs and translate them into monetary terms and quantifiable figures. The following list is by no means complete, but it serves as a starting point for this analysis. It is important to understand that these costs will not be the same for each startup; they depend on the individual characteristics of each different venture.

Limited quality and variety of services and products offered. A major value addition of the incubator is its ability to reduce transaction costs through its extensive networks or in-house capabilities. The flip side of this, however, is that the incubator may limit the choice for the startup. In-house incubator services may reduce monetary costs to the startup but may prove counterproductive if the quality of the service is compromised. Likewise, receiving services from the incubator's supplier is not always optimal. This problem is enhanced in the *keiretsu* model.

Compromising independence. In most cases, incubating requires that the startup give up a certain amount of control over the enterprise. Even in the best-case scenario, this means that the founders may not always agree with the direction the company takes. More importantly, however, differing incentives and conflicts of interest may result in disagreements between the founders and the incubator. In these situations, the value of the enterprise may be reduced.

Maintaining corporate culture. The most important asset of a startup is its human capital. Maintaining the corporate culture is instrumental to any organization and is crucial in startups (where the people *are* the company). Incubating involves exposing the startup to a powerful external culture that can compromise the culture already established within the organization.

Operational flexibility. Although the incubee may overlook this cost, incubating generally leads to reduced flexibility. Whereas the incubee's objective is to maximize its own value, the objective of the incubator is to maximize the total value of its different incubees. As a result, conflicts of interest may result that lead to a reduced level of operational flexibility.

➤ Benefit Analysis

The value of the benefits offered by an incubator depends on the match between the incubee and the incubator, and should be evaluated accordingly. For example, the network provided by an incubator would be more valuable to a startup that depends on alliances with leading content providers for the success of its business model than to one that does not. The following list highlights some of the important benefits provided by the incubator that must be converted into monetary terms by the potential incubee (see Table 2.1 for a summary):

Speed to market. Part of the value an incubator provides is increasing speed to market. Speeding up the processes of developing an idea into a company increases the odds of being a first mover and allows a company to reach critical mass faster.

Networking. The incubator helps open doors to potential partners, customers, suppliers, and investors. For different startups, the value of this

Table 2.1 Why incubators?

Costs	Benefits
• Monetary costs of becoming an incubee	• Economies of scale
• Limited choice of services	• Networking
• Compromised independence	• Management focus
• Flexibility and independence	• Time to market
• Cultural sovereignty	• Low transaction costs

network is different, so each company has to assess the quality of this service and the value it brings to the incubee.

Incubator management expertise. Most incubators will participate in developing the incubee's strategy. The value of this service is determined by the supply of such expertise by the incubator and the demand for this service by the startup.

Lower transaction fees. The access of the incubator to a variety of service providers reduces costs.

Economies of scale. The incubator's ability to share resources among incubees leads to economies of scale and lower expenses.

➤ Calculating the Value of Incubators

Once the entrepreneur has carefully identified and quantified the different costs and benefits that will result from incubation, the expanded transaction theory can be used to assess whether involvement with an incubator is appropriate.

Using Equation 1 and the expanded transaction theory, the value of incubating can be defined as follows:

Value of incubating = Benefits of incubating
                   − Monetary cost of incubating
                   − Nonmonetary cost of incubating

Equation 2

Because Equation 2 measures the incremental costs and benefits over the nonincubator model, the startup should incubate if the value of incubating is greater than zero.

■ SELECTING AN INCUBATOR

The entrepreneur must take three steps to evaluate both the need for an incubator and the type of incubator needed:

1. Startup evaluation: The entrepreneur evaluates the startup against specific criteria (explained in this section). This step provides the entrepreneur with a clear picture of the startup's internal and external operating environment.
2. Incubator evaluation: The entrepreneur evaluates the types of incubators and other alternative providers of capital that are available. This stage is intended to provide the entrepreneur with a clear picture of the types of incubators available and the resources provided by each.
3. Matching of supply and demand: After evaluating the startup's demands and the existing supply of funding sources, the entrepreneur chooses the model that provides the most value for the venture.

➤ Startup Evaluation

When considering the option of an incubator, the entrepreneur should first evaluate the startup's need for expertise and resources. Different management teams have different levels of experience and industry (or domain) expertise. A significant part of the incubator's value-add is its ability to complement the skills of management, and the incubator can be assessed for its ability to bring management and industry expertise to the startup. A startup is made up of a team of individuals who bring together different skill sets needed for the venture. The greater the variety of management, the more complete the in-house skill set and the lower the need for an incubator to complement these skills. An in-depth understanding of the domain in which the startup will operate is crucial. If management lacks this knowledge, an incubator that is focused on a specific industry may provide this expertise.

The second dimension along which the startup should evaluate itself is its need for resources. The following list should be used when considering the need for external resources:

- *Importance of speed to market.* The greater the importance of speed to market for the specific startup, the greater the requirement for additional resources.

- *Importance of network.* Startups operating in a space that requires a high level of networking/alliances should be more inclined to seek external resources.

- *Access to capital.* The greater the access to capital for a startup, the lower the value of commodity services, such as physical infrastructure, and professional services that can be purchased on the open market. Consequently, startups with high access to capital have a lower need for external resources.

Entrepreneurial Models

After the self-evaluation is complete, the potential incubee should be able to determine where it lies on the diagram shown in Figure 2.2. To illustrate this process, we describe various startups with different characteristics and then map their positions.

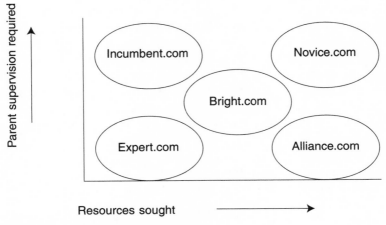

Figure 2.2   Evaluating the startup.

- **Expert.com** requires little management supervision and resources (e.g., MyCFO.com).
- **Bright.com** requires a little more supervision but a lot more resources (e.g., Ethnicgrocer.com).
- **Alliance.com** requires little supervision but a great deal of networking (e.g., SurePayroll.com).
- **Novice.com** requires a great deal of both supervision and resources (e.g., Efrenzy.com in April 1999).
- **Incumbent.com** requires a low level of resources and a high level of supervision (e.g., vertical marketplace operated by major car manufacturers).

➤ Incubator Evaluation

When evaluating your choice of incubator, we suggest using two key criteria: the resources provided by the incubator and the incubator's level of involvement with the incubee. Incubators offer startups some or all of the following services.

Infrastructure. Incubators can provide incubees with receptionist services, office space, high-speed Internet access, meeting rooms, office peripherals, and so on. Government- and university-related incubators have traditionally focused on these services. Most of these services are too lumpy and expensive to be used by one startup, so combining them in an incubator provides benefit to all participating startups. Additionally, the incubator provides more flexibility to the startups as the business grows without the considerable expenses of relocation.

Research and development. Both academic incubators and high-tech corporate incubators focus on providing this service to the entrepreneur. Academic incubators generally focus more on the practical applicability of fundamental research. Corporate incubators generally focus on companies that have links with the incubators' core technology and products.

Capital. An incubators may have a fund that it uses to invest in ventures. This is the traditional focus of venture capital funds.

Access to capital. Some incubators link incubees to other providers of capital. Traditional incubators that have offered this service have focused on providing access to debt capital. More recently, incubators have focused on links to venture capital firms and investment banks, because these sources are more valuable to the entrepreneur.

Access to a network. Incubators add value to startups through their extensive networks. Such networks consist of other startups (the community idea), potential investors, technology partners, marketing partners, and so forth. The ability to create the right alliance or attract the right capital is crucial to the startup and is leveraged by the incubator's network. These services are also referred to as "leveraging the Rolodex."

Synergies. By creating "eco-nets," in which the incubator maintains a controlling interest in its fledgling companies, startups can complement each other and increase their total value.

Professional services. Startups often do not have the scale necessary to hire employees who provide professional services. Furthermore, the unifying characteristics of many of these services mean that the experienced incubator can effectively leverage its past experience and accumulated expertise to benefit the new company. Also, as most of these services are in high peak demand (like hiring a CEO or negotiating a bank loan), the incubator can share the peak loads among the startups and increase capacity utilization. Therefore, the value added is a result of the incubator's know-how and the economies of scale that arise from centralizing these services. Professional services include financial services, legal advice, marketing services, public relations and Web design, business development advice, and strategic advice.

Level of involvement. Incubators should also be evaluated on the basis of their level of involvement with the incubee. By *involvement* we refer to management supervision and participation in the decision-making processes of the incubee. Though it is true that different startups require different levels of an incubator's involvement, incubators have distinct philosophies and management styles pertaining to their involvement with the startup. Level of involvement can be categorized as follows:

- *High level of involvement.* Incubators that provide a very high level of supervision and are integrally involved on a micro level in shaping the incubee's strategic and tactical decisions.

- *Medium level of involvement.* Incubators that participate more peripherally in the incubee's decision-making processes and strategy formulation. For instance, a traditional venture capitalist helps manage the business periodically from the board level.

- *Low level of involvement.* Incubators that supply capital and other resources but are not actively involved in supervising the incubee. These include incubators that act as match makers linking entrepreneurs and investors.

Incubator Models

Now that we have defined the two evaluation criteria, we can characterize the different type of incubator models. As discussed earlier, the boundaries between the activities of each type have become blurred. However, this categorization provides a useful framework for classifying different suppliers of services.

Match makers. Match makers provide a meeting platform for entrepreneurs and service providers. An example is Garage.com, which provides an Internet-based platform where entrepreneurs can post their business plans, and investors can analyze these plans, deciding whether or not to invest. Assistance in obtaining seed-level financing is Garage.com's primary objective, and it succeeds in compressing the entrepreneur's "concept to cash" time via mentoring and a high-quality investor network. This allows the entrepreneur the time needed to focus on building the business. Garage.com also provides member entrepreneurs with expert advice, research and reference materials, and topical "forums" to help them launch and grow their startups.

Offroad Capital's business model is slightly different because it standardizes the equity offering memoranda and provides market pricing of securities. The match-maker model is, on average, the model with the least involvement from the incubator. Mostly the incubator just enables the contact and stays hands-off thereafter.

Government- or university-linked. Government and academically related incubators were the first models to appear. The rationale was to use the institution's academic research for practical benefit. The majority of these incubators are not-for-profit; rather, their objective is to create jobs, support economic development, and foster technology usage. An example is the Los Angeles County Business Technology Center, whose mission is to support regional economic revitalization by assisting in the development of startup and early-stage high-technology firms. Another example is a joint venture between the city of Evanston and Northwestern University: the Evanston Research Park. The mission of this organization is to accelerate technology transfer from the laboratory to the marketplace by means of a research environment that combines the resources of a major university, a progressive community, and private industry.

Venture capitalists (VCs). It is difficult to generalize about venture capitalists, as a wide variety of firms are classified as VCs. The venture capitalist category includes firms such as Kleiner, Perkins, Caufield & Byers, as well as "boutique" VCs. The differences between firms are enormous; some provide access to a network of alliance partners, industry expertise, infrastructure, and professional services, whereas others just provide capital. To complicate the matter, a traditional VC, such as Accel Partners, may also branch out into pure incubation, where it works with concept startups of three to four people to help develop the nascent groups into real businesses.

Corporate incubators. Corporate incubators are divisions of established companies that invest with strategic intent, aiming to create and expand new markets for the company's products or services. For example, Intel Capital began by investing in companies whose products and services helped fill the gap in Intel's product line, capabilities, and capacity. Intel's investment scope expanded to a broad range of Internet companies that were creating exciting new content and capabilities.

Accelerators. The accelerator category includes various models. For example, idealab! identifies, creates, and operates Internet businesses. Idealab! currently has 50 businesses in various stages of development; it generates ideas for new Internet businesses and then creates, capitalizes, and operates a separate company to conduct each new business. Actively participating in the ongoing operations of its network companies, through board representation, information sharing, and facilitation of collaboration among the companies, idealab! also recruits management to oversee the day-to-day operations, thus letting senior management concentrate on executing the business plan. Additionally, idealab! provides each operating company with a full range of operational support services, including office space and the accompanying network infrastructure, technology, graphic design, marketing, recruiting, competitive research, legal, accounting, and business development services.

Accelerators also include firms that combine significant technology expertise with powerful creative design teams. These firms act as consultants and/or investors and allow Internet firms to expedite the launch process. An example of a firm in this category is IXL Enterprises. IXL helps businesses identify how the Internet can be used to their competitive advantage and uses its expertise in creative design and systems engineering to design, develop, and deploy advanced Internet applications and solutions. IXL's objective is to enable its customers to gain faster time to market, increased brand awareness, and new revenue opportunities.

Keiretsu. The *keiretsu* model is best described by the example of divine interVentures, which acquires a stake in a number of companies and then fosters collaboration among these companies by providing cross-selling and marketing opportunities. Unlike a VC model, divine interVentures locates many of these companies in its own facilities. In addition to providing its partner companies with capital, the firm offers them a comprehensive array of strategic and infrastructure services. The *keiretsu* model is designed to promote collaboration among the partner companies by helping them gain significant networking, cross-selling, and marketing benefits.

With these models in mind, the incubator landscape can be visualized as in Figure 2.3.

➤ Matching Supply and Demand

After evaluating the characteristics of the startups and those of the incubators, the entrepreneur is now better positioned to select the best provider of capital. Although each specific incubator is unique, this framework provides a rational method for understanding which supplier is most appropriate (see Figure 2.4).

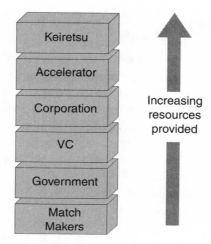

Figure 2.3   Ranking of incubator models.

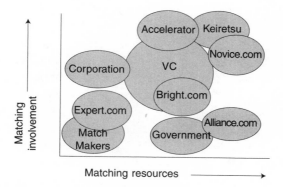

Figure 2.4   Matching supply and demand.

Capacityweb.com Incubated by Divine InterVentures

Capacityweb.com was founded by two Kellogg MBAs in 1999. Both founders were new entrepreneurs with a powerful business-to-business concept. However, their lack of experience necessitated a high level of supervision and, correspondingly, an increased level of resources. At the time this book was written, Capacityweb.com best fit into our schematic as Novice.com, searching for a *keiretsu* model of incubator that could provide the necessary services.

While the founders sought venture capitalists and other providers, they focused on obtaining two critical services. First, the majority of their customers were Midwest-based and the company needed access to the network. Second, speed to market was critical. Divine fit perfectly. Not only was Divine able to provide strong regional resources, but it also had a wide array of in-house services that have helped Capacityweb.com to scale dramatically. As Arvind Kapur, Capacityweb's co-founder put it, "Given what Divine has accomplished in the last seven months, we were confident that they can provide us with the essential speed to market we require. Although we only have 15 professionals working full-time, with Divine's staff it feels more like 55."

Divine provides Capacityweb.com with all of the internal resources necessary to get to market quickly. In addition to housing Capacityweb.com physically, divine provides it with technical, marketing, financial, legal, and other personnel.

Only a few months after incubation, Capacityweb has made significant progress. Arvind acknowledges that "relative to what we gave up, we have got a tremendous deal. Not only has this dramatically improved our chances for success but also significantly increased the total pie."

■ NEW INCUBATOR MODELS

The rapidly evolving Internet economy is driving continuous change in the incubator industry. Two new models have recently emerged: self-incubation and incubating the incubator.

Under self-incubation, a number of noncompeting startups share the same resources and office space, and entrepreneurs from the varying firms provide advice for each other and leverage their networks. The main advantage of this concept is that there are no costs associated with self-incubation. However, the model lacks a formal incubator team to lead the startup and accelerate speed to market. This is a controversial model that, according to Dinah Adkins, executive director of NBIA, is a case of "a bunch of people who know nothing about business passing along misinformation to each other." Ms. Adkins adds, "There needs to be an incubation manager who puts the companies through the paces and does a real critique of the business."

Although self-incubation has its flaws, it provides an inexpensive and somewhat effective way of increasing the resources of a company and creating economies of scale. Theoretically, sharing suppliers and other service providers reduces transaction costs and creates value. With respect to the framework presented in this chapter, self-incubation provides a valuable solution to startups that do not seek adult supervision but require resources.

The model of incubating the incubators was prompted by the multitudes of new incubators entering the marketplace, which leads one to ask: Just how much experience and knowledge do these new incubators have, and how much value can they add? This question encouraged entrepreneurs with the necessary experience to sell their services to new incubators. Companies that fall within this model are Incubator.com, KnowledgeCube, and The Atlantic. These companies are spreading the commercial model of incubation by teaming up with and training local management teams that will then establish their own incubators, which eventually will become part of the global incubator network.

■ WHAT'S NEXT?

The evolution of the incubator model and the increase in the size of this industry are in every way linked to the expansion of the global network economy. This activity, which in our view will only increase, has led to the identification of a new incubator model: the meta-incubator, where the local incubator model will shift to a global model, allowing ideas created in one area of the world to scale quickly and

influence the global market. There are several advantages of the meta-
or global-incubator model:

Zero to global. Companies such as eFrenzy, which have developed a
U.S. business, need to go global immediately following the U.S. launch.
By focusing exclusively on their own countries, startups with innovative solutions are essentially destroying value. Chatri Trisiripisal,
founder of eFrenzy, claims that IXL is playing a lead role in helping
move its business model across countries.

Reduction of local risk. The advantage of being global for the incubator
is that it has more companies to choose from. This clearly allows the
incubator to maximize its value, as it can incubate the world's best
companies as opposed to only one country's best companies. Additionally, it minimizes the inherent local risk (for example, the volatility of
the U.S. IPO market).

Ability to share ideas. The global incubator model enables the principals
of the incubator model to share ideas globally. This will allow business
ideas to be built from a global perspective from day one.

National competitive advantages. This is perhaps one of the greatest
advantages of a global incubator—taking advantage of national competitive strengths. The United States, for example, is the leader in
marketing, whereas India has emerged as being effective in building
technology.

A number of firms are already applying the meta-incubator model
to their businesses. In February 2000, Andersen Consulting, now
Accenture, announced a global network of 17 "dot-com launch centers," which will provide e-commerce startups with the tools and coun-
sel they need to quickly become viable, revenue-producing businesses.
Andersen seeks to nurture young companies that already have a nucleus
of management and $1 million to $2 million in financial support. Once
primarily a computer distributor, Softbank now has stakes in more than
100 companies worldwide and plans to expand that number to 780 in
5 years. It uses its global network to turn its U.S. holdings into foreign
businesses. Typically, it takes a U.S. company business model and clones
it in a foreign market. In January 2000, Pacific Century CyberWorks
and CMGI teamed up to form a joint venture that will serve as a Hong

Kong-based holding and management company for 18 of CMGI's U.S.-based Internet subsidiaries. Additionally, CMGI has invested 5 percent in Divine InterVenture. This is indicative of the growing trend of incubators investing in other incubators to achieve local and global scale. Accel Partners, the incubator of walmart.com, formed a joint venture with KKR, a leveraged buyout firm. This demonstrates rather forcefully that the whole world of venture capital and incubators is being turned upside down. These examples are exactly the type of business combinations that will allow New Age companies access to global scale. Benchmark has adopted a different strategy: rather than buy, it has opted to make. Benchmark recently unveiled plans to open a London office and create a $500 million fund aimed solely at Europe.

Other Silicon Valley firms looking to expand globally include Garage.com, Guy Kawasaki's early-stage venture company; and Draper Fisher Jurvetson, which recently announced plans to open offices in London, Hong Kong, and Singapore. "The Internet is a global phenomenon," says Warren Packard, partner at Draper Fisher. "We'd be too local in thinking it's only a U.S. phenomenon."

For existing and future incubators, the key success factors remain clear. Incubators must focus on noncommodity services, because transaction costs will be reduced to minimal levels. Noncommodity services include advanced high-tech abilities, in addition to a powerful net work that allows for internal synergies as well as access to participants outside of the network. Ultimately, long-term success requires any business to provide long-term, sustainable value. Incubators that can provide this competitively, and thereby build successful, valuable companies, will succeed. Those that cannot will find the shakeout of the year 2000 to be an unfortunate validation of old-fashioned business essentials, even in the midst of the New Economy.

■ REFERENCES

Adkins, Dinah. "New Reports Find the Keys to Entrepreneurial Success." National Business Incubation Association press release (June 10, 1999).

Adkins, Dinah. "New Study Shows Business Incubation Has Significant Economic Impact." National Business Incubation Association press release. 1999.

Agoston, Jennifer, and Meredith Erlewine. "Incubation Sensations." National Business Incubation Association press release, 1999.

Aragon, Lawrence, and Julie Landry. "How a Farming Town Hatched a New Way of Doing Business." *Redherring.com* (January 19, 2000).

Blackburn, Nicki. "Jerusalem Global to Fund Three Incubators." *The Jerusalem Post* (November 17, 1999).

Burger, Frederick. "Business Incubators: How Successful Are They?" *Area Development Online* (January 1999).

"Finding a Business Incubator." *MoneyMinded* (January 2000).

Gerstenfeld, Dan. "Nurturing the Seeds of Success." *The Jerusalem Post* (January 2, 2000).

"Get Hatched: An Insider's Guide to Incubators." *Redherring.com* (January 2000).

Grande, Carlos. "Ernst & Young Backs Start-Ups." *Financial Times London* (December 8, 1999).

Hayhow, Sally. "A Comprehensive Guide to Business Incubation." National Business Incubation Association, 1996.

"Incubators Embrace Fledglings Seeking Success." *South China Morning Post* (November 5, 1999).

Lichenstein, Gregg A., and Thomas S. Lyons. *Incubating New Enterprises: A Guide to Successful Practice*. The Aspen Institute, 1996.

Malik, Om. "Hatch Them Young." *Forbes Magazine* (December 15, 1999).

Masterson, Victoria. "Hatching Out the Fledgling E-Firms." *The Scotsman* (November 2, 1999).

Newsweek. Special issue (August 2000): 32.

Robinson, Sara. "One Way to Play Start-Ups." *New York Times* (November 28, 1999).

Sinton, Peter. "Andersen Launching Dot-Com Incubators." *San Francisco Chronicle* (February 9, 2000).

Soref, Ezer. *Israel Venture Association 1998 Yearbook, A Survey of Venture Capital and Private Equity in Israel*. Giza Group, 1998.

Stirland, Sarah Lai. "Who Will Incubate the Incubators?" *Redherring.com* (April 10, 2000).

University of Michigan, National Business Incubation Association, Southern Technology Council, and Ohio University. *Business Incubation Works*. 1999.

Chapter

The Startup Graveyard

10 Lessons for Avoiding Failure and Secrets for Success

■ INTRODUCTION

It is estimated that more than 75 percent of Internet startups that reach any stage beyond having an initial business plan will end in *absolute* failure—and these daunting numbers arose before the 2000 shakeout in the technology marketplace. VCs understand these facts and, on average, fund less than 1 percent of the business plans they receive for consideration. Once a company moves beyond the conceptual and planning stage, it must make several management decisions that will prove critical to sustained success and viability. Companies that make strategic errors during this crucial time often do not survive long enough to rebound.

In this chapter we hope to help readers understand the various ways in which startup companies can fail, so as to build a foundation for avoiding devastating mistakes. To give insight into how a new company can maximize its chances for sustained profitability, we will examine the characteristics of successful startup firms. Also included is a unique diagnostic tool to help entrepreneurs assess their own businesses and identify existing or potential problems. See Appendix A at the end of the book. Although the lessons discussed in this chapter apply to companies during any stage of the life cycle, the early stages (i.e., before sustainable revenue and/or profit generation) are the most critical, because missteps taken during this time have a "snowball" effect for young companies.

■ VIEWS OF FAILURE: VC VERSUS ENTREPRENEUR

Depending on your perspective, failure can range from lack of funding to an inability to hire new employees. After extensive discussions with those that represent the proverbial two sides of the coin—VCs and entrepreneurs—a common theme emerged: There are many ways to fail in this marketplace and each depends on the goals that have been targeted for the company. (See Table 3.1 for a summary.)

From the perspective of the VC, investing in a startup is a failure if the firm generates a below-target return. As early-stage investors willing to assume a large amount of risk, VCs often have return objectives of several multiples of their investment. Such a lofty target makes it easy to see the discontinuity that exists between the views of the average stock market investor and the highly specialized VC institution. If a venture firm provides backing for a new idea that returns only 25 percent, that firm's view will be that those same funds could have been used instead to seed the next Yahoo! Opportunity costs are large in seed-stage investments, so the payoffs must be high.

Secondly, a VC might classify a deal as a failure when the relation-

---

Table 3.1 What constitutes failure?

VC

1. Below-target IRR/ROI.
2. Bad relationship with entrepreneur.

Entrepreneur

1. Lack of funding.
2. Lack of value, either as stand-alone or adjunct proposition.
3. Inability to attract or retain talent.
4. Emotional/ego disappointment.

ship with the entrepreneur turns sour. A brilliant new idea might appear to be a potential financial boon to the investor, but sometimes a rift develops between the two parties. Whether the rift is caused by differences in philosophy or simply a personality clash, the resulting falling-out can cause the VC to walk away, forcing the entrepreneur to reinitiate the search for funds. Additionally, the entrepreneur has destroyed a valuable relationship, which could hurt any chance for future backing. In early-stage ventures, the quality of a startup is often perceived to be the quality of its management. In the tight VC community, a manager with a bad reputation will have difficulty funding the next venture.

For entrepreneurs, the classification of failure is much more diverse, but the most fundamental is lack of funding. Despite the wide range of investment opportunities available today (some of which you have been or will be introduced to in this book), actually securing an initial meeting with a VC firm is a tough proposition. When this hard-earned event occurs, the startup has only a short time to convince the VC that the startup firm's concept and implementation plan are stellar. In addition to the challenge of obtaining financing, there is also the concern that once funded, the startup will run out of money before the market opportunity fully presents itself.

A lack of financing is often the result of an entrepreneur's failing to convince potential investors of the value the firm will bring to the marketplace—the company's value proposition. Every startup management team imagines that they have discovered a new idea with great prospects for phenomenal growth. Nevertheless, there are those who fail to execute their plan effectively and convert their concept into a revenue-generating business. In several instances, companies that have modest value propositions on their own have gained significant value as adjuncts to other businesses—the business-versus-application issue. As a stand-alone, free, electronic card service that had no revenue but remained one of the 10 most trafficked sites on the Web, Bluemountainarts.com had limited financial value for its owners. This changed considerably once the site was sold to Excite@Home, which could cross-sell its other products and services to Bluemountainarts.com users.

If a new firm cannot attract and retain talent, the entrepreneur might view the business as a failure. The increased number of startups, in combination with the hot job market this has created, makes attracting and keeping top talent a challenge.

Finally, as with the VC, an emotional or subjective element can cloud the entrepreneur's view of success. An entrepreneur may have overcome all the roadblocks and built a valuable enterprise—only to be removed from the company. It is not uncommon for a company to outgrow its founder, and on these occasions the firm's VC-influenced board might elect to remove the founder. For entrepreneurs, who still profited from their startup experience, an ousting becomes an emotional failure.

■ WHAT CAUSES FAILURE: THE FACTS, THE SUSPECTS, AND THE SURPRISES

The causes of failure are numerous and disparate, but fall into three main categories:

1. *The facts:* Factors that the entrepreneur or management team has direct control over through their daily business decisions. These include people and management, market opportunity, funding, and details of the product and service.

2. *The suspects:* Factors that the entrepreneur or management team can seek to understand and adjust their business to deal with, but on which they do not have any direct effect. These include competition in the marketplace for a product or for talent (future employees), future funding, technological advances or upgrades, and customer preferences.

3. *The surprises:* Factors that are beyond the scope of the entrepreneur's purview. These include paradigm shifts, such as technological advances; new business models; and divine acts. The firm's ability to adapt to these unexpected occurrences will determine whether the surprise is fatal, as well as offering insight into the viability of the company.

This chapter focuses on the business challenges over which managers have the highest level of control: the facts.

■ EVALUATING THE FACTS

In its most fundamental form, the success or failure of a startup is based on the decisions and actions that occur during the developmental stages of the venture, in four key areas:

Management expertise. The most critical component of any business, this aspect encompasses the vision and passion of the founder and the management team; the experience and skill set that the management team brings to bear on the venture; management's ability to execute the plan and adapt to a changing market environment; and management's success in attracting and retaining human capital.

Market opportunity. Market opportunity reflects the caliber of the business model (i.e., its adaptability, scalability, revenue- and profit-generating ability, defensibility), the competitive market position, and the market potential of the idea.

Funding. The term *funding* includes the amount of capital and the quality of the company's investors.

Product and service. This aspect refers to the degree to which the product addresses customer needs, the selection of technological support, and the fulfillment of client needs.

➤ Management Expertise

This book stresses the importance of intellectual capital to the sustained success of a business. We have already noted the importance of the founding team's management expertise and personal network. Indeed, the business probably will not get off the ground without these qualities. Furthermore, although a primary cause of startup failure is the inability to bring an expert team to the company, several other areas concerning management also prove to be challenges to a young company. The following six lessons explore the relationship between management, the organization, and the marketplace.

Lesson #1: The founding team must sustain vision and passion for the company over the long term. A company founded by an individual who is motivated by profit or stock price will fall prey to shortsightedness. The entrepreneur needs to remain passionate and display a limitless devotion to the idea. Founders whose focus is only on the post-IPO stock valuation will not be prepared to meet the challenges of growing a profitable business in a rapidly evolving marketplace.

Lesson #2: Management must possess skill sets appropriate to the needs of the firm. In the early life of a startup, the participants usually consist only of the founder and the immediate team. Particularly when the idea for the company was the brainchild of only one person, it is essential to back the idea with a team of experts who can execute the business plan and manage operations. Having a well-rounded team allows the entrepreneur to remain focused on the company's goals and give the proper direction to the firm.

Lesson #3: Management and organization must be congruent or strategically aligned. Congruence and *strategic alignment* are terms and concepts stressed by organizational design experts in all industries; they are often determining factors in business failure for companies in all sectors. There must be a fit between the type of people leading a company, the tasks that must be accomplished, and both the formal and informal structures that allow these people to perform their jobs.

Lesson #4: The company's culture must remain sensitive to the speed of the market and be supported by management. This is similar to the preceding lesson, but can be applied to the organization as a whole, rather than just to the connection between management and employees. The unique culture within startups is legendary and almost a requirement for a business that thrives in creative environments and whose "big idea" is its value proposition. Efforts are thwarted when startups enter a growth stage and suddenly are asked to take on the demeanor of a mature company. These shifts in culture and the transitional problems they cause dilute the organization's ability to respond to the changing marketplace. When John Morgridge assumed the CEO position at Cisco Systems in 1989, he changed a long-standing Cisco tradition: free soft drinks. He reduced the number of available flavors from around 50 to 24. Morgridge, widely known for controlling costs that did not directly enhance product development or customer relations, viewed the change as inconsequential. The company ground almost to a standstill as employees exchanged vitriolic e-mails concerning the decision. Within a week, the decision was reversed—and a small aspect of the original culture was preserved.

The inability to preserve a culture and organizational design that have proven successful for a business has caused some of America's most renowned corporations to fail when they tried to enter the Internet marketplace. This problem has been dubbed the "Parent Trap," because the rules imposed by parent companies on their offspring sometimes serve only to limit their success. Online communities present a fine example of the "Parent Trap" problem: Several top companies thought this was the best place to gain a foothold in the Internet sector and almost all failed. CompuServe (H&R Block), Genie (GE), Pathfinder (TimeWarner), and Prodigy (IBM and Sears) all fell prey to a smart young startup from Virginia called America Online. These giants of American industry failed because they were held back by corporate infrastructures that slowed them down operationally—a terrible liability in an era where speed means everything.

A classic example of a startup failure that managed to get more than one of these areas wrong is Pointcast, a pioneer in streaming content-push technology. Pointcast ignored the fact that its technology could be easily imitated. Furthermore, the technology for the system they developed created a nightmare for users, as the service swamped networks with traffic and caused many crashes for dial-up users. Finally, Pointcast was never able to monetize the customers who were not intimidated by these problems. Pointcast did not fully understand its market, and thus failed to build an appropriate revenue model.

Lesson #5: Revenue models must be clear and adaptable; there can be no missteps with regard to technology choices and responsiveness to customer needs. This lesson is clear and concise. Management must focus on each of the "4Cs:" company, customers, competitors, and collaborators. The firm has to have a scalable revenue model that is supported by its technology choices and customer service philosophy. The streets of Silicon Valley are littered with the remains of companies that failed to address each important aspect of their business, and last year's dip in technology stocks has begun a winnowing process that will have devastating effects on companies with weak business models.

Lesson #6: Lack of focus can wipe you out. For years, Michael Porter has instructed managers that a company has to pay attention to its source of competitive advantage, then concentrate resources toward this end. Losing this direction diverts attention from achieving a primary goal, and causes employees to become confused about their purpose. Entrepreneurs who think that pursuing several goals improves the chances of success will actually find that the opposite occurs. *Wired* magazine failed to prosper under the guidance of its original founders for this very reason. Instead of creating a magazine that focused solely on the cultural aspects of the Internet age, the startup aspired to be a multimedia octopus, with tentacles reaching in several directions. Said one former employee, "There were probably a dozen visions—so you eventually end up cross-eyed."[1] Eventually, competitive pressures forced *Wired* to forgo its book-publishing business and concentrate its efforts on the high-growth portal arena, with the support of Lycos. The magazine was then sold to Condé Nast, an organization more inclined to put the proper resources in place for the magazine succeed.

➤ Market Opportunity

The second major area where failure can develop lies in market opportunity. Many companies fail because they have chosen a market that simply does not have the critical mass to support a high-growth startup.

Lesson #7: Being first is good only if there is a market for your product or service, if you can capitalize on your advantage, or if you can keep recreating that first-mover advantage. First-mover advantage, the goal of many Internet startups, is a term that has long existed in the business lexicon. The rise of startups today is the direct result of a paradigm shift toward new ways of doing business, creating the chance for smart, fast companies to move into new or even established markets and quickly build a brand. Though there seem to be limitless opportunities to create this advantage, too many companies realize too late that being first is good only when there are enough buyers to warrant a new segment. If the market is indeed large enough, one must also be able to capitalize on this advantage before the inevitable competition sees the potential too and moves into the market. Nothing attracts new players like a profitable new idea, especially one that is easily copied.

➤ Funding

Funding is where it all begins—or ends, depending on how capital is sourced and sustained during a company's pre-IPO stages. The 1999 market drop in technology stocks signified that capital was no longer king where tech startups were concerned, and CEOs were urged to revisit the basics of their businesses (as described earlier in this chapter).

Lesson #8: "Zombies" should be put to rest. Zombies stay alive by eating the flesh of unsuspecting living victims. In the Internet world, these walking corpses have taken the form of startups that just will not die, devouring capital while trying to sustain ideas whose time has come and gone. *Cash burn* is a popular term among startups with limited means, which must pay strict attention to how quickly they are using their resources to get something to market. The negative connotation applies only when this money is used improperly, or to keep an unsustainable business afloat.

Lesson #9: "Smart money" is better than "stupid money." Two common terms heard in the world of early-stage companies are *smart money* and *stupid money*, and there is a large difference between the two. Smart money is cash that will not only help pay the bills, but also help a company find the right strategic partners, recruit top-notch talent, and learn from people who have vast information about all aspects of the Internet economy. Stupid money brings no such resources to the table. This type of money can be even more harmful than not having money at all, if it adds to the costs of supporting these relationships or deters smart-money investors from contributing to the business. This is not to say that this source of capital has no place in the startup field. Often angel investors are the only money source available, and if the entrepreneur believes that the business is smart enough to manage these relationships wisely until smarter money comes along, there is every reason to believe the firm will succeed.

➤ Product and Service

The last key aspect of potential failure stems from problems with the actual product or service being offered. This failure is often linked to a lack of expertise on the part of the management team, causing a lack of congruence or alignment between marketing and operations.

Lesson #10: Fulfillment and customer service are critical. Entrepreneurs are often idea generators, constantly looking for markets appropriate for new business ventures. But the customer must always be part of this equation. From the beginning, the startup needs to consider how the customer will be satisfied at every point in the value chain, from information search to postpurchase service. This process must be scalable as well. Failure can result from lack of planning for growth, when existing structures cannot keep pace with the market's appetite. Marketing could launch an advertising blitz, but a lack of communication with operations will break down the planning process. A good example is the infatuation of Internet companies with Super Bowl XXXIV ads in 2000. These ads generated a tremendous buzz and drew huge amounts of traffic to Web sites. However, in several cases, the sites were not ready for the demand, and long access times angered potential customers.

■ AVOIDING FAILURE

The 10 lessons from the preceding section offer a clear framework for improving the startup's chances of success. First, there must be a clearly defined set of goals. Once these are established, successes and failures can be evaluated relative to the goals. The entrepreneur should have full control of the *facts*, be aware of and proactive about the *suspects*, and build enough flexibility into the business model to react successfully to the *surprises*. These lessons offer important strategies for the startup firm to avoid failure; the next section examines what the startup should do to maximize its chances for success.

■ SUCCESS: FINDING THE PROMISED LAND

As with failure, what constitutes success depends on perspective. The VC is still concerned about return, and points to the need for a high ROI. Depending on the VC, the return objective could be 2x, 5x, 10x, or even 50x return on investment. In addition, a VC may emphasize nonmonetary evaluative criteria, such as market dominance and the accompanying prestige. Prominent VC shops point with pride to their Internet startups that have become household names.

Entrepreneurs also want to benefit financially and enjoy the profit and power that success provides, whether through an IPO or an acquisition by a larger company—the methods of achieving this goal are numerous. Beyond monetary success, a startup that turns into a viable, sustainable business is often the primary goal for the founder. Other entrepreneurs strive to create a growing business that will triumph even in economic downturns. Finally, there are altruistic entrepreneurs, who start companies not only for the love of the experience, but also for the chance to make a contribution to society.

Whatever the motivation to start a company, the entrepreneur needs to focus on several criteria to be successful. Although these criteria are essential, they each have a different priority within the firm. An inability on the part of the startup to meet many of these objectives will increase its odds of failing. Conversely, companies may do well in spite of missing some of these elements. The startup that recognizes the need for each of these items and addresses them all is in a better position to succeed over the long haul than the startup that does not understand their importance.

First-tier priorities include having a visionary leader (usually the CEO), having management expertise (usually the president, who handles the operations of the company), and seizing a market opportunity. Second-tier priorities for startup firms are having a high-caliber workforce, a solid business plan that is adaptable and scalable, profit potential, and the ability to execute. Third-tier priorities concern organizational culture, brand, quality of funding, the ability to stay ahead of the competition, responsive customer service, and satisfactory fulfillment.

Amazon.com, though no longer considered a startup today, is a prime example of a firm that has consistently focused on all of these priorities. Although Amazon encountered substantial obstacles during the year 2000, and many analysts wondered about its long-term viability, the company certainly succeeded throughout the formative, startup phases to become the dominant online player it is today. As such, Amazon represents an ideal case for learning how to avoid early-stage failure and build a substantial enterprise:

First-tier priorities: CEO Jeff Bezos provides visionary leadership for the firm. COO Joe Galli executes the company's business plan and monitors its daily operations. Amazon.com continues to tap into previously unseen market opportunities, first with its book-selling business and now with its extended products and services.

Second-tier priorities: Amazon.com's location in Seattle enables it to take advantage of the local ecosystem and the quality workforce. With a well-conceived business plan, the company extends and leverages its customer base through affiliate programs. The business model is adaptable, as evidenced by strategic investments in relationships with retail partners such as Drugstore.com as well as the advent of the "Z-shops" where Amazon captures a part of each transaction conducted in connection with the site. Furthermore, the model is scalable: more than 17 million customers in 160-plus countries generated more than $1.6 billion in sales in 1999. Finally, by positioning itself as an online shopping portal, Amazon.com is able to add complementary business units over time.

Third-tier priorities: One of the most recognizable online brands, Amazon.com continues to leverage its name and image by recreating its first-mover advantage through such innovative services such as the affiliate program, the One-click program, and personalized recommendations. The company is the last word in online customer service. It is the most popular online retailer and 73 percent of its business is from repeat customers. Fulfillment is strong, with 99 percent of 1999 holiday orders shipped on time.

■ DIAGNOSIS: SUCCESS

We have shown how to define success and failure, and have discussed the main attributes of each. To help firms apply these lessons, we created a diagnostic tool, based on extensive field research and dialogues with investors. (See appendix A at the end of the book.) This diagnostic tool represents the elements of success against which VCs evaluate potential investments. The tool acts as a checklist for the entrepreneur and covers all the major criteria discussed in this chapter. The diagnostics are broken into early- and later-stage investment periods, because the entrepreneur and the VC must focus their energies on different factors at different growth stages of the venture. VCs and entrepreneurs weighted the different categories—management/people, market opportunity, funding, and product and service—against the importance each played in their investment decisions or business development processes.

To attempt to quantify the focus of the VCs and entrepreneurs, we presented more than 25 VCs and entrepreneurs with the diagnostic tool and had them provide input as to how they actually allocated their time or what time allocation they advocated. The results of that diagnostic analysis (see Figures 3.1 and 3.2) indicate that in the early stages of a company's life, VCs placed much more emphasis on putting together the right management team and accessing the right skills and experience than on the entrepreneur. In this sense, early-stage invest-

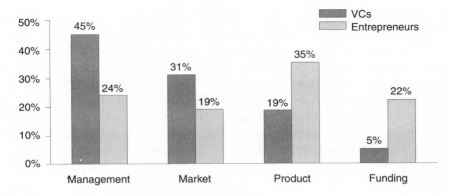

Figure 3.1   Early-stage investment period.

ment was more of a bet on the team and its ability to execute than on the idea or business model. In contrast, the entrepreneurs focused most of their time on developing the business model or the product or service offering.

Over time, this difference flattened out, with the entrepreneur's focus becoming much more aligned with that of VC. This result came about either through greater interaction between the entrepreneur and the VC community, or through a natural progression of the business, with management realizing that it needed to focus more of its time on building the company.

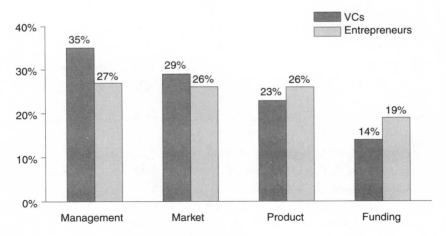

Figure 3.2   Later-stage investment period.

In today's fast-paced business environment, a startup venture faces many daunting challenges in its quest to survive and prosper. Although the basic tenets of building a successful business—strong leadership and management, good people, a solid business plan, and a product that people want to purchase—have not changed, the speed with which a company must achieve some degree of success has increased greatly. Fast money demands fast returns. Building an idea into a successful business venture, however, defines success. Entrepreneurs must ensure that they do not commit any of the fatal errors that can destroy their visions. Management teams that are too slow to act, fall prey to their own egos, or lack the skills necessary to meet the demands of the business will fail. Those that can identify problems as they occur and react with the proper remedies will lead their companies to growth and prosperity.

■ NOTE

1. Susan Moran, "*Wired* Looks for Niche in a World It Once Defined," *Internet World* (May 18, 1998).

■ REFERENCES

Amazon.com, Inc. "Amazon.com Announces Profitability in U.S.-Based Books, Financial Results Fourth Quarter 1999." Press release (February 2, 2000).

Balu, Rekha. "Starting Your Start-up: Unit of One." *Fast Company* (January 1, 2000).

Beste III, Fredrick J. "25 Entrepreneurial Death Traps." Speech at the Pittsburgh Growth Capital Conference, Pittsburgh, Pennsylvania, June 20, 1995.

Bunnell, David. *Making the Cisco Connection*. New York: John Wiley & Sons, 2000.

Case, Tony. "Condé Nast Gets *Wired*." *Folio Magazine* (June 1998).

Chan, Marcus. "Channel A Demystifies Asian Symbolism for American." *San Francisco Chronicle*, February 11, 1997, C4.

Channel A. "Channel A Launches First Internet Service in U.S. to Capitalize on Unmet Demand for Asian-Related Content, Products and Services." Press release, PR Newswire, September 24, 1996.

Coughlin, Kevin. "Hackensack's IDT Hopes to Find Magic in Genie." *The Start-Ledger*, September 23, 1996, 19.

"Disconnected, Wired Up, H&R Block Sheds Distraction." *Omaha World-Herald*, September 9, 1997, 14.

"The Failure of Nets, Inc." *Webcentric* (November 1997).

"The Fall Guys." *Business 2.0* (July 1999).

Gartner Group. "Group Identifies Five Pitfalls for eBusiness." *NUA Internet Surveys* (October 1, 1999).

Gove, Alex. "Telling Secrets." *Red Herring Magazine* (September 1997).

Greiner, Larry E. "Evolution and Revolution as Organizations Grow." *Harvard Business Review* (May-June 1998).

Harmon, Amy. "How Blind Alleys Lead Old Media to New." *New York Times*, January 16, 2000, 1.

Harvey, Phil. "Toysrus.com, eToys Buckle Under Pressure." *Red Herring Magazine* (December 29, 1999).

Hatlestad, Luc. "How Cabletron Failed." *Red Herring Magazine* (October 1999).

Hoye, David. "Can Prodigy Save a Sinking Ship? Its Future on the Web." *Arizona Republic/Phoenix Gazette*, February 5, 1996, E1.

Kovatch, Karen. "Nets Creditors Fight Jim Manzi Payment." *Pittsburgh Business Times*, week of March 16, 1998.

Loizos, Constance. "Reload." *Red Herring Magazine* (December 1997).

Lowenstein, Roger. "Being There First Isn't Good Enough." *Wall Street Journal*, May 16, 1996, C1.

Lynch, David J. "A $1.2 Billion Debacle. How Prodigy Fell from Envy to Near-Ruin." *USA Today*, May 30, 1996, B1.

Maloney, Janice. "Why *Wired* Misfired." *Columbia Journalism Review* (March/April 1998).

McManis, Sam. "Losing the Start-Up Gamble." *San Francisco Chronicle*, December 10, 1999, b-1.

Meeker, Mary, et al. "Public Internet Company Data." Morgan Stanley Dean Witter & Co., February 18, 2000.

Moore, Geoffery. "Why Companies Fail." *Red Herring Magazine* (October 1999).

Moran, Susan. "*Wired* Looks for Niche in a World It Once Defined." *Internet World* (May 18, 1998).

Patterson, Lee. "Taking it Five Ways." *Forbes ASAP* (June 2, 1997).

Pfeiffer, Eric W. "The Story of a Prodigy." *Forbes ASAP* (October 5, 1998).

Rybeck, Dan. "Conventional Rethinking: Upon Examination, Old E-Business Sayings Just Aren't What They Used to Be." *Star-Tribune Newspaper of the Twin Cities Minneapolis–St. Paul*, February 7, 2000, D3.

Seidemann, Tony. "The Fall Guys." *Business 2.0* (July 1999).

Semansky, Anna C. "Reload: Channel A Goes Off the Internet for Good." *Red Herring Magazine* (December 1998).

"When Startups Become Blowups." *Forbes.com* (February 23, 2000).

Willis, Clint. "Try, Try Again." *Forbes ASAP* (June 2, 1997).

Williams, Mark. "Pointcast of No Return." *Red Herring Magazine* (September 1999).

Chapter

4

Valuation Techniques for Internet Firms

■ INTRODUCTION

Despite the fact that most Internet companies were not generating earnings, optimism about future possibilities caused investors to fall in love with these firms. Through the beginning of 2000, this love affair resulted in unprecedented valuations and veritable investor frenzy. Some experts labeled this behavior "irrational exuberance;" others claimed that these companies were valued fairly, if not perhaps even undervalued. What was driving these valuations? How does the Internet illustrate the potential impact of economy-wide paradigm-shifting technologies on the establishment of market valuations? More generally, what yardstick is needed to fairly measure value during times of great change? During the Internet hysteria, analysts every-where scrambled to develop methodologies to explain and forecast valuations. To this end, they incorporated more qualitative metrics and subjective methods into their analyses, which naturally led to controversy in the industry. This chapter examines and analyzes cur-rent methods of valuing Internet companies and delivers a more refined, although preliminary, approach to valuing such companies in the midst of great uncertainty.

■ METHODS FOR VALUING OLD ECONOMY COMPANIES

The main methods used for valuing public Old Economy companies are discounted cash flows (DCF) and comparable company multiples. Other methods of valuation include comparable transaction multiples analyses, leveraged buyout (LBO) value, liquidation value, and EVA. DCF and comparable company multiples are the methods most frequently used by practitioners. The objective of this section is to give a brief overview of each method and then assess its applicability to the valuation of Internet companies.

➤ Discounted Cash Flows

Cash drives the value of traditional companies. A DCF approach analyzes the cash available to all capital holders before any financing. A DCF valuation is strongly tied to the fundamentals of the company, because it models the cash flow from a specific set of operating assumptions, such as growth in revenues, operating margins, capital expenditures, and working capital.

DCF is difficult to apply to the valuation of Internet companies, for several reasons. First, although DCF valuation is strongly tied to the company's fundamentals, stock prices are not; they are based on fundamentals and momentum. Second, the current pace of change in the technology sector is breathtakingly swift. Predicting next year's cash flow for a business with a very short operating history is a significant challenge. Finally, the DCF models lack flexibility.

➤ Comparable Company Multiples

To determine comparable company multiples, we look for companies with operational and financial characteristics similar to those of the company being valued. Relevant multiples for this set of comparable companies can be calculated using:

- Firm value or market value/net sales
- Firm value or market value/EBITDA (earnings before interest, taxes, depreciation, and amortization)
- Firm value or market value/EBIT (earnings before interest and taxes)
- Firm value or market value/net income (P/E)

The average or a mean of these multiples calculated for a set of comparable companies is applied to the operating results of the company being valued. However, there are several problems with using multiples for valuing Internet companies. Given the strong differences in business models, it is very difficult to find truly comparable companies. Most Internet companies have negative EBIT and net income. The only multiples that can be applied are revenue multiples.

■ CURRENT METHODS FOR VALUING NEW ECONOMY COMPANIES

Because traditional valuation methods have proven ineffective for understanding the skyrocketing stock prices of Internet companies, new approaches are being introduced to perform Internet valuation. Valuation of New Economy companies is a dynamic process, with different stages. We will first discuss pre-IPO techniques, and then look at the IPO process itself, before finally addressing current, post-IPO valuation techniques.

➤ Pre-IPO Valuation Methods

Startup companies go through a long and tedious process before they can be introduced on the stock market. The first step is to obtain initial financing from angel investors and to develop a concrete and executable business plan. Entrepreneurs then require additional financing from venture capitalists. Venture capitalists exchange financing for an equity stake in the business, based on their review of the business plan and a due diligence process. Determining a value is more art than science. Christine Comaford of Artemis Ventures described the process as "80 percent emotional, 20 percent pragmatic." To determine their equity stakes, venture capitalists look mainly at the addressable market size, recent comparable deals done by venture capitalists in the company's market, and the expected return. They also assess the entrepreneurs' ability to attract angel investors and their bargaining power (number of term sheets signed with other recognized VC firms[1]).

In a report entitled, "Three Ways to Obtaining Venture Capital," PricewaterhouseCoopers studied the required return to venture capitalists and its link to the amount of equity ownership held by the venture capitalists. Table 4.1 demonstrates the broad model, which can be refined based on the company's specific market and its competitive advantage.

As you can see from Table 4.1, to realize a 30 percent return on an investment of $2 million, a venture capitalist would need to own 24 percent of a company with an estimated market value of $40 million in 6 years. The venture capitalist needs to determine whether the company will have a $40 million valuation, based on a revenue multiple, at the end of the 6 years.

In addition to these technical parameters, other, more qualitative, factors are considered by venture capitalists in assessing a nascent company's potential. These include the company's technology, sales and marketing experience, recruiting ability (employees, board of directors, advisors, and university professors), operations, and the close-

Table 4.1 Ownership required by venture capitalists to support a 30 percent return.

Estimated future market value of a company in six years (in millions of $)	20	40	60	80	100
Millions of dollars invested			Ownership %		
$2	48%	24%	16%	12%	10%
$4	96%	48%	32%	24%	19%
$6	N/A	72%	48%	36%	29%
$8	N/A	96%	64%	48%	38%
$10	N/A	N/A	80%	60%	48%

ness of the product to shipping (and the degree to which that product is desired by consumers).

➤ Valuation Methods for the IPO Process

After finding a venture capitalist, a successful company then goes through several rounds of financing before finally going public. The value of the company increases at every round of financing and the founders' ownership gets diluted. The IPO gives rise to a new valuation of the company. At this point, venture capitalists exit and the public market takes their place, ensuring future funding and liquidity.

A prestigious bank's endorsement is essential for the success of the IPO if they are to broker the deal to investors and to have initial returns. The prestige of the investment bank is a valuable signal to investors about the capability of the new company's management, which is particularly important in times of uncertainty and when traditional metrics of value (profitability, products . . .) are not available. Investment bankers, who are willing to be the lead managers for the IPO, assess the quality of management by considering, among many parameters:

- The prior working histories of the entrepreneurs (such as the scope of their responsibilities in well-established firms)
- The progressive path to the point of the IPO (good advisors as members of the board, quality of angel investors, well-recognized venture capital firms)
- The strength of current relationships with upstream, horizontal, and downstream partners (such as a key distributor)
- The heterogeneity among the management team (leads to functional diversity and signals the ability to make strategic decisions successfully)

Conversations with venture capitalists and entrepreneurs in Silicon Valley confirm the conclusions of Monica Higgins and Ranjay Gulati of the Kellogg Graduate School of Management that, to be the successful entrepreneur of a high-growth firm, it is critical to get solid general management training and learn the trade before entering the high-technology domain. Besides gaining experience, the entrepreneur also develops key relationships and affiliations that will positively influence the decisions of third parties when he or she launches a startup.

➤ Post-IPO Current Valuation Methods

Once New Economy companies are quoted on a stock market, numerous valuation methods can be employed, including multiples analysis, metrics, qualitative factors, and backward DCF valuation.

Multiples Analysis

Multiples are ratios derived from the financial statements and the stock price. The most common multiple used to compare Internet companies and arrive at a price multiple is the revenues multiple (defined as market value or firm value/revenues). This multiple measures how many times its revenue the company is worth. Table 4.2 shows examples of revenue multiples assigned to portal companies. The use of revenue multiples is widespread because most Internet firms do not have earnings, so multiples such as P/E cannot be used. In addition, in today's hyper-growth environment, market share is a key driver of value, and revenue is a good indicator of market share.

There are limitations to revenue multiples, however. First, no matter how revenue recognition methods differ, if we want to apply multiples to revenue numbers, we must take steps to ensure that these

Table 4.2 Revenue multiples for portal companies.

Company	Mkt Value/ LTM Rev	Mkt Value/ 2000 Rev	Mkt Value/ 2001 Rev
About.com	63.6	14.4	6.6
AOL	27.4	19.3	18.6
Ask Jeeves	248.9	44.9	21.1
Excite@Home	60.8	18.5	10.7
Goto.com	276.2	60.2	31.1
Looksmart	78.6	31	17.7
Lycos	48.2	26.6	N/A
Yahoo!	156.7	106.8	78.9
Minimum	**27.4**	**14.4**	**6.6**
Mean	**120.1**	**40.2**	**26.4**
Median	**71.1**	**28.8**	**18.6**
Maximum	**276.2**	**106.8**	**78.9**

Source: Deutsche Bank.

revenues are recurring. There are five red flags to watch for when using revenue multiples:

1. Earnings versus cash flow disparity—when net income is much higher than cash flow from operations
2. Unsustainable sales—nonrecurring sales that generate one-off revenue streams
3. Large reserves—companies setting aside income to bolster flagging earnings later
4. Deferred expenses—timing mismatches between revenue and expenses
5. Acquired profits—earnings growing due largely to acquisitions

All these factors point to potentially unsustainable earnings that require further examination before multiples are applied to the reported numbers. In general, the matching principle, which stipulates that revenues be recognized in the same period expenses are incurred, should be applied. Otherwise, a company might be overvalued. In late March 2000, MicroStrategy's stock price dropped by 60 percent in a single day when the company announced a restatement of its prior years' income, because of violation of the matching principle.

Another limitation is that revenues multiples do not reflect other key value drivers, such as gross margins, as can be illustrated by comparing eBay and Ubid. Both eBay and Ubid are considered auction houses. They had comparable 1999 revenues: $225 million for eBay and $205 for Ubid. Yet eBay currently trades at 80x revenues, with a market cap of $18 billion, whereas Ubid trades at just over 1x revenues with a market cap of $320 million. eBay is a virtual marketplace that has very high margins (approximately 85 percent), as it earns commissions on products sold through its site and never takes possession of the goods sold (nor does it take responsibility for delivery of the goods sold). This business model is extremely scalable, and does not require increasing amounts of working capital for the company to grow very quickly. In comparison, Ubid is an e-tailer of computer-related products and carries a large inventory on its books. Ubid has low margins (approximately 9 percent), significant inventory risk, and requires large infusions of working capital to sustain its high growth rate. The market has recognized the difference in these business plans and valued them accordingly.

Metrics

In addition to examining revenue multiples, an investor needs to analyze several other metrics to refine and adjust a valuation. *Metrics* are
ratios that usually do not involve figures from financial statements;
rather, they look at key operational value drivers of the company. For
example, some of the most commonly followed metrics are enterprise
value/unique users, as well as the reach of a Web site. Examples of
four business models (portals, ISP, B2B, and B2C) are shown in Table
4.3. The lists are by no means exhaustive for any of these categories,
but do show a few of the more important metrics being used.

To understand which metrics to apply, the analyst must look at what
drives a company's revenues, as well as its business model. It is important to understand which areas should be growing the fastest and what
the expectations are for these metrics.

An important metric in this context is *unique user multiples*. This
method is based on the monthly statistics in the United States and MMXI
in Europe that are published by MediaMetrix, Inc. These companies
provide data on the number of different individuals who visit a Web

Table 4.3   Business model/metrics comparison.

Business Model	Revenue Driver	Types of Metrics Used
Portal	Advertisement	Ad revenue/page viewed; Ad revenue/registered user; Ad revenue/advertiser; Number of advertisers and reach
ISP	Subscriptions and advertisement	Subscriber addition; Time spent on site/subscriber; Firm value/subscription
B2B	All B2B (selling and market makers)	Revenue/customer; Revenue/transaction; Gross profit per order
B2B and B2C	Selling companies	Purchase frequency; Customer acquisition cost; Customer maintenance cost

site in a given month, counting them only once regardless of the number of times they visit during the month. *Reach* is defined as the number of unique users divided by the total number of home Internet users in the given territory; it shows the amount of penetration by a Web site within a region and is an important metric in understanding how attractive a Web site is to advertisers.

Another closely followed metric for many new Internet companies is *customer acquisition cost*. This metric is defined as the amount spent on sales and marketing divided by the number of customers or subscribers. Almost three-quarters of all Internet company expenses involve sales and marketing, so this metric is key in gauging the success of a firm's ability to attract consumers and is of particular importance for B2B and B2C companies.

Qualitative Factors

Qualitative factors are emerging as an increasingly critical component in determining the valuation of a firm. They are used by analysts to temper and justify the enthusiasm (or hype) associated with Internet valuations. Qualitative factors can be classified into four main categories: top-line growth, customer base and human resources, business model characteristics, and the quality of management.

Top-line growth. Top-line growth addresses revenue growth potential and includes several different facets: market size, strong industry growth, a growing customer base, relationships with key customers and suppliers, and low employee turnover.

The size of the market is one of the strongest indications of a company's potential revenue. The bigger the market, the better the revenue-generating prospects. Firms operating in a large and growing market are often awarded a premium that is directly linked to their growth potential. "For the seeable future, almost all B2B market makers are likely to continue to appear small relative to the huge market opportunities they address. Investors will ascribe extremely high multiples to the companies for which potential market opportunities look far from saturation."[2]

Overall industry growth and growth in certain subsectors of the market are important as well. Indeed, much of the valuation of individual companies reflects the strong anticipated growth of the entire sector.

Customer base is defined as the number of users of the company's

Web site, and is one of the key determinants of long-term success. A growing customer base indicates successful scalability of the product. Estimates are that it is 20 times more expensive to attract a new customer than it is to keep an existing one, so attracting and maintaining a large customer base is clearly a strong indicator for expanding sales of new products and services.

In terms of valuation, high-quality customers that generate a large number of transactions at relatively higher margins are more valuable than those that are less profitable or more costly to serve. Dividing the value of transactions by the number of transactions (*average transaction value*) allows an estimate of how much money a company can potentially earn per transaction.

In addition to growing the overall customer base, retaining key customers and selling them more services are important to every line of business (*penetration*). Losing a key customer can be devastating. Higher value is placed on companies that are able to secure positions with strategic customers, or on companies that have a relatively small individual customer risk because they have numerous customers. Concerning supplier power, we would place more value on industry leaders that have a large number of weak suppliers, because they can take advantage of opportunities to secure better terms from these suppliers, thereby enhancing profitability.

Employee turnover is notoriously difficult to track, especially at the programmer level. Abnormally high employee turnover, particularly at the management level, can be interpreted by the market as a sign of internal distress and can ultimately spook investors. Attracting and retaining computer-savvy talent at the programmer level is no easy task in today's Internet-frenzied and tight labor market.

Business model. Thorough analysis of the business model itself is central in determining the potential value of a company. The winning equation for the business model seems to be based on a limited number of characteristics:

- Easy to understand and implement
- Scalable
- Able to handle a large number of transactions
- Number 1 or number 2 in its space; has a first-mover advantage

- Adaptable to sectors with high-value transactions, such as the auto and electronics industries

Management. In our view, companies will be rewarded for the same factors that leading offline entities have mastered. These include skill in logistics, efficient sales force management, good supplier relationships, effective customer retention strategies, and an ability to use strategic partnerships as vehicles to enter noncore markets. The unifying force integrating these different areas is management.

The sidebar featuring Merrill Lynch's top 10 questions to B2B market makers is an example of the type of qualitative screening a leading investment bank uses to assess the value of an Internet company. It shows that the 10 key questions traditionally asked by Merrill Lynch include several designed to size up the company's management.[3] In short, however, according to most VCs and investors there is no strict method for linking qualitative factors and quantitative valuation. Weighted coefficients are generally not used to value the different qualitative factors (such as the number of years of management experience in the industry, the number of managers having a startup background, etc.).

Merrill Lynch's Top 10 Questions to Ask B2B Market Makers

(*Market makers* are intermediaries and include catalogs, auctions, exchange, and communities.)

1. **How large is the industry (gross sales, U.S. and worldwide)? How much of it do you think will be transacted through a B2B market maker? Why?**

Many market makers just assume that 10 percent to 40 percent of gross sales will go through market makers. In many cases, though, especially in industries with low fragmentation, there is little reason to use a market maker. Market makers must

(continued)

(i) solve specific, identifiable problems and (ii) add value to both the buy and sell side of the supply chain, or the industry will just ignore them.

2. **How fragmented are the buy and supply sides of the industry?**

Industries with a high level of fragmentation on both the buy and sell sides are the best for market-maker adoption, because a market-maker can add value simply as an aggregator.

3. **How inefficient are procurement, sales, and distribution in the industry?**

The promise of the marketplace is, in part, to cut the fat. Thus, it helps if the industry is chubby to begin with.

4. **What specific industry problems can a third party solve for the buy and sell side?**

The best market-makers will identify specific buy- and sell-side problems that they can solve, as well as future problems that they expect to be able to solve. Using a market maker requires a change in corporate behavior, and changing behavior is difficult. As a result, market makers who show that they can "ease pain" immediately (provide obvious, identifiable, and quantifiable advantages) will likely see faster adoption than those that do not.

5. **How much of a change in behavior does using your marketplace require on the part of suppliers and buyers?**

The less the better, unless you can convince the company to pay millions of dollars for software licenses and installation. In that case, it will be easy to force changes in behavior, because the company risks losing its investment otherwise.

(continued)

6. **What are your transactions today? How are they ramped? What is the strategy for generating industry-leading liquidity (transaction volume through the marketplace)?**

The slickest, most highly functional marketplace is worthless if buyers and sellers congregate to do business somewhere else.

7. **What portion of your management team is from the industry you address? Do senior people have strong relationships at the highest level with industry players?**

Even in the Internet industry, people like to do business with people they know and like. This is especially true in the case of market makers, which initially might seem to be less friend than foe.

8. **How do you intend to induce the participation of suppliers, particularly large ones?**

Big suppliers are usually critical to gaining liquidity (who wants to shop at a market that does not carry most of the products?). They are also the least likely participants to need a third-party market maker, especially early on. Having clear strategies for signing them up is therefore critical to success.

9. **Are other B2B market makers addressing this industry? Are you ahead of or behind them in terms of transactions, revenues, and buyer and supplier relationships? Why?**

This question will likely lead to a winner-take-most game. The aim is to identify the market leader as quickly as possible and to put your eggs in its basket.

10. **Do middlemen in the industry add significant value? If so, how do you plan to work with them? Have you partnered with the key distribution and logistics providers?**

(continued)

> You can buy and sell things all day long, but when you are
> done transacting, you still have to ship the products. Depend-
> ing on the industry, some intermediaries will continue to add
> value in a market-maker world; others will not. The best mar-
> ket makers will partner with intermediaries who add value, and
> slowly but surely, take away market share from the ones who
> do not.

➤ **Backward DCF**

Backward DCF is used mainly as a reality check to verify the multiples
and metrics used to value firms. Backward DCF takes the stock price
of a company and uses it as a base to determine what hypotheses have
been used to come up with that stock price. Analysts can therefore
determine the key parameters used, such as revenue growth in the su-
pernormal growth period, the gross margins, the discount rate used,
and the growth rate of earnings in perpetuity.

■ REAL OPTIONS

In the New Economy, managerial decisions fundamentally affect a
company's success—venture capitalists themselves admit that their
decisions to invest are often driven by the quality of the management
team. Recognizing this, investors and venture firms are paying increasing attention to the real options approach to valuation of Internet
startups. This approach takes into account managerial flexibility to
delay, modify, or expand decisions beyond the value determined by
DCF; in essence, the real options approach to valuation attempts to
quantify managerial flexibility. This is a powerful tool because of its
promise to precisely price flexibility in uncertain environments. The
research of Fischer Black, Robert Merton, and Myron Scholes on value
options revolutionized the financial markets. If these same concepts
can be transferred from finance to valuation of companies, flexible
managerial decisions can be priced as part of a portfolio of well-defined options.

McKinsey & Company has previously applied option pricing to a
variety of asset option situations in which flexibility was critical. In one
case, the option value of a large mineral lease was 100 percent higher

than its simple net present value (NPV). The option to defer development until the mineral price rose made the value much higher than indicated by NPV analysis. Similar methodology can be applied to valuing Internet startups, as companies that venture into the vast unknown can be thought of as having a portfolio of real options.

In financial markets, an option gives its owner the right, but not the obligation, to buy or sell a security at a given price. Likewise, a company that owns a real option has the right, but not the obligation, to make a potentially value-adding decision to invest, expand, defer, or abandon. For example, Amazon.com's e-commerce expertise and customer franchise in the book business gave it valuable real options to invest in the e-commerce markets for music, movies, and gifts. The key here is to remember that the options are not exercised when they are not valuable, so the maximum downside loss is known but the upside is virtually unlimited.

This chapter does not intend to delve into all the technical issues surrounding the pricing of real options. Real options modeling and pricing are extremely complex, and are currently the topics of study by full-time mathematical and financial researchers (who are experts in stochastic calculus and statistical theories). Rather, our objective is to give an overview of this powerful approach, discuss its various strengths and weaknesses, and give a very straightforward valuation example. The chapter will wrap up with a discussion of the applicability of real options in New Economy company valuation.

➤ Real Option Models and Inputs

We can account for at least four types of real options in valuing any company:

1. Option to abandon: a managerial option to divest a given venture or project.

2. Option to defer: call option to invest in the future if a given venture or project is deemed valuable for additional investment; the value of "wait and see."

3. Option to expand or contract: option to commit further if a given venture or project is deemed valuable or to scale down investment in the future if not.

4. Option to switch: ability to change amongst modes or states of operation.

Whichever model we use for valuing options, we need a minimum of five basic inputs to calculate the price of an option. The first is the *strike price*, which is the exercise price of the option. The second is *time to expiration*, which is the time limit in which the option can be exercised. The third is *volatility*, which is the market-perceived variation in price for a given security within a given timeframe. The fourth is the *spot price*, which is the price of the security at time of option transaction. The last is the *risk-free interest rate*.

As an example, let us assume that you wish to buy an option to purchase 100 shares of Microsoft, expiring in 3 months. The strike price is the price at which you can exercise the option. Suppose that Microsoft is now trading at $120, and your strike price is $145—you will exercise the option in 3 months if and only if the traded price of Microsoft is above $145. Time to expiration is the second component of the option, defining the timeframe in which you can exercise the option—three months in this case. Volatility is given by the market's anticipation of the fluctuation of the Microsoft stock price in the next three months. This determines how likely it is that the price of Microsoft will wind up above $145 within 3 months. Spot price is the current value of Microsoft's stock, which is $120. The risk-free interest rate is usually determined by the U.S. Treasury yield curve; in this case it would be the rate of the three-month Treasury bill.

➤ Pricing Real Options

In pricing derivative securities for equities, bonds, foreign exchange, and commodities, the five basic inputs are relatively easy to determine. The strike price and the time are defined by investor preference, option volatility is actively traded in the free market, and the spot price and interest rate are readily available market information.

In pricing managerial flexibility, however, these parameters are much more difficult to define. For example, how would you know what the strike price is under an option to expand operations? How would you determine the volatility of an option to defer an investment decision? Nevertheless, if we want to delve into the practical issues of actually quantifying managerial flexibility, a systematic way of determining these inputs is absolutely critical. Hence, a discussion of the methods of and difficulties in determining these five inputs in pricing real options is in order.

1. *Determination of strike price.* Unlike the over-the-counter (OTC) financial options market, where market players can simply choose discrete option strikes, a real option strike price must be determined through a disciplined approach. The concept that managers possess flexibility in decision making is nothing new, but the problem is actually defining the exact flexibility they possess so that we can quantify the portfolio of flexibility.

   Take a hypothetical example. Thomson Company, which specializes in selling travel maps, decides to go into the business of selling online maps through the Internet. Based on its sales forecasts, Thomson believes that the online business can generate up to $8 million in revenues from 1 million customers per year. Further assume that Thomson needs to generate at least $5 million per year for this to be a viable business. In valuing the exit option regarding the Internet business, management can determine the strike price of its option to abandon the project if the revenue for the first year is less than $5 million.

2. *Determination of time to expiration.* Again, in OTC option markets, the expiration date of options can be chosen at will, but managerial real option expirations are chosen through a disciplined process. In this case, the manager must determine exactly when a decision must be made before the start of a project.

   Let us go back to our Thomson example. Under the exit-option scenario, the time to expiration (when the manager must make a decision to continue or abandon) is one year. This is a deliberately chosen date upon which the manager will assess the situation and take a disciplined action.

3. *Determination of volatility.* In OTC option markets, individual option volatilities are actively posted and are traded like other financial securities with bid/ask spreads. In real options, the volatility of a decision is determined through comparables.

   If we return to our hypothetical Thomson Company, we can determine the volatility through comparable businesses—specifically, the volatility of revenues. In mathematical terms, we need to determine the standard deviation of the next year's revenue stream. We can do this by checking the historical volatility of earnings with similar online companies. The more similar the operations, the better the information. If there are no directly comparable companies (i.e., no map companies have ever sold maps online), then we will need to research across different companies to deduce our volatility. For instance, we might take a cross-section of B2C companies that have target markets of 1 million customers, and a cross-section of B2C companies with approximately $8 million revenues to assess their revenue volatility. These kinds of analyses are similar to existing project finance methodologies in determining appropriate discount rates.

4. *Determination of spot price.* OTC markets are efficient enough to have spot markets for trading of individual companies. In our real options example, the spot price must be determined through forecasts and data from comparable companies.

   In the Thomson case, the spot price would be the discounted cash flow value in one year. That is, we calculate the present value of the cash flow from the expected revenue in one year. The expected revenue can be determined by the combination of using Thomson's best estimates and using revenue information from comparable companies. In addition, we can also use regression analysis to obtain the expected revenue after researching for the right independent variables from comparable companies.

5. *Determination of risk-free interest rate.* Both the OTC market and real options use the same risk-free rate. We can easily determine this by looking up the current interest rate of the three-month U.S. T-bill.

In our example, Thomson Company appears to be a company that has had fairly predictable operations but is now forming an Internet arm that carries an exit option. How do we value the company?

The valuation can be seen as valuing the sum of three parts: (1) valuation of Thomson's traditional business, using DCF; (2) valuation of Thomson's Internet arm, using DCF; and (3) valuation of Thomson's exit option.

Value of Thomson's traditional business. This part is relatively easy. We can look at historical earnings, project the growth of the business, and then choose a comparable discount rate for a DCF value. The DCF method was discussed in some detail in the previous section, so we will not restate it here. Assume that after our analysis, the traditional business is valued at $200 million.

For parts 2 and 3, the value of the Internet arm is simply the sum of discounted cash flow plus its portfolio of real options. In this case, the option is the exit option. Of course, many options exist within a company, and it is simply a matter of discipline that we identify them one by one. For simplicity of illustration, we assume that Thomson has only one option.

Value of Thomson's Internet arm excluding option values. The methodology is roughly the same as for the valuation of the traditional business (part 1 of our analysis). The problem here is that most Internet startups have DCF values close to zero, or even negative. That is because DCF ignores option values completely. For part 2, assume that we obtain a value of $2 million after DCF.

Value of Thomson's exit option on its Internet arm. Now we go back to our five basic inputs in real option pricing: strike price, time to expiration, volatility, spot price, and risk-free interest rate.

1) Strike price: $5 million
2) Time to expiration: 1 year
3) Volatility: comparable B2C companies have very volatile revenue streams. The average volatility is 50 percent.
4) Spot price: after scaling for size differences of comparable B2C companies, the expected revenue for the first year is calculated to be $8 million. This must be discounted back to year zero. Assuming a comparable discount rate of 55 percent, the spot price is $5.16 million.
5) Risk-free interest rate: 3-month T-bill is 5.8 percent.

According to Table 4.4, the option is worth $769,000. In sum, Thomson Company is worth $200 + $2 + $0.769 = $202.77 million. In our example, we assumed that Thomson has one real option, but most New Economy companies possess a whole portfolio of real options. If we can use a disciplined approach to identify a given company's obvious real options, we will probably find that these companies are comprised mostly of real-options values.

Table 4.4   The basic Black-Scholes model.

$$d_1 = \frac{\ln(S/X) + (r + \sigma^2/2)t}{\sigma\sqrt{t}}$$

$$p = Xe^{-rt}N(-d_2) - SN(-d_1)$$

$$d_2 = \frac{\ln(S/X) + (r - \sigma^2/2)t}{\sigma\sqrt{t}} = d_1 - \sigma\sqrt{t}$$

The exit option is priced as a European Put Option, so our general equation is the second equation. The actual calculations:

Spot	5.160	*Put Price:*	*0.769*
Strike	5.000	Put Delta:	−0.334
Volatility	0.500		
Interest rate	0.058		
Time	1.000		

LN (S/X)	Vol^2/2	d_1	$N(d_1)$	$N(-d_1)$
0.0315	0.125	0.429	0.666037	0.334

d_2	$N(d_2)$	$N(-d_2)$	exp(−rt)	
−0.071	0.4717	0.5283	0.9436	

➤ Issues with Real Options

There are generally three major difficulties with valuation using the real options approach. The first is the difficulty in defining exactly what managerial flexibility a company possesses. The second is the difficulty in determining input variables for option valuation, because of the lack of comparables in New Economy companies. The third is complexity. In our Thomson Company example, we simplified many variables; in valuing a real company, however, the analysis will be far more complex.

In valuing managerial flexibility, the first prerequisite is to understand and define exactly what options the company possesses. Of course, this is often easier said than done. For example, what flexibility does Amazon.com have, given that it has 6 million customers? It can obviously go into other B2C businesses, but what exactly would those businesses be? Saying that we wish to value the entire portfolio of managerial real options is almost like saying we want to value all possible contingencies. The only solution is to value some of a company's major options.

The second difficulty is in determining exactly what the five inputs should be, even after we have clearly defined our real option. For example, what if a company has a completely new business model such that no real comparables can be found?

The third difficulty is complexity. Valuation of real options is tremendously time-consuming and complex. It is also expensive—there are not many people in the world who truly understand real option theories, so hiring a team of specialists would be extremely costly. Therefore, instead of performing all the complex analyses, individuals applying valuation methods tend to prefer the simplicity of revenue multiples and qualitative metrics.

■ WAVE THEORY

Wave theory is another interesting method that is currently used on the trading floor—but not by research analysts. We believe this theory provides insight into valuing Internet companies because it allows for the rapidly changing competitive landscape, technological advances, investors' psychology, and the huge uncertainties involved in early startups.

➤ Background of Wave Theory

Wave theory is not new. Ralph Nelson Elliott invented it in the 1930s. In 1927, Elliott compiled and began analyzing every bit of hourly, daily, weekly, and monthly stock market data he could find, some of it dating back to the 1850s. After a few years of painstaking research, he began to fit together the missing pieces of a fascinating puzzle. Elliott observed, "[H]uman emotions are rhythmical. They move in waves of a definite number and direction. The phenomenon occurs in all human activities, whether business, politics, or the pursuit of pleasure. It is particularly evident in those free markets where public participation in price movements is extensive."[4]

Elliott isolated five types of different waves in the stock price that showed the investors' psychological impact on stock performance. For example, when a new trend begins, a few well-informed or lucky traders will spearhead the market in what will later be seen as the start of a larger move, which will move the stock price up. After a subsequent downward trend, caused by hesitancy and doubts as to whether the trend will be dominant, the traders who were left out become convinced by the trend and decide to buy into the rally, thus fueling the premium of the stock price. This is precisely the situation of the current stock premium given to high-tech firms. This theory shows that "mankind's progress (of which the stock market is a popularly determined valuation) does not occur in a straight line, does not occur randomly, and does not occur cyclically. Rather, progress takes place in a 'three steps forward, two steps back' fashion."[5] It also implies that mass psychology has significant influence on social behaviors. As mass psychology moves from optimistic to pessimistic and back to optimistic again, stock traders can take advantage of the waves and make profits. Therefore, this theory has been widely applied in the technical analysis of stock markets.

➤ Application to Valuation

If we agree that there are patterns in Internet economies, how can we isolate those patterns and quantify their momentum? Let's examine whether there are any similarities between Internet economies and waves. From physics, we know that velocity = wavelength x frequency (see Figure 4.1). We found we could draw an analogy:

"Internet Madness" = Potential of technology application × Frequency of technology innovation and speed to market

Equation 3

We found a similar property with the interaction of waves. Figure 4.2 shows a constructive interference example. When two waves of the same wavelength and frequency occur in the same place, they will affect each other. If their crests and troughs occur in the same place, the end result can be calculated by adding the two waves together: the resulting wave will have increased amplitude. Analogously, we think the rekindling of investor interest, occurring concomitantly with the advancement of high technology, sparked the high-flying valuation of high-tech firms such as Ariba and CommerceOne.

However, when multiple waves come together, they do not always create positive effects. Figure 4.3 is an example of destructive interfer-

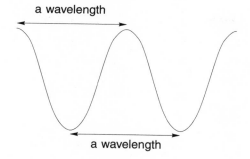

Wavelength
The distance between a vibrating particle and the nearest one to it in the same place (the identical point on an adjacent wave). This is also the distance between two troughs or two crests.

Frequency (f)
The rate of reoccurrence of vibration, oscillation, or cycle. This can be considered the number of complete oscillations in a vibrating system that occur in unit time.

Wave velocity (c or v)
The speed of the wave in the direction it is traveling. The velocity of a wave will depend on the medium in which it is traveling. (For example, you can feel the vibration of a train coming on the tracks far sooner than you can actually hear the train.)

Figure 4.1 Wavelength.

ence. If the crest of one wave occurs at the trough of another and the waves have the same amplitude, they will cancel each other out and the resulting wave will be zero. Analogously, if the current business models are built solely on the existing technology, when the technology infrastructure leapfrogs existing technology, the business models will soon become dinosaurs if they cannot proactively adapt to the new environment. Similarly, for many people, it is difficult to conceive that

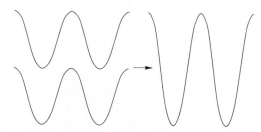

Figure 4.2 Constructive interference.

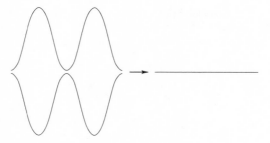

Figure 4.3   Destructive interference.

the B2C segment lost its luster so soon. We can ascribe this to destructive interference between two differently timed waves that resulted in a significant decline in interest in the B2C segment.

➤ The Power Law

A 1999 article in the *Wall Street Journal* described a new pattern discovered by Michael Mauboussin, chief investment strategist at Credit Suisse First Boston (CSFB), who considered the valuation of Internet stocks relative to one another. Among Internet stocks, he said, "There is literally a mathematical relationship between the ranking of the stock and its capitalization." If we do not try to justify the high prices investors are willing to pay for Internet stocks as a group, we can see how so much of the stock-market value of Internet companies is clustered into just a handful of companies. A mere 1 percent of the 400 companies in the sector account for 40 percent of its $900 billion value in the stock market (see Figure 4.4.)

Mauboussin graphed the companies' values and rankings (relative to one another) on an ordinary chart and found that the results gave a hockey-stick-like pattern: a couple of companies in the multiple-billions of dollars, and everything else clustered close to zero. Using some slightly different but relatively simple math, he found that each company's value bore a predictable relationship to the others. He could not find a pattern like this in any other sector. "I don't know why it works for this sector, but it suggests a couple of things," Mauboussin said. "One, there is a little method to the madness of how the market values these things. More important, these are winner-take-all or winner-take-most markets." The pattern emerges when the companies'

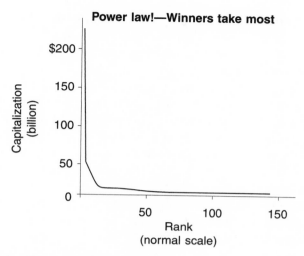

Figure 4.4   The power law.

values are plotted along with their market-capitalization ranks on a logarithmic chart. On such a chart, each inch equals a similar percentage change. For example, the distance between 100 and 1,000 is the same as that from 1,000 to 10,000, because both moves represent a 900 percent increase. This is the characteristic of a "power law," normally found only when measuring natural or social phenomena. Mauboussin's colleagues looked for something similar in eight other sectors, including financial companies and utilities. They found the pattern in spots, but nowhere as consistently as with Internet stocks. CSFB's research was inspired in part by work at the Xerox Palo Alto Research Center, which found a power-law relationship between Web site usage and ranking. It found that the top 0.1 percent of sites got 32 percent of usage, the top 1 percent got 56 percent, and the top 10 percent got 82 percent. The values of the companies themselves followed the same pattern. Mauboussin's new theory is still controversial. However, he found that the key takeaway of his analysis is that Internet stocks are correctly valued relative to each other—rather than boldly stating that the overall sector is appropriately valued. But he also suggested that his analysis indicated that the Internet sector is not as overvalued as most analysts warned. Although the average value of an Internet company at the time of his analysis was about $500 million, that figure was distorted by the enormous values of a handful of entities. The median value was just $53 million—suggesting that the market indicated that the vast majority of Internet companies were actually worth much less. Mauboussin's argument that the Internet sector might not have been as overvalued as many analysts contended seems to have been contradicted by the massive falloff in valuations during the last three quarters of 2000. His first assertion, however, merits more consideration. It could very well be that Internet-related companies were fairly valued *relative* to each other, but were buoyed overall by the Internet hysteria. In retrospect, the sector "madness" reflected the combination of significant uncertainty with the accurate but vague realization that the economic changes arising from the Internet revolution were real and substantial. Although reality seems to have returned by late 2000, it is unclear to what extent the markets have developed effective mechanisms to achieve more accurate long-term valuations for companies in sectors characterized by significant uncertainty. In examining the period discussed by Mauboussin, if we say that B2C and B2B are different waves of different segments of the New Economy, we could say that the newly found power law would allow us to estimate the height of the crest of the wave. If it is a winners-take-most situation, we could try to identify which firms will be the top players in each segment and value them accordingly. The timing of valuation is critical to accuracy, because the current Internet companies are "floating" on a wave that goes up and down not year by year, but month by month. Valuation based on this model is much more difficult to perform than if using a straightforward DCF approach. However, the power law may offer alternative insights, whereas the DCF method does not seem to tell the entire story.

■ A PRELIMINARY APPROACH TO VALUING AMAZON.COM

Having considered the current valuation methodologies used by research analysts, we developed our own approach to valuing New Economy companies, which we will demonstrate by analyzing Amazon.com. First, we will perform a top-down approach, and then apply a bottom-up approach to check for convergent modeling and refine the results.

In applying the top-down approach, we use detailed qualitative analyses to refine the price/revenue multiples assigned. No matter how successful some companies are, they all possess very different management teams, business models, costs, margins, and so on. Through rigorous qualitative analysis, we can further refine the multiples to resolve more subtle differences between comparable companies' values. The second step is to use the bottom-up approach to cross-check and improve the valuation accuracy. The bottom-up approach provides accurate numbers from financial statements so that we can determine the company's current financial health. In today's fast-paced environment, these historical numbers are not always indicative of the future, but the approach is useful when combined with the top-down approach to justify the multiples or growth rates. The top-down approach offers a big picture of the company's value, assuming that the current information reveals predictions for the near future. We then build on this insight using the more precise bottom-up approach to refine the result. By combining two approaches that focus on different stages of a single company, a more accurate value can be achieved than with only one. The following example calculates the value of Amazon.com in December 1998—a period in which the company sold only books. We then show a historical valuation exercise to verify the accuracy of our calculations for the market capitalization of Amazon.com for that time period.

➤ Top-Down Approach

The top-down approach consists of assessing the value of a company by starting with an estimate of the overall market size and then determining the market capitalization of the company (see Table 4.5).

Here are the steps used for the top-down approach:

1. Estimate the total market size of online book sales in 2005 of $8.9 billion.

2. Estimate the market share of Amazon in 2005 for books of 40 percent. This estimate is based on the current online books market share of 70 percent and the increasing competition estimated in the next years.

3. From the total market size and the market share of Amazon.com, we obtain Amazon.com's revenues in 2005.

4. We determined a revenue multiple in 2005 using a benchmark of comparable companies, which we estimated at 20. (See the next section, "Qualitative Analysis.")

Table 4.5 Step-by-step using top-down valuation approach.

Description	(Books only)
Amazon's addressable market size online 2005	$8.9 billion
Amazon's market share of online market	40%
Amazon's revenues 2005	$3.6 billion
Revenue multiple	20x
Market capitalization 2005	$71.2 billion
Discounted market capitalization 2000[†]	$16.6 billion

All estimates are from Salomon Smith Barney.
[†]Discount rate based on the CAPM formula:
$$Re = rf + (rm - rf)Be = 5.795 + (7\% * 2.48) = 23.16\%$$

5. We obtain the market capitalization of Amazon in 2005 of $71.2 billion.

6. Discount this market capitalization for five years at an appropriate discount rate. The discount rate of 23.16 percent was calculated using the capital asset pricing model (CAPM).

7. The value of the market capitalization, as of December 1998, is estimated at $16.6 billion.

➤ Qualitative Analysis

Amazon.com was founded on the notion that it could compete in the book retail business, and the firm possesses all the positive qualitative aspects of a promising Internet business. As the first significant player on the Internet, it was at the forefront of a large and rapidly growing market. The competitive landscape at that time was also promising; investors' confidence was very high and that confidence drove the stock value up. Further, Amazon.com's business model was relatively straightforward and its site was designed for ease of use. Compared to traditional retailing, Amazon.com's business model had strong competitive advantages (namely, purchase convenience, large variety of products, and price). Amazon.com also clearly secured the first-mover advantage (largest customer base and the best brand awareness in the book e-tailing business). In addition, Amazon's business model was very scalable, because it could easily expand its retail activity to other products, such as CDs and videos.

On the management side, Amazon.com possesses a strong team. The operating model focuses on serving customers, and the team has strategic vision and proven ability for execution. Jeff Bezos, founder and CEO, showed his vision and leadership by pushing the company's concept and operations through various critical strategic phases, such as the diversification of e-tailing products and services. All key positions are held by experienced managers with proven track records in blue-chip companies. Among them are Joe Galli, COO, who during his 19 years with Black & Decker served as president of the Worldwide Tools and Accessories division; Warren Janson, CFO, who gained valuable experience as CFO and vice president of Delta Air Lines; and Rick Dalzell, CIO, who came to Amazon.com after serving as vice president of information systems at Wal-Mart. Other members include David Risher, vice president of product development, who managed Microsoft Access and founded Microsoft's Web site for personal investments before going to Amazon; and finally Jeff Wilke, Amazon.com's general manager of operations, whose background includes time spent as general manager of AlliedSignal's Pharmaceutical Fine Chemicals unit.

➤ Bottom-Up Approach

In addition to the top-down approach, we calculated the market capitalization of Amazon.com using a bottom-up approach. The bottom-up approach starts at the micro-level (i.e., using metrics) to determine the market capitalization of the company. As described in Table 4.6, we first estimated the number of sales per customer at the end of 1999 at $100, and then multiplied this number by the number of customers at the end to obtain the sales figures in 1999, $1,544 million. A multiple of 10 times next year's sales (1999) determined the market capitalization of $15.4 million at the end of 1998. The valuation of $16.6 million performed under the top-down approach is in line with the valuation of $15.4 billion calculated by the bottom-up approach.

➤ Applying Wave Theory to Quantify Momentum

The value of a company is not static, but rather floats on waves. Because using multiples is a popular approach in valuation, we believe the specific multiple we apply to a company should also change to reflect

Table 4.6 Bottom-up approach to valuation.

$ in thousands except customer ratios, margins, and stock price

	1996	1997	1998	1999 (est.)	2000 (est.)	2001 (est.)	2002 (est.)
Net sales	15,746	147,787	609,820	1,543,946	2,704,560	3,931,916	5,511,481
COGS	12,287	118,969	476,155	1,243,682	2,151,921	3,066,895	4,298,955
Gross profit	3,459	28,818	133,665	300,264	552,639	865,021	1,212,526
Operating expenses	9,866	60,201	194,699	623,908	868,331	990,843	1,157,411
Inc. mktg. expenses	6,081	40,075	132,704	408,809	527,249	629,107	771,607
Operations net	(6,407)	(31,383)	(61,034)	(323,644)	(315,692)	(125,822)	55,115
Customer accounts	180	1,510	6,200	15,512	22,920	31,047	40,034
New accounts	180	1,330	4,690	9,312	7,408	8,127	8,987
Sales/customer	87	98	98	100	118	127	138
GP/customer	19	19	22	19	24	28	30
Sales & mktg/cust	34	27	21	26	23	20	19
Gross margin	22%	19%	22%	19%	20%	22%	22%
# outstanding shares	333,000	333,000	333,000	333,000	333,000	333,000	333,000
	1996	1997	1998	1999	2000	2001	
Expected stock price given 10x next year's sales	4.44	18.31	46.36	81.22	118.08	165.51	
Total market cap. (in $billions)	1.48	6.10	15.44	27.05	39.32	55.11	

where on the wave the company currently finds itself. Although long-term stock prices ultimately reflect fundamentals, the wave of technological madness has driven valuation to levels that are not easily explained by fundamentals alone. Further, it is meaningless for us to estimate the value of a company over a long period of time, such as five to ten years. So, in applying wave theory, changes in a top company's sales multiples (market capitalization over sales) can be tracked over the different time periods of a wave (inception, peak, and decline). After eliminating other abnormal effects of stock price, and assuming that its fundamental part is constant, a model indicating the change of investor psychology over a period of time reflected by the change of its sales multiple emerges.

This valuation method rests on several key assumptions:

1. That the market capitalization of each segment, the market capitalization of each top player in that segment, and the sales revenue of each top player all have relationships expressed by some multiples, and that these multiples evolve over time and can be measured.

2. That historical waves, such as the B2C wave, can be used as references to value B2B, application service providers (ASPs), wireless, or other future waves.

3. The power law applies to the valuation of different players within the same segment. If assumptions 1 and 2 hold true, then we would refine the multiples (P/S or P/E) using historical waves to value individual segments or firms at a certain point in time to obtain a more accurate valuation.

If total discounted market size of each segment, total segment market capitalization at the time of valuation, and total sales of the segment all have a constant relationship, we will have a very interesting tool to estimate revenue multiples at a specific time. For example, last February, the discounted market size of online B2C was $100 billion, and total market cap of B2C was $60 billion. Similarly, Amazon.com's market cap was $30 billion, and its sales were $30 million. Thus the sales multiple was 100, the market capitalization of the segment over the market capitalization of the top player was 2, and the segment market size over segment market cap was 3.3. We then tracked these multiples for all subsequent months. After observing the entire wave of B2C from its inception until its decline, we will have accumulated a sample of multiples for top B2C players that characterizes how revenue multiples evolve over time in the B2C wave. If we then assume that investor psychology is similar, we can use these multiples for valuation of B2B companies.

To clearly observe how historical multiples evolved, we need to keep all other variables that affect market capitalization constant. Of course, to make this model practical, you must perform additional research, such as clearly defining what constitutes the B2C wave, what B2B segments exist in the market, and so on (see Figure 4.5). Then statistical analyses can be used to eliminate other factors affecting stock price to calculate "normal" aggregate market capitalization of a segment over time. In addition, the top players' market capitalization, outstanding shares, sales, and revenue multiples over time will have to be tracked before a reference model of multiples for one segment can be established.

■ FUTURE OUTLOOK FOR VALUATION MODELS

We foresee a growing trend toward convergence of Old- and New Economy firms, as recently demonstrated by the AOL–Time Warner merger. Valuing these hybrids will present a set of new challenges. Although traditional techniques, such as multiples of EBIT and DCF, will become increasingly useful in valuing profitable companies as the high-tech industry matures, we are confident that the wave and mo-

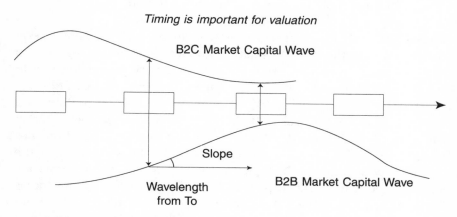

Figure 4.5 Timing of valuation.

mentum theories described in this chapter will apply equally to post-New Economy firms that are fortunate enough to find themselves positioned on the next big wave. Therefore, these alternative models should be considered as tools to help delineate market activity and valuation during times of great uncertainty and change. Looking forward, the pace of technology change—and therefore economic change—is likely to become ever more volatile. Thus, understanding market activity under conditions of uncertainty will become even more important.

■ NOTES

1. Professor Lestina, "Private Equity and Venture Capital Financing," Discussion at Kellogg Graduate School of Management, April 1, 2000.
2. Henry Blodget and Edward McCabe, *The B2B Market Maker Book*, Merrill Lynch, February 3, 2000.
3. *Ibid.*
4. www.elliottwave.com.
5. *Ibid.*

■ REFERENCES

Amram, Martha, and Nalin Kulatilaka. *Real Options: Managing Strategic Investment in an Uncertain World.* Boston, Mass.: Harvard Business School Press, 1999.

"Analyst Discovers Order in the Chaos of Huge Valuations for Internet Stocks." *Wall Street Journal*, December 27, 1999.

Archibold, Raimundo C., Susan Walker White, and Tom Wyman. "Amazon.com: An eTailing Megabrand Is Born." *JP Morgan Research Report* (December 9, 1999): 1–28.

Bahramipour, Lilly, Thomas Berquist, Jamie Friedman, Steven Kahl, Anne Meisner, Michael Parekh, and Rick G. Sherlund. "B2B: 2B or Not 2B?" *Version 1.2: The Tech Conference Edition, Goldman Sachs E-Commerce/Internet Report* (January 2000): 1–16.

Berquist, Thomas, Daniel Degnan, Jamie Friedman, Vik Mehta, Anthony Noto, Tonia Pankopf, Michael Parekh, Sood Rakesh, Coralie Tournier Witter, and Jimmy Wu. "Internet Quarterly: Expanding Mainstream

Usage into 2000." *Goldman Sachs Technology Report* (January 2000): 1–30.

Blodget, Henry, and Edward McCabe. *The B2B Market Maker Book.* Merrill Lynch, February 3, 2000.

Cibula, Michael, and Lauren Cooks Levitan. "Amazon.com, Inc." *Robertson Stephens Research Report* (February 3, 2000).

Cocroft, Constance, and Andrew W. Roskill. "Business-to-Business e-Commerce: Making the B2B Connection." Warburg Dillon Read Global Equity Research (January 2000): 3–53.

Coopers & Lybrand. "A Message to Entrepreneurs—Three keys to obtaining venture capital." March 2000.

"Cultivating Real Options in Silicon Valley (and within BigCo)." Corporate presentation, Origin Group, Inc., 1999.

De Neufville, Richard. "Motivation for Options: Valuation of Flexibility in Systems Design." Class lecture slides from the MIT course "Strategic Dynamic Planning." Massachusetts Institute of Technology, 1999.

Digital Frontier Conference, January 21-22, 2000. Valuation Panel.

Dixon, Christopher, James Preissler, and Paul Kim. "Valuing new media." PaineWebber, January 13, 2000.

Gulati, Ranjay, and Monica Higgins. "Getting Off to a Good Start: The Effects of Top Management Team Affiliations on Prestige of Investment Bank and IPO Success." 2000.

Laderman, Jeffrey M., and Geoffrey Smith. "Internet Stocks: What's their real worth?" *Business Week*, December 14, 1998.

Lestina, Prof. "Private Equity and Venture Capital Financing." Discussion at Kellogg Graduate School of Management, April 1, 2000.

Lowell, Nicholas, Geoff Ruddell, Michael Wand, and Alex Newman. "Pan European Internet." Deutsche Bank, January 25, 2000.

Mauboussin, Michael J., and Bob Hiler. "Cash Flow.com." Credit Suisse First Boston, February 26, 1999.

Meeker, Mary. "Amazon.com: Inflection! Amazon.calm!" *Morgan Stanley Dean Witter Research Report* (February 3, 2000).

PricewaterhouseCoopers. "Three Ways to Obtaining Venture Capital." 1999.

Salomon Smith Barney. "Amazon.com." December 1999.

Schappe, Jeffrey. "E-Business Next Wave: Principles for Internet Investing in 2000 and Beyond." Georges K. Baum & Company, January 19, 2000.

Stephens, Robertson. *The Web Report* (Internet Stock Group). January 28, 2000.

Triantis, Alexander J. "Real Options: Basic Concepts, Tools and Applications." Working paper, University of Maryland, 1999.

Trigeorgis, Lenos. *Real Options in Capital Investment.* Westport, Conn.: Praeger Publishers, 1995.

Walravens, Patrick. "Understanding B2B E-Commerce." Lehman Brothers, January 14, 2000.

Winston, Wayne L. "Pricing of Options and Real Options for Arbitrary Distributions." Working paper, Indiana University, 1999.

www.elliottwave.com.

Chapter

New Economy Metrics

Measuring Intellectual Capital

■ INTRODUCTION

In a speech at Grand Valley State University, Alan Greenspan stated, "Ideas have replaced physical bulk and effort as creators of value." He also noted that "[m]ost of what we currently perceive as value and wealth is intellectual and impalpable." Although everyone accepts the fact of its existence, extensive debate continues over how to measure and manage intellectual capital. Some insist that the accounting profession must emerge from the Middle Ages and recognize these assets on financial statements. Others argue that intangible assets are not measurable in dollar terms. The continuing debate has yet to spawn a generally accepted method of measurement; as a result, difficulty in valuation and lack of awareness of intangible assets are leading managers to make partially informed investment decisions. The goal of this chapter is to analyze currently available methods of measurement and to recommend approaches that will enable managers to consider these important assets more fully. A complicating factor in the assessment of intangible assets, particularly in Internet-related companies, is debate over valuation techniques and benchmarks for these companies in general.

Current attempts to quantify intellectual capital recognize that the difference between the market capitalization of a firm and the replacement value of the firm's tangible assets lies primarily in the firm's intellectual capital. The replacement value of assets can be difficult to measure, so we use book value as a proxy for replacement value. In 1999, the average market-to-book ratio for the S&P 500 companies reached 6.25—for high-tech companies, the ratio is even larger. This widening gap between market and book value illustrates the high proportion of corporate market value that knowledge assets create. For example, the book value of Microsoft's core revenue-generating assets is $20 billion; however, its market capitalization was $474 billion as of February 25, 2000. How can this more-than-20-fold difference between the revenue-generating assets on the balance sheet and the market capitalization be explained? Much of this difference between book value and market value can be attributed to intangible assets. For this reason, the market-to-book ratio can be used (with some limitations) as a simple, albeit crude, measure of the ratio of tangible to intangible assets (see Table 5.1).

■ WHAT ARE INTANGIBLE ASSETS?

Intangible assets, like physical assets, create shareholder value when they are expected to generate above-average returns. A defining characteristic of firms with a high proportion of intangible assets is their reliance on employees' knowledge and the management of knowledge assets to add value to their products and relationships. *Knowledge assets* are a type of intangible assets that possess three unique qualities physical assets lack: they can be deployed simultaneously in multiple locations and for multiple projects; they experience increasing returns; and they have an inherent feedback mechanism that leads to a self-propagating "virtuous circle."

■ INTELLECTUAL CAPITAL DEFINED

It is easy to get lost in the maze of terminology surrounding intellectual capital. *Knowledge management, organizational learning, intangible assets,* and *invisible assets* are just a few of the current buzzwords. In this chapter *intellectual capital* is used as an umbrella term. Renowned business writer Thomas A. Stewart defines *intellectual capital* as "the sum of everything the people in the company know which gives a

Table 5.1 Overall measures of intellectual capital.

Measure	Components			Comments
Market-to-book ratio (p/b)	Market value ÷ Book value			Very crude; relies on accounting data as a proxy for value of tangible assets.
Tobin's Q ratio	Market value ÷ Replacement cost			Improvement over p/b; however, difficult to estimate replacement cost for some firm-specific assets.
Calculated intangible value (CIV)	3-year average pretax earnings	× Industry average ROA	× Firm's tangible assets	Good indicator of efficiency of assets relative to competitors, but relies on accounting conventions (ROA).

(continued)

Table 5.1 *(continued)*

Measure	Components			Comments
Knowledge capital earnings (KCE)	Modified average 3-year historical normalized earnings	− Portion of earnings attributed to financial assets	− Portion of earnings attributed to capital assets	Can also be used to calculate total value of intellectual capital by dividing KCE by average return of knowl-edge rich industries.
Pricewaterhouse-Coopers LLP Overall Value	Tangible assets	+ DCF of intangible assets	+ Goodwill (options of firm)	Unique approach incorporates DCF valuations for each asset and real options theory to price goodwill.

competitive advantage in the market."[1] Another definition is knowledge that can be converted into value. We prefer a three-part definition of *intellectual capital* that includes human, relational, and structural components.

Employee competence is marked by the ability to act in a wide variety of situations to create both tangible and intangible assets. These are the employees who contribute knowledge and ideas. All employees are human capital, but not all employees are knowledge workers. An individual who works on an assembly line is considered human capital because of his or her potential for improving the process, but one who spends the lion's share of his or her time generating, managing, and converting knowledge to value is a *knowledge worker*. The employee is an asset, but is perfectly mobile and cannot be owned. The workers' importance to the New Economy is reflected in skyrocketing compensation packages. To reduce turnover, many firms are including equity and employee stock option plans with vesting periods. We know that key employees such as the CEO add tremendous value to organizations, as often shown by the fall of a stock price after a resignation announcement. In startups, especially in the dot com world, a company's market value can be comprised almost solely of the value of the management team. Note, too, that although both of these examples illustrate the value of key personnel, the value of the collective sum of human capital is much harder to estimate.

Relational capital encompasses the external revenue-generating aspects of the firm. Branding, reputation, strategic alliances, relationships with customers and suppliers, and even a firm's list of blue-chip clients all have revenue-generating potential. Customers will pay more for the Coca-Cola brand than for a generic-label brand.

Structural capital refers to the enabling structures that allow the organization to exploit its intellectual capital. Items of structural capital range from complete intangibles, such as the culture and spirit of the organization, to more tangible items, such as copyrights, trademarks, patents, internal databases, computer systems, and company intranets that manage knowledge.

■ HISTORICAL TREATMENT OF INTELLECTUAL CAPITAL

Intangible assets do not readily lend themselves to easy measurement, especially by historical cost or even by dollar figures. Current accounting standards do not permit their inclusion on the balance sheet. Accountants recognize the intangible assets of a firm only when the firm is sold at a premium over the book value; historically, accountants have used a plug called *goodwill* to reconcile the difference between book and market value. This is slowly changing because the SEC now requires more detailed information on the breakdown of this premium. The current system is better suited for capturing the value of capital assets in an industrial economy than to measuring intangible assets in the New Economy.

Current financial reporting methods are hindered by the process of measuring assets according to their original cost. The choice of depreciation method is arbitrary in that it does not strive to accurately reflect market or replacement values. Possible changes include replacing book with market value on financial statements and the reporting of more intangible assets on the balance sheet (which the SEC advocates). Whereas most capital assets decline in value over time, intangible assets frequently increase in value, as knowledge workers improve their skills and level of experience and employ better methods of using their environment. In addition, firms are able to leverage this knowledge many times over by building on it and distributing it throughout the company.

There are two difficulties in accepting the difference between market and book value as an accurate measure of intangible assets. First, shareholders buy and sell stock based on factors outside the scope of the company's assets or activities. A significant amount of variation in share prices does not correspond to the firm's performance. Although the volatility of a stock is an important measure, it may have nothing to do with the firm's intangible assets.

Second, book value is often understated. Because firms depreciate assets for tax considerations, these assets may be undervalued, causing book value to be understated. Somewhat ironically, a firm's skilled management of depreciation may be considered an intangible asset that is rewarded by a larger spread between market and book value.

Tobin's Q is a ratio, developed by Nobel Prize–winning economist James Tobin, that seems to resolve the difficulty posed by varying depreciation practices. The ratio compares the market value of a firm with the replacement cost of the firm's assets. The denominator—replacement cost—is improved by adding accumulated depreciation to the reported value of the company's fixed assets, and by accounting for inflation. Tobin's Q discounts the management's treatment of depreciation and, more importantly, over time reveals the diminishing returns of a firm relative to other firms. A Tobin's Q of 2 means that the firm's market value is twice as large as the replacement cost of its assets. A large ratio relative to comparable firms can be interpreted to mean that the firm is receiving great returns on its assets without suffering the effect of diminishing returns. This measure reveals more compelling results when compared to other firms over a constant period of time.

The spread between market and book value has fluctuated historically but has increased in recent years as market enthusiasm has pushed stock prices higher. One common measure used today as discussed in the previous chapter is DCF analysis. The cash flow of younger, high-growth firms tends to be much more volatile than that of established firms. DCF analysis takes into account the expected growth of cash flows. Today's analyst also applies such metrics as relative multiple evaluations, P/E and PEG ratios, and industry-specific ratios to assess value in the current landscape. Although many industries have evolved a "traditional" set of metrics designed to accommodate the nuances of that particular business line, New Economy firms have yet to create a formalized set of metrics.

■ ALTERNATIVE ACCOUNTING FOR INTELLECTUAL CAPITAL

Alan Benjamin, former director of the SEMA Group, one of Europe's leading computer services companies, created an alternative income statement that acknowledged the creation of knowledge and cash instead of after-tax profit. Benjamin's accounting method measures a firm's knowledge bank and endeavors to reverse the current accounting methods that capitalize PPE and expense labor and training. The capitalization of salaries, training, and R&D costs all depends on how much of the employees' work is devoted to current tasks versus future training, research, and development. The long-term investments are intellectual. For instance, the entire salary of a clerk would be expensed, but some of the salary for a marketing professional would be capitalized, as it affords the firm future benefit. Most of a new hire's pay would be capitalized, because most of that time would be spent learning how to add future value to the company; all of the salaries paid to researchers would be booked as an asset on the balance sheet.

Benjamin estimated R&D value by taking the net present value of new products discounted at the firm's cost of capital and subtracting likely deductions from failure, competition, and unforeseen costs. The net present value of the remainder would be booked as an asset. All capitalized salary, training, and research costs would then be depreciated over time as tangible assets. The art of Benjamin's accounting method relies on thoughtful analysis of the present versus future value afforded by employees' efforts.

■ MEASURING INTELLECTUAL CAPITAL AT THE FIRM LEVEL

We have already introduced two preliminary measures of intellectual capital: the market-to-book ratio and Tobin's Q ratio. Now we will introduce several more current approaches to measuring the overall intellectual capital of a firm.

The NCI Research group, in Evanston, Illinois, has developed a measure of intangible assets that is valuable in its comparison of market-to-book ratios. NCI measures the calculated intangible value (CIV) of firms by comparing a three-year average earnings figure to year-end tangible assets. The difference between this three-year modified ROA and the industry average ROA is the firm's CIV (refer back to Table 5.1). This intangible value is not the firm's market value, but is a measure of a company's ability to use its intangible assets to outperform the other companies in its industry. NCI found the CIV figure to be relevant in measuring both firm value and operations management. Falling CIV often accompanied a declining market-to-book ratio and stock price. In contrast, if the CIV rose while the market indicators fell, the company was often considered undervalued. NCI also found CIV to be a telling statistic from an operational standpoint. On the one hand, a declining CIV indicated that a firm was spending too much on bricks and mortar and not enough, perhaps, on R&D or brand building. A steadily rising CIV, on the other hand, may indicate that the company is building the infrastructure to produce future cash flows before that future earning potential is reflected in the market valuation. By taking the dollar amount of the firm's CIV and dividing it by an appropriate discount rate (such as the firm's cost of capital), the NPV of the firm's earnings attributed to intangible assets can be determined. One benefit of this measure is that it allows us to compare CIV across industries, because it incorporates industry average ROA as a basis for the measure.

Baruch Lev and Marc Bothwell of BEA-Credit Suisse Asset Management developed a unique approach to measuring the overall value of intellectual capital, which has now been applied to 27 chemical companies and 20 pharmaceutical companies. Their method is based on the assumption that firms utilize three different types of assets to earn profits: physical, financial, and knowledge assets. Their method assigns ownership of a portion of earnings to each of these three assets. By taking the product of the book value of financial assets from the balance sheet and an appropriate rate of return on financial assets (4.5 percent in this case), they determine how much of the earnings can be attributed to the financial assets. They then follow the same procedure for the physical assets (7 percent in this case). An average of normalized three-year historical earnings and three-year expected future earnings is taken, and the portion of earnings attributed to financial and physical assets is subtracted. The remaining portion of earnings is attributed to knowledge assets. At this point they divide this figure by a proxy for an appropriate knowledge assets discount rate. They use 10.5 percent, which is an average rate of return for three knowledge-rich industries (software, biotechnology, and pharmaceuticals).

Calculating the knowledge capital earnings (KCE) and knowledge capital assets (KCA) creates a broad range of metrics and ratios. Examples are knowledge capital margin (KCE/sales) and knowledge capital operating margin (KCE/operating income). This model is more robust than the previous methods because it breaks out valuation among the three different types of assets. In addition, one need not know the market value of the entire concern to determine the KCE; it is a bottom-up approach that adds flexibility to the valuation.

Marc Vermut of PricewaterhouseCoopers's Intellectual Property Valuation Practice stresses the importance of identifying where the value lies in the organization before determining which components will drive the valuation. The first step in the process is to perform a traditional business analysis to identify the value drivers. He applies this approach primarily when a transaction has occurred and the overall value of the concern is known. The total value must then be allocated across different business units or specific assets, stressing future potential income (discounted cash flow) or market-comparable methods, to value individual assets. In Mr. Vermut's opinion, the sum of tangible and intangible assets does not perfectly equate to the market value of the firm.

He attributes the gap between all assets (including intellectual) and the market value of the firm as goodwill, and he sees the value of goodwill in the alternatives or options available to the management team. Valuable options include entering (and exiting) new markets or lines of business or introducing a new product. This type of valuation is called *real options theory* and applies options pricing concepts to real-world business situations. Real options theory has been gaining popularity in recent years and lends itself to the highly competitive climate of the New Economy. Using goodwill to represent an option also helps to explain volatility in stocks when there are no noticeable changes in tangible or intangible assets.

Although Tobin's Q, Calculated Intangible Value, and Knowledge Capital Earnings are good overall indicators of whether the value of intangible assets is increasing or decreasing, these indicators have three drawbacks: they are backward-looking; they incorporate accounting measures or ratios that may be arbitrary and perhaps are not ideally suited for valuing intellectual capital; and, because these overall measures are broadly based, they do not expose specific problem areas to management.

■ MEASURING INTELLECTUAL CAPITAL AT THE OPERATING LEVEL

The manager's challenge is to leverage the firm's intellectual capital on the operational level so that capital markets will reward it. How can we develop a model for measuring intellectual capital that includes the characteristics that add considerable value to a company, such as employee morale, strong management leadership, and a creative environment?

The Balanced Scorecard is the first widely recognized method of evaluation that measures intellectual capital in addition to traditional financials. A practical management philosophy co-created in 1992 by Harvard Business School professors Robert Kaplan and David Norton, the Balanced Scorecard measures four different areas: traditional financials, customers' view of the firm (relational capital), internal processes (structural capital), and organizational learning/growth of the knowledge base (human capital). One important aspect of the Balanced Scorecard is that it focuses on only a few critical measures, so companies do not get distracted by measuring too many things. The scorecard also forces senior managers to consider the company's important operational measures in their entirety, so that improvements in one area are not made at the expense of another area. The Balanced Scorecard, though the first widely used management evaluation methodology to incorporate intellectual capital, does not clearly delineate specific metrics that could be incorporated into a valuation model.

Intellectual capital gurus Leif Edvinsson and Michael Malone have developed a reporting model that includes financial, customer, human, process and renewal, and development indicators. Because elements of intellectual capital are difficult to measure, there is no formal model for or external reporting of these assets in companies' financial statements. However, many companies use these measures internally, and some are beginning to include intellectual assets on their balance sheets. In fact, Swedish companies such as Skandia are leading the way. Skandia's value scheme breaks intellectual capital down into human capital, customer capital, and organizational capital, all of which interact with each other to create value for the company.

➤ Human Capital Measures

As the scale tips from tangible to knowledge assets, creativity and knowledge, the ability of the workforce to convert these assets into revenue become increasingly important. The firm must concentrate more on hiring, training, and retention. Most of the value in a knowledge firm is generated by human capital. The value reaped from relational capital also would not exist without the human capital. Because people ultimately make the company, human capital is a firm's most important intangible asset. Venture capitalists often base their funding decisions solely on the strength of a company's management.

Innovation is the most revealing indicator of a firm's human capital. Some firms compare the percentage of new sales against existing sales to demonstrate innovation. This proportion is often misleading because it ignores any cost-benefit analysis of new products. Because the percentage of a sales figure does not capture the price premium or price leadership of new, innovative products, the gross margin of these new products is really a better measure of innovation. Truly innovative products that reflect the creativity of the firm's employees demand a price premium to stay ahead of falling prices. The best measure of employee innovation, therefore, is to compare the gross margin of new products to that of the old.

Although innovative products may be measured using financial data, many quantitative measures of human capital are also of critical importance to the firm's management. Skandia's Karl Sveiby suggests three such indicators for the classes of intangible assets: growth and renewal, efficiency, and stability. Based on its understanding that the firm's human capital provides critical insight into future earning potential, management must constantly reevaluate the state of its most important asset. The "horsepower" of a firm's employees (most importantly of its revenue-producing employees) can be measured through an analysis of employees' tenure, turnover, experience, and learning. The total number of years in the profession of a firm's workforce is a measure of the skill and experience of the professional body. Although this measure may not prove informative at a particular point in time, its *change* over time may dramatically illustrate the success of the firm.

The educational level of the professionals in the firm also indicates competence, as education can serve to weed out underperformers. Another possibility for measurement lies in the costs associated with professional development programs. Firms that keep track of how much they have invested in certain employees may be better informed when comparing costs to output. Another way to assess the effect of professional competence within the firm is to track employee turnover and analyze how it affects the overall competence of the firm. Sveiby argues that a healthy knowledge firm's proportion of nonrevenue-producing employees should never exceed 10 percent.

Lastly, the attitudes of employees reveal a great deal about the value of a firm's human capital. Surveys are the tool most frequently used within companies to measure employee satisfaction. An improvement over the intraoffice survey—where input may be colored by the fear of negative feedback and its consequences—would be to have all surveys administered by a third party that offered absolute privacy.

➤ Structural Capital Measures

Companies store information in their computer systems and databases while protecting their intellectual property in the form of patents, trademarks, and copyrights. More and more companies are also valuing legally protected intellectual capital and including it on their balance sheets. Structural capital exists to facilitate the interaction between the company and the world. A firm's systems connect it more closely with the customer, but also with other external structures.

Trademark & Licensing Associates (TLA), which specializes in valuing structural assets, assigns such assets to one of three bundles. A technical bundle includes trade secrets, formulas, proprietary test results, and the like. A marketing bundle consists of copyrights, logo, advertising, trademarks, and so on. A skills and knowledge bundle includes databases, quality control standards, asset management processes, and proprietary information management systems. Once the assets have been categorized, they are valued in three ways. Is the asset differentiated? Does the asset have a value to someone else? If so, how much would someone else pay for the asset?

Although a level of subjectivity will always be present in valuing intangible assets, there are demonstrable ways for any company to utilize structural capital to improve operations. For instance, Wal-Mart, which is not considered a knowledge company, has been a dominant retail player primarily because of effective inventory management practices. Wal-Mart's use of technology and information systems illustrates the all-important lesson that technology by itself does not create economic opportunities, but it improves efficiency. Technology should not be used for technology's sake, but rather to streamline distributive networks.

Wal-Mart has become a dominant retailer worldwide by successfully managing its structural capital and benchmarking its progress. The growth and renewal of structural capital may be measured by a firm's investments in internal systems. Investing in new methods, in systems, and in equipment such as information-processing systems indicates a firm's dedication to structural improvements.

Trademarks and Copyrights

The value of copyrighted and trademarked assets makes intellectual property protection a top priority for companies in the New Economy. After polling 45 companies with some of the world's best-known trademarks, Forrester Research recommended three levels of asset management. In Level 1, *asset cataloging*, intellectual property is organized and managed internally to ensure availability for updates, distribution, and other uses. In Level 2, *distribution*, assets are made available to an external audience. As a general rule, the more valued the content, the more important it is to manage where the asset is disseminated. Level 3, the *monitoring* phase, identifies and assesses use of trademarked assets.

Management of these trademarked assets will shift the paradigm from control to use. Right now, the emphasis is on the property owner's rights. As a result, royalty and licensing fee structures are high, piracy is common, uncertainty abounds, and one-to-many models result in ad hoc usage. The trend is shifting from a focus on ownership rights and control to a focus on property use. Front-end, flat fees will become commonplace, piracy will decline because of devaluation, and many-to-many models will create intellectual property-based communities.

Patents

Patents are another intellectual asset that affects a company's valuation. Baruch Lev suggests a correlation between patents and profits. In his research, Lev learned that companies with frequently cited patents are likely to see their stock rise more rapidly. The patents are usually of high financial value, and the companies that own them benefit from the commercial exploitation of their intellectual property. Active management of a company's patents is another area in which resources can generate revenue. Gordon Petrash, central recordkeeper for Dow Chemical Corporation's 29,000 in-force patents, found that Dow exploited less than half its patents. His group worked with the business units to reorganize the patent portfolios, saving the company more than $1 million in maintenance costs in the first 18 months. Over 10 years, Petrash projects that Dow will save $50 million in tax, filing, and other maintenance costs. Furthermore, he believes that by exercising some valuable but previously unused patents, the company will increase its annual patent revenue from $25 million, in 1994, to $125 million by the end of 2000. According to Petrash, "The long-range goal is to extend the work of knowledge management into less defined, and more valuable areas of intellectual capital—'art and know-how,' trade secrets and technical expertise worth billions of dollars."

➤ Relational Capital Measures

One important subset of relational capital is customer capital. Customer capital includes relationships with suppliers and other players along the value chain; most importantly, though, it involves a firm's relationship with its customers. Loyalty and increased business are critical measures of customer relationships.

What is a loyal customer worth? According to Frederick Reichheld of Bain & Co., "Raising customer retention rates by five percentage points increases the value of an average customer by 25 to 50 percent." The basis of Reichheld's assertion is that long-term customers tend to make bigger purchases and pay higher prices than new customers, who often are shopping for discounts. Existing customers create less debt and buy more items over time, in an attempt at one-stop shopping. Most importantly, these long-term customers create additional business through referrals. Another critical aspect of Reichheld's study is that on average, firms spend more to acquire new customers than to retain old ones. A firm must segment its customers according to their expected value to the firm.

The Danish management consulting firm PLS-Consult segments its customers in three categories: whether they contribute to image and provide beneficial references, whether they pose challenging questions that can increase learning, and whether the project will benefit individual consultants working on the project or add to the structural capital of PLS. Any customer that ranks strongly in all three categories is considered the ideal customer. Logically, high-ranking customers also generate strong earnings for the firm. Another way to analyze attractive customers is to measure their earning potential. How do they compare to their peers? Are they growing faster than their industry? How much of their total business do you receive?

The growth and renewal of customer capital may be measured by profitability per customer. Surprisingly, Sveiby reported that 80 percent of customer sales are often not profitable. This happens because many companies track the cost of products instead of customer profitability. Careful analysis of individual customer P&L accounts may lead to dramatically improved earnings. As with all measures of assets, firms do not want to become too reliant on any group of customers. Sveiby argues that as a general rule, no more than 50 percent of sales should come from the top 5 customers. The true test of customer satisfaction is the level of information shared between buyer and seller. How much information about future demand does your customer share with you, and how much information do you share with your customer? The efficiency of customer capital may be measured in the short term with satisfaction polls, but in the long term, the best indicator of customer satisfaction is retained business.

Measuring Brand Equity

Brand equity is a form of customer capital for which well-established valuation methods exist. One way to value the strength of a brand is to look at the premium price it enjoys over other similar products and assign a value to the brand based on that premium. Another valuation method is to take an income-based approach and measure the expected cash flow generated by the product or service for some period in the future. Studies show that market values of well-known companies consist more of intangible than tangible assets, implying that a portion of this difference can be explained by the value of the brand of the well-known companies. The Coca-Cola brand name, for example, is the world's most valuable at about $39 billion.

Online, with no merchandise to touch or taste, a company's brand is its strongest link to customers, and the level of consumer involvement with that brand is more important than the questionable measurements of brand awareness and recall. Audits & Surveys Worldwide will extend its market research into measuring consumer involvement by monitoring the number of personal home pages with tributes to brands, as well as the number of discussions or forums devoted to trademarked products.

■ METRICS FOR VALUING INTELLECTUAL CAPITAL

There is a plethora of metrics that can be used to measure components of intellectual capital at the operating level. The usefulness of individual metrics varies across industries and between firms in the same industry. The first step in using such metrics is to determine which metrics are best indicators of value and weakness in your industry. A list of potential metrics follows; in the following examples we have taken three firms from different industries and have applied either human, relational, or structural capital metrics, depending on which was the most relevant.

Human Capital Metrics

Cost of employee/training expense	How much does the firm pay the employee in salary and equity relative to comparable employees? Exercise caution when using training expenses; they do not indicate

	the effectiveness of the training. A good benchmark is to compare similar training to other firms in the same industry.
Revenue generated by employee	The discounted cash flow generated by the employee-client relationship.
Market capitalization per knowledge worker	This ratio is interesting to use as a year-over-year measure to spot trending.
Education level of employees/type of degree	Education includes academic achievement, on-the-job training, and the challenging nature of completed projects. These three measures are closely linked and measure the level of education of knowledge workers. These figures are useful for comparison with competitors, in addition to benchmarking year over year.
Value of area of expertise	Linked closely to education level. What is the employee responsible for within the firm? How important is that area to the success of the firm?
Knowledge worker turnover	These workers possess valuable knowledge regarding the firm, products, clients, processes, and systems. They also appreciate in value from year to year (to a certain point). Therefore, it is important to measure their rate of turn over. Newer knowledge workers turn over more frequently; a measure of the ratio of workers with tenures of more than two years also makes sense to measure knowledge worker satisfaction.
Knowledge to non-knowledge worker ratio	This measure is useful for making comparisons between companies

in the same industry. It can be in terpreted in two ways: If the ratio is low, it could either be a sign that the firm is leveraging knowledge workers, or it could be a sign that the firm is falling behind the competition in terms of proportion of knowledge workers. Other measures must be used in conjunction to interpret this one.

Conversion ratio

The ratio of workers that an organization converts from non-knowledge workers to knowledge workers. This ratio measures the effectiveness of the ongoing learning and development within the organization.

Employee network

Client relationships of employee. Overlaps with relational capital.

Number of years' experience in profession

This measure reflects the cumulative number of years of experience in the profession of the organization's knowledge workers. This figure is useful as a year-to-year comparison to gauge if a firm's knowledge base is growing.

Ratio of learning projects

Another measure of an employee's competence and development is the number of projects that the professionals feel challenged them and added to their level of knowledge.

Relational Capital Metrics
Customer retention

The devotion of customers represents significant value to a company in the form of future expected cash flows and reputation effects that can lead to new customers (and additional revenues).

Customer acquisition costs	The rate at which a company acquires new customers—and the cost of acquiring customers—demonstrates the value of its customer capital. It measures the effectiveness of advertising and the company's brand recognition.
Market share	Percentage of the market a firm controls. The greater a firm's market share, the greater the competitive advantage it enjoys, which results in higher profitability and valuation.
Brand equity	Elements of a brand's image have the ability to shift economic demand for a brand. These elements include the product or service represented by a brand, its authority as a brand, the approval conferred on the consumer of the brand, and how the customer identifies with the brand.
Customer satisfaction index	Getting feedback from customers as to their satisfaction with a firm's product or service is easier in the Net Age. It is important for companies to know customers' perceptions of quality. Companies that show an interest in customers' opinions can generate higher customer retention.
Prestige of client base	For companies in the New Economy, acquiring high-profile clients such as Microsoft, IBM, Amazon, or Intel leads to considerable value in the form of ability to attract new customers (and new revenues) and to establish brand recognition by association with blue-chip clients.

Number of exclusive client relationships	The number of exclusive client relationships results in value creation for a company by securing future cash flows from locked-in clients.
Strength of relationships with customers/information sharing ratio	Companies that can develop close relationships with their customers—and persuade them to share information—are better able to serve those clients and attract new customers. The percentage of customers who share information can indicate loyalty and result in operational efficiencies, leading to higher profitability.
Strategic alliances	Similar to the prestige of client base, forming strategic partnerships and alliances with high-profile companies can generate considerable value for a company. For a company like Greenlight.com, which is trying to enter enter the fiercely competitive car e-tailing market, partnering with Amazon.com for $82.5 million over 5 years resulted in brand recognition and customer traffic it otherwise could not have afforded.

Structural Capital Metrics

Culture	The pattern of beliefs, values, practices, and artifacts defines who the firm's members are and how they do things. Is the culture of the firm consistent with its goals? Does the firm have buy-in from its employees?
Frequently cited patents	Research by Baruch Lev found a direct correlation between a company's patenting history and

	its stock price. A typical U.S. patent cites about eight earlier U.S. patents, one or two foreign patents, and one or two non-patent items. The patents that are frequently cited by others are usually of high financial value. Companies with frequently cited patents are likely to see their stock rise more rapidly.
IT investment	Information technology is a key tool in a knowledge-based economy.
R&D Investment	Expenditure on R&D generates value, and it is reasonable to regard such expenditure as an investment.
Knowledge Management Infrastructure Spending	Expenditure in this area is representative of a firm's investment in effectively disseminating knowledge throughout the company. There is tremendous value in capturing and leveraging a company's collective knowledge.
Trademarks	A company's trademarks contribute to its brand equity and top-of-mind awareness in the market place.

■ MEASURING RELATIONAL CAPITAL AT EBAY

Online auctioneer eBay had a market capitalization of $23.5 billion (as of April 7, 2000) and physical assets of $111.8 million, based on its most recent annual report. When you consider eBay's value proposition, the concepts of *brand*, *community*, and *customer service* immediately come to mind. One can argue that almost all of eBay's high-flying valuation can be attributed to its relational capital. Even following the substantial fallout of the 2000 tech market crash, eBay maintains a substantial valuation. By scoring eBay on this set of relational capital metrics, we can understand why it is one of the most successful companies in the New Economy.

Customer retention. eBay scores very high in customer retention because it is very easy to register and post items in its system. Conversely, this ease of use makes it conducive to browsing by customers who simply click through the site and do not buy or post items. eBay works hard to make sure that customers have a positive first experience, so they will continue to use the site and become an active part of the community. eBay's strong sense of community also gives it a very high customer retention rating. Community features such as chat rooms, bulletin boards, and "About Me" pages encourage consumer loyalty and repeat usage.

Strength of relationships with customers/information sharing ratio. eBay is a prime example of a company developing close relationships with its customers; this sharing of information enables eBay to serve its customers better and attract new visitors.

Customer acquisition costs. In the world of e-commerce, companies are spending billions to drive traffic to their Web sites, and it is important for companies to measure their costs of acquiring new customers. From December 31, 1998, to December 31, 1999, the number of registered eBay users grew from approximately 2.1 million to more than 10 million, while eBay spent $96 million on sales and marketing. eBay has very low customer acquisition costs compared to similar firms in the e-commerce space.

Customer satisfaction index. eBay's Feedback Forum encourages every eBay user to provide comments and feedback on the other eBay users with whom they interact, and offers user profiles for providing feedback ratings. eBay does an excellent job of utilizing the Web and its large database of users to ask customers for their opinions. This leads to increased customer satisfaction and helps build community.

Brand equity. eBay's brand equity can be measured by the premium it enjoys over its competitors. Many auction sites have cropped up in the wake of eBay's success, and many offer their services for free. However, eBay can continue to charge a small fee for posting items because it reaches such a large community. Consumers know that the strong brand name of eBay brings more traffic to their offerings and increases their chances of generating interest in their auction items.

Reputation. Reputation is a very strong aspect of eBay's brand equity. Consumers are sharing a lot of information about themselves, including credit card information and home addresses, and they must trust eBay to be responsible with this information. The company has developed a number of programs aimed at making users more comfortable about dealing with unknown trading partners over the Web. eBay has responded to fraud issues by implementing a Safe Harbor program and escrow service. The company has also developed an extensive set of rules and guidelines designed to educate users and help implement eBay's prohibition on the sale of illegal or pirated items. eBay's increase in market value over the last year can be linked directly to its improvements in safety (see Figure 5.1).

Market value of eBay = $23.5 billion		
	Intangible assets = $22.7 billion	
Equity (tangible assets) $852.5 million	External structure (relational capital) = Approx. 90% of intangible assets = $20.4 billion	Internal structure (human and structural capital) = Approx. 10% of intangible assets = $2.3 billion

Relational Capital Metric	Assigned Weight (% of Relational Capital Value)	Contribution to Value ($Billions)
Customer retention	20.0	$ 4.085
Strength of relationship with customers	10.0	2.043
Customer acquisition costs	5.0	1.021
Customer satisfaction index	15.0	3.064
Brand equity	25.0	5.106
Reputation	20.0	4.085
Prestige of client base	0.0	0.000
Strategic alliances/partnerships	5.0	1.021
Total	100.0	$20.425

Figure 5.1   Market value of eBay.

Prestige of client base. For eBay, the prestige of its client base is not an essential component of its valuation, as it targets the individual consumer. For eBay, the sheer size of its customer base, not the prestige or quality of those customers, makes it appealing to strategic partners, advertisers, and service providers.

Strategic alliances/exclusive partnerships. Although many companies are using strategic partnerships to increase brand awareness and attract customers, eBay is more a target for other e-commerce players than the one seeking out such relationships. eBay has a strong alliance with AOL as the preferred provider of personal trading services on AOL's proprietary services AOL.com, Digital Cities, ICQ, CompuServe, and Netscape. The AOL partnership is very valuable to eBay (it paid $75 million for the contract) because it gives the company access to AOL's subscriber base of 20.5 million.

By applying this set of relational capital metrics to eBay, one can generate a rough estimate of how the company's market value can be derived, assuming a reasonable level of market efficiency. The key to using this framework is that the company must measure these attributes over time and assess areas for improvement. For example, although eBay's reputation as a safe trading environment is now a source of positive value for the company, the fraud problems it encountered in 1999 would have been a negative drain on the market value. Figure 5.1 illustrates the breakdown of eBay's market value and how the various relational capital metrics contribute to total market value.

■ MEASURING STRUCTURAL CAPITAL AT PFIZER

Pharmaceutical company, Pfizer, Inc. had a market capitalization of $153.2 billion and physical assets of $20.57 billion, based on its most recent annual report. Considering Pfizer's mission to achieve and sustain its place as the world's premier research-based health care company, one can argue that most of Pfizer's valuation lies in its structural capital. By scoring Pfizer on this set of structural capital metrics, we can understand why it is one of the world's most successful pharmaceutical companies (see Figure 5.2).

Patents. Pfizer, Inc., scores high in this area because of the vast number of U.S. and foreign patents the company owns or licenses. These pat-

Market value of Pfizer = $153.2 billion		
	Intangible assets = $144.4 billion	
Equity (tangible assets) $8.8 billion	Structural capital = Approx. 80% of intangible assets = $20.4 billion $115.5 billion	Human and relational capital = Approx. 20% of intangible assets = $28.8 billion

Structural capital (Pfizer)	Assigned Weight (% of Relational Capital Value)	Contribution to Value ($Billions)
Patents	20.0	$ 23.1
Trademarks	20.0	23.1
IT investment	15.0	17.3
R&D investment	35.0	40.42
Culture	10.0	11.58
Total	100.0	$115.5

Figure 5.2   Market value of Pfizer.

ents cover pharmaceutical products, pharmaceutical formulations, product manufacturing processes, and intermediate chemical compounds used in manufacturing. According to Pfizer, the company's patent and related rights are of material importance to its businesses in the United States and most other countries. Based on current product sales, and considering the vigorous competition, the patent rights Pfizer considers most significant in relation to the business as a whole are those for Norvasc, Cardura, Zithromax, Zoloft, Diflucan, Glucotrol, XL, Viagra, and Trovan.

IT investment. According to Pfizer's Web site, the company must be willing to invest in new technologies to reap their ultimate benefit: a reduction in the cost of disease. An immense amount of capital has been invested in the information technology sector, and the result has been steadily lowered costs, improved quality, and increased access to technologies.

R&D investment. Pfizer is primarily a research organization, and its R&D investment is the wellspring of its growth and profitability. The company's central research component—7,000 professionals working in more than 30 countries—constitutes an R&D program of tremendous breadth. Pfizer's R&D investment has exceeded $2 billion annually. Pfizer currently supports research on three continents involving 180 research projects across 31 major disease groups. According to its Web site, discovery researchers may test millions of chemical compounds to find a dozen candidate drugs, of which one might result in an approved medication. The time from discovery to approval can be as long as 15 years, and the average cost of bringing a pharmaceutical product to market is half a billion dollars.

Trademarks. In Pfizer's 1998 annual report, the company listed a total of 134 trademarks: 46 pharmaceutical patents, 42 over-the-counter product trademarks, and 46 animal health trademarks.

Culture. The Pfizer culture is dedicated to helping humanity and delivering exceptional financial performance by discovering, developing, and providing innovative health care products that lead to healthier and more productive lives. The values at the foundation of Pfizer's business include integrity, innovation, respect for people, customer focus, teamwork, leadership, performance, and community.

By applying this set of structural capital metrics to Pfizer, one can derive a rough estimate of its market value. Again, the key to using this framework is that the company must measure these attributes over time and assess areas for improvement. Figure 5.2 illustrates the breakdown of Pfizer's market value and how the various structural capital metrics contribute to its total market value.

■ MEASURING HUMAN CAPITAL AT MERRILL LYNCH

The investment bank Merrill Lynch had a market capitalization of $38.1 billion (as of April 10, 2000) and physical assets of $12.4 billion, as of its latest annual report. Much like other successful investment banks, Merrill Lynch's intellectual capital dwarfs its book value. Although investment banks' products could be considered a commodity, the market recognizes dramatic differences in the values of banks' intellectual capital. Although Merrill Lynch has significant relational capital, we argue that the firm's human capital differentiates it from its competitors. If the senior banking professionals with important client relationships left the firm, so would the clients. That is why banks pay so much for talent (see Figure 5.3).

The first step in valuing human capital, regardless of industry, is to ask what role the employees play in driving the value of the business. What makes a firm distinctive? What do customers pay for? The newly founded private equity arm of Merrill Lynch is a good example of an entity whose people add critical value. The group's success depends totally on the ability of its partners to raise and invest capital. Once the critical assets—in this case the partners—have been identified, the firm may begin to value its resources and better manage its human capital.

Cost of employee/training expense. How much does an employee cost Merrill Lynch in salary and future options? Is the employee replaceable? What is the asset's replacement cost? In the case of the private equity group, the partner who raised the most capital from limited partners is not replaceable in the eyes of those who contributed the funds. In most cases, the replacement cost of an employee will equal

Market value of Merrill Lynch= $38.1 billion		
	Intangible assets = $25.7 billion	
Equity (tangible assets) $12.4 billion	External capital (relational capital)= Approx. 25% of intangible assets = $6.4 billion	Internal structure (human and structural capital) = Approx. 75% of intangible assets = $19.3 billion

Human capital (Merrill Lynch)	Assigned Weight (% of Relational Capital Value)	Contribution to Value ($Billions)
Revenue generated by employee	30.0	$ 7.710
Education level of employee	15.0	3.855
Area of expertise	20.0	5.140
Knowledge worker turnover	10.0	2.570
Employee client list	25.0	6.425
Total	100.0	$25.700

Figure 5.3 Market value of Merrill Lynch.

the going market rate. For instance, if any firm is willing to pay more than another firm to attract talent, that price will become the market rate, because every firm will have to adjust its pay scale to retain personnel.

Revenue generated per employee. The income approach estimates an asset's future earning potential in the same way as a discounted cash flow analysis. In the case of an investment banker, it may be appropriate to measure the banker's worth to the firm by the revenue generated from that banker's clients. What is the expected life of the cash flows? Has the employee signed a noncompete clause that precludes the individual from taking the client list to another bank? What is the risk associated with those expected cash flows? Each industry and firm within each industry must consider different factors in answering these questions.

Education level of employee. Managers may accurately measure the education level of new employees. Does the addition of an employee increase or decrease the average academic achievement of employees? Perhaps a single employee who graduated from the school of hard knocks instead of Kellogg is good for a firm's street smarts, but a trend of decreasing academic achievement means trouble.

A manager should consider more than just the academic achievements of the company's employees. On-the-job learning is often more meaningful than a classroom education. Managers should measure what kind of projects an employee undertakes. Does an employee receive a variety of assignments? Are the projects challenging? Is the employee gaining new skills? The answers to these questions will enable managers to more effectively measure and manage their human capital.

Value of area of expertise. As employees gain experience on the job, managers may designate them as "owners" of an information area. The goals of promoting employee ownership of interest areas are twofold. The firm benefits because employee ownership creates a reliable, single source of updated information for the rest of the firm. Secondly, a manager may create a sense of accountability in employees that will also make them more valuable over the long term. The investment banking industry provides an interesting case study for information ownership.

Investment banks place their junior analysts in industry-specific groups so as to create areas of expertise within the firm. In addition to industry segmentation, investment banks also encourage functional areas of expertise. Analysts are encouraged to build databases of information that are used across industries. For example, defensive strategy tactics are an important product offered by investment banks to all industries. By encouraging a single employee's ownership of the defense database, a manager may increase the worth of that individual employee to the firm. This provides a global firm with a single source of updated information, keeping individuals from having to repeat the same work. The "owner" employees benefit from exposure within the firm, and the opportunity to prove themselves.

Value of employees' network. Employees can add significant value to a firm through a network of external contacts. A manager can value this set of relationships in several ways.

Continuing with the investment-banking example, senior bankers are compensated by how much revenue their client contacts generate. A fault with this measurement is that it fails to account for the contribution of the team working for the senior banker. The revenue generated by each client may be a better measure of the team working on the deal than of the individual banker.

Another measure of the value of relationships is to estimate what the firm would lose in revenue if that employee were to leave. For instance, if Merrill Lynch hired the child of a prominent CEO, the value of that employee would not be limited to his or her actual work product, but would also include the revenue generated from the firm's relationship with the parent's firm.

■ CONVERTING KNOWLEDGE INTO VALUE

Intellectual capital represents the conversion of knowledge into value for a firm. Thus, intellectual assets (people, patents, processes, brand names) are the "debits" and intellectual capital is the "credit" or the equity invested in intellectual assets. Because human capital and relational capital are transient, companies must strive to convert these assets into permanent structural capital. Managing intellectual capital is almost synonymous with managing a New Economy firm. The proportion of intellectual capital to book value of a knowledge firm is much higher than in a traditional firm, so the management of the knowledge firm should be concentrating its efforts on evaluating, building, and nurturing knowledge assets.

There is no Band-Aid solution to managing intellectual capital within the operating context of an organization. An expensive knowledge management consulting project is only a starting point. If the expense of such a project is a deterring factor, keep in mind that the internal cost of implementing effective intellectual capital management will probably be a multiple of this figure. Appointing a director of knowledge management does not ensure success. The nurturing and management of intellectual capital must be done in every division and at every level of the organization. The management of intellectual capital places human resources management front and center; however, elements of that management are embedded throughout other areas of management research. An example is the concept of continuous process improvement in Total Quality Management, or the "Create, Convert, Capture" concept from management strategy. Only by converting and capturing the inherent knowledge of the firm will an organization be able to compete in the Knowledge Economy.

Is the notion of intellectual capital merely a management fad? Certainly not—it took many years before discounted cash flow valuations became widely accepted for valuing firms, but they are now the standard. Compared to discounted cash flow valuations, the management of intellectual capital is still in its infancy. We are seeing intellectual capital management make the transition from being a management fad to a strategic necessity at every level of the organization. Intellectual capital will increasingly become embedded in the culture and management policies and processes of firms. Intellectual capital management requires a real and strong commitment from senior executives, who have for the most part been slow in acceptance and adoption. Nonetheless, the rewards for an effective long-term commitment to valuing and managing intellectual capital as a discipline could be enormous, and ultimately essential.

■ NOTE

1. Thomas A. Stewart, *Intellectual Capital: The New Wealth of Organizations* (Doubleday, 1999).

■ REFERENCES

Aaker, David A. *Building Strong Brands*. Free Press, 1995.

"An Intellectual Accounting: Why Do Intellectual Capital Measures Focus on the Wrong?" *KMWorld Magazine* Archives (January 1, 1998).

Brooking, Annie. *Intellectual Capital: Core Assets for the Third Millennium.* International Thomson Computer Press, 1996.

Burkowitz, Wendi R., and Ruth L. Williams. *The Knowledge Management Fieldbook.* Financial Times/Prentice Hall, 1999.

Colvin, Geoffrey. "How to Get Your Head Around Measuring Minds," *Fortune* (December 20, 1999).

Davidow, William. "Accounting Systems Are Completely Wrong." *Red Herring* (January 1995).

Dyson, Esther. "It Comes Down to Two Things." *Forbes ASAP* (April 7, 1997).

Glaser, Perry. "The Knowledge Factor." *CIO Magazine* (December 15, 1998).

Greenspan, Alan. "Reflections." Speech at Grand Valley State University, September 8, 1999.

Henig, Peter D. "Internet Valuations Get Even Nuttier." *Redherring.com* (May 22, 1999).

"Intellectual Capital: Key to Value Added Success in the Next Millennium." *CMA—The Management Accounting Magazine* (January 2000).

"The Intellectual Property Mess." *The Forrester Report* (April 1999).

Jurvetson, Steve. "From the Ground Floor." *Red Herring* (no. 77, April 2000): 86.

Kaplan, Robert S., and David P. Norton. "The Balanced Scorecard: Measures That Drive Performance." *Harvard Business Review* (January/February 1992).

Kaplan, Robert S., and David P. Norton. *The Balanced Scorecard: Translating Strategy into Action.* Harvard Business School Press, 1996.

Karlgaard, Rich. "SEC Loves IC." *Forbes ASAP* (April 7, 1997).

Kelly, Kevin. *New Rules for the New Economy.* Penguin Books, 1998.

Lambe, Patrick. "When the Fad Hits the Firm." *Business Times Singapore* (January 25, 2000).

Lev, Baruch. "Knowledge and Shareholder Value." January 2000.

———. "The Old Rules No Longer Apply." *Forbes ASAP* (April 7, 1997).

Malone, Michael S. "New Metrics for a New Age." *Forbes ASAP* (April 1997).

Mattson, Beth. "Executives Learn How to Keep Score." *City Business* (August 9, 1999).

Mazzie, Mark. "Intellectual Capitalism: Turning Knowledge into Profit." *CIO Enterprise Magazine* (October 15, 1999).

McIntosh, Jennifer. "A Crucial Business Imperative: Leveraging Human Capital." *KMWorld Magazine* Archives (January 1, 1998).

Microsoft Corporation. *Annual Report.* 1999.

"New Way to Calculate Future Earnings." *Business Times Malaysia* (October 5, 1999).

PricewaterhouseCoopers. "Report." April 2000.

Schrage, Michael. "On the Job: Brave New Work, How the Bell Curve Cheats You." *Fortune Magazine* (February 21, 2000).

Stewart, Thomas A. *Intellectual Capital: The New Wealth of Organizations.* Doubleday, 1999.

Sveiby, Karl. "The Invisible Balance Sheet." White paper, Umea University, 1989.

Sveiby, Karl. *The New Organizational Wealth.* Berrett-Koehler Publishers, 1997.

"Vikings of Intellectual Capital." *Business Times Singapore* (November 9, 1999).

Winston, Paul D. "Brand Risk Management Adds Value." *Business Insurance* (November 1999).

Chapter

Wireless
E-Business

Identifying the Next Killer App

■ INTRODUCTION

Wireless networks and the Internet are converging to bring consumers and businesses a new type of commerce: mobile commerce (m-commerce). In this new exchange medium, mobile handheld devices will be used to communicate, inform, transact, and entertain. Numerous estimates put the number of Internet-enabled handsets at 500 million by 2003; it appears that a large and vibrant global market for new mobile applications and services is emerging.

Though the consumer implications of wireless technology are tremendous, larger and more immediate market opportunities exist in the corporate arena. B2B e-commerce is expected to reach $1.4 trillion by 2004. To realize their full economic potential, companies will have to adopt mobile Internet applications to accelerate the pace of business, because these applications will eliminate the constraints of time and location on business. The value of wireless technology comes from its:

- Mobility/ubiquity—it offers anytime/anywhere access
- Speed—it requires no plug-in time and has high data rates
- Tracking/localization capabilities

- Personalization—mobile interfaces are the most personal
- Ease of use, with no physical connections—it is easy to tap into the infrastructure
- Safety—the user is never alone and can stay within a safe distance

Although the wireless data industry failed to reach the mass market several times through the 1990s, growing demand for mobile access to the Internet, intranets, and e-commerce has finally propelled wireless technologies into business and consumer markets. What is more, it is foreseeable that the business market will drive further technological advances and market penetration, fueled by an increasingly mobile workforce that relies on the Internet, intranets, and extranets for day-to-day business activities.

IDC forecasts that the mobile workforce will reach 47 million workers by the end of 2003; Dataquest estimates that the U.S. wireless data market (including telephones, personal digital assistants (PDAs), laptops, etc.) will grow from 3 million subscribers today to 36 million subscribers in 2003. At a global level, the projections are even more compelling. Nokia predicts that by 2002, a greater number of people will be linked to the Internet via wireless connections than via land lines. In the same year, Nokia expects that the numbers of both wireless and Internet subscribers will overtake those of traditional telephone subscribers. Further, Ericsson foresees that four out of every ten online users will have wireless access to the Internet, suggesting that 2003 will be the year in which the wireless web will overtake the hard-wired one. This is not an unfathomable concept, given that for every Internet user today there are three mobile subscribers worldwide.

The purpose of this chapter is to evaluate the potential for wireless business applications in the ever-changing technological and economic landscape. Cahners In-Stat Group forecasts that wireless data users in enterprise segments will multiply more than tenfold, from 784,000 in 1999 to nearly 9 million in 2003. Felix Lin, the CEO of AvantGo, calls this the "Second Coming of the Internet." Currently, a handful of custom software development houses are writing applications for specific corporate client needs, and customers are already using them. Success in this arena, however, is being measured in the dozens of seats, not thousands, and adoption remains slow. AvantGo, the largest company in this space, believes that 10 percent of the Fortune 500 companies are its customers. CEO Lin estimates that enterprise applications bring in $150–200 in revenue per seat. In the future, e-commerce players will be compelled to move into the wireless market if they are to fulfill their potential.

■ IDENTIFYING THE NEXT KILLER APP

After considering the caliber of available wireless technologies and their applicability to the needs of business, the three applications that qualify as potential "killer" apps are mobile application service providers (ASPs), wireless medicine, and mobile asset management. These applications have several things in common:

- Mobile communication is the key. These applications could not exist in the hard-wired world, and as such they represent a paradigm shift in their respective markets.

- The applications are designed to meet customer needs and were, above all else, customer-focused. This quality is an essential element in any business application, and in the case of our killer apps is critical to sustaining success in their respective markets.

- The applications passed robust filtering criteria, which gives them the maximum chance of surviving as sustainable business models.

■ APPLICATION SERVICE PROVIDERS

Field service/dispatch mobile *application service providers* (ASPs) for small businesses are designed for small business owners who cannot commit to the infrastructure investments required to support mobile office facilities for field service personnel. Because these businesspersons often work independently and are away from the office for much of the time, they either lose sales or must employ personnel to schedule their work on a day-to-day basis. If they knew their work schedule ahead of time, they could plan their routes better and work more efficiently. Further, depending on the nature and requirements of their business, field service personnel can look at customer records, diagnostic information, and/or inventory in real time. The introduction of such services will enable small business owners to have 24x7 access to low-cost business services such as workflow management, billing, and point-of-sale services.

The target market for mobile office applications are in the areas of:

- Transportation (delivery of food, oil, newspapers, cargo, courier services, towing trucks, taxis)
- Utilities (gas, electricity, telephone, water)
- Field service (computer, office equipment, repair persons)
- Healthcare (visiting nurses and doctors, social services)
- Security (patrol, alarm installers and monitors)

Based on customer needs, the ASP solutions will be wireless-enabled (through the Wireless Application Protocol or WAP), Web-based, and connected to a call center interface. Small business customers can connect through the call center or access the Web site to fill in the order form. The order form and invoice are then sent to the field service professionals through WAP interfaces. Additionally, the field professional can be sent the relevant maps and most efficient routes to get to the next location. After the order is filled or the service performed, the professional can update the invoice in the central database, which resides on centrally hosted servers. The advantage of having the database live on the central server is transparency—it allows both the field professionals and their customers to look at the data.

The market potential for ASP in the small business arena is very healthy. According to the Yankee Group, the field service industry employs more than 7 million mobile technicians in the United States. In a recent report, Cahners In-Stat Group forecasts 10 percent growth annually in small business spending, from $142 billion in 1998 to more than $200 billion by 2002. The strong economic forecast is due in part to the fact that there are 2.2 million small businesses. Almost one-quarter of these technology expenses can be attributed to communications and are expected to grow steadily over time.

Technologically mature companies that make up only 6 percent of small businesses but spent upwards of $28 billion in 1998 also drive spending. These companies have their own information technology (IT) staffs, Internet access, distributed computing, and one or more non-PC servers. This indicates that there is a huge market to deliver services to the other 94 percent of businesses that do not have access to their own IT staffs, but still have scheduling and other IT needs. Another driving force in this market will be technologically advancing companies. These firms buy additional PCs, network hardware, and wireless services and equipment. They also spend significant amounts on long distance, especially as competition heats up. This group, which makes up about 61 percent of small business, spent about $103 billion in 1998.

Once these markets are tapped, growth in the use of this application will come from reaching consumers who see the Web as their access to services. As the application gains acceptance among the field service workers themselves, there will be an increasing chance of matching consumers to the service provider of their choice. Another component will be providing access to businesses to call in for customized help services.

➤ Business Model

There is certainly no dearth of companies building new applications for the mobile world. The next step is to find a user base for these applications and to identify new segments. Although current applications are aimed at bigger corporations, it is inevitable that the next wave will be aimed at small businesses. In that context, mobile ASP will survive on the strength of its revenue model, its partners, and its ability to capture a substantial user base. In this section we discuss each of these components of a business model.

Revenue Model

The revenue model for ASP applications will be solely transaction-based. Be it pizza delivery or a call for taxi service, every service request that goes through the call center or Web site is chargeable. Similarly, the small business or mobile professional will also be charged for service. We predict that this will be a winning proposition for small businesses, as it will effectively replace calling services in some cases and secretarial help in others. At a minimum, the service will ensure that the professional does not miss any calls and will help him or her organize a better schedule. In the beginning, the key will be to capture a significant installed base by going through professional organizations and unions, perhaps by giving away the application for free. Because the user base consists of small businesses, it will be crucial to convince the users of the service utility before launching other applications on the same platform. For example, services highly targeted toward a particular professional community and its customers can be launched. As the service becomes widely accepted, another revenue stream might come from licensing the service to different wireless carriers. This could also be viewed as a strategic alliance to increase penetration. This leads us into our next topic, partnering.

Partnering

Because the service is being rolled out as a horizontal service across many verticals, it is necessary to ensure fast acceptance. This can be done through alliances with professional organizations and service organizations such as janitorial services. Another way to consolidate the fragmented demand would be to work with establishments that serve individual contractors, such as Home Depot.

Small businesses are often strapped for time, money, and expertise. The smaller the business, the more important service and support become. As a result, small businesses rely primarily on offline retail outlets, where service and support are more readily available. Cahners In-Stat sees support mechanisms as important tools to move these businesses to online purchasing. Even without the service, nearly 20 percent of small businesses currently buy computer hardware, and more, online. Offline retailers with online selling capabilities will have a significant advantage in reaching small businesses through the Internet, and they will drive the growth of this channel.

Those are some of the positive aspects of ASP business applications. Potential barriers to success include the threat of larger, established firms entering this space, and security and trust issues, in that small businesses may be reluctant to hand over their records and operating data to a service provider.

➤ Competitive Landscape

The ASP market consists of the user base, service providers, infrastructure enablers, and the interactions among them. The success of the mobile ASP market will be driven by its ability to link service consumers with service providers, by offering both parties custom-tailored, convenient, cost-effective, domain-specific service bundles. Early observations indicate that ASPs will distinguish themselves by building deep, domain-specific franchises that can deliver localized solutions with a high quality of service. To achieve this, the mobile ASPs must rely on enabling infrastructure solutions from companies that generate low-cost, scalable services for generic tasks across multiple domains. These companies typically fall into one of two categories: mobile data service providers and integrated contact centers.

Mobile data service providers supply the key components for building mobile field service systems, including network communication systems, wide area network (WAN) technologies, rugged mobile computers/handhelds, and application-specific software. Companies such as Telxon, Mobile Data Solutions (MDSI), and Aether Systems will help mobile ASPs build integrated mobile network and information management solutions for robust field service and dispatch applications. These services may include mobile workforce management, work order scheduling, inspections, mapping/GIS, collections/compliance, work order processing, warehousing and inventory tracking. In this area, specialists are emerging. Pointserve.com, an Austin, Texas-based company, not only gives consumers an Internet solution, with the convenience of scheduling a service online, but also gives field dispatch service providers a scheduling solution, complete with appointment times, technician skill sets, and consumer locations.

Integrated call center solution providers, such as Oracle and Kana/Silknet, help third-party call center service companies to which mobile ASPs can outsource customer interaction management. With the help of these firms, field service personnel will have a complete picture of each job ticket and each customer, regardless of how that customer chooses to communicate with the company. By easily leveraging expertise and information from multiple sources throughout the company database, field representatives will be able to solve problems quickly and effectively.

With these infrastructure services in place, we observe two types of mobile field/dispatch ASPs emerging: field service enterprise software solution providers, and industry-specific, mobile field-centric ASPs. The focus of this chapter is on the latter, so we will discuss these ASPs in greater depth while recognizing the existence of the former.

Mobile ASPs are in the business of building service networks that aggregate domain-specific expertise. To generate value for target customers, these mobile ASPs are aggregating supply in local, fragmented markets to deliver a customer experience that entails lower search costs and enables higher quality of service. A drawback of such businesses is that they are harder to scale. Markets must be developed locality by locality. We believe that this business model is more likely to emerge city by city, like Ticketmaster Online, rather than en masse, like eBay.com.

➤ Signposts

Given the nascent nature of the small-business, user-oriented, mobile ASP endeavor, it is helpful to have a few signposts that will mark positive growth in this market. They are:

- Widespread adoption of cost-effective, platform-independent handheld devices: Handhelds such as WAP-enabled telephones or wireless Internet-ready personal digital assistants (such as the Palm or Handspring devices) must get sufficient penetration into the small business market. Because field service/dispatch is a carrier-independent application, carriers will not subsidize the handsets. Mobile ASPs will have to come up with creative business models to bear the cost of handsets or pass them on to end users. This may limit adoption unless the most aggressive projections for mobile phone penetration come true and deliver the economies needed to reduce the device cost of high-end mobile phones to less than $100 per unit.

- Emergence of next-generation customer relationship management (CRM) software: As CRM software applications (from companies such as Oracle and Siebel) integrate pre-sale functions (marketing and sales) with post-sale functions (service delivery and customer care), field dispatch and maintenance-repair-overhaul organizations will increasingly be connected to their customers in a databased environment that supports customer-driven decision making. Channel integration and access to customers via a common platform that enables customer interactions over the Web, via call centers, or via mobile field channels (voice, WAP, SMS) will enable seamless interactions with customers and boost service levels. This will expand the productivity frontier and enable companies to provide one-to-one provisioning of services, capital resource tracking/logistics, and billing solutions that increase customer loyalty and bolster revenue growth.

- Branded service portals successful at aggregating a fragmented, localized customer base: The ultimate test of this business model will be in the establishment of outstanding, vertically focused, branded service portals that offer deep industry expertise and local specialists who offer a high level of accountability and quality of service.

It is safe to say that the mobile ASP business of providing wireless application-based services to small businesses is bound to explode. As soon as the penetration of smart mobile handhelds reaches critical mass and cost of connection becomes economical, this emerging market space will take off.

■ WIRELESS MEDICINE

The benefits of wireless technology to the healthcare industry are clear. Quality care depends on fast, reliable data exchange. The number of data points generated in this industry is simply mind-numbing. Each diagnosis and subsequent treatment plan depends on numerous elements of a patient's history and examination. This includes not only medical information, but also the patient's demographic, insurance, and billing information. In fact, one-third of all value-added service in the healthcare field relates to information, according to Evans and Wurster, the authors of *Blown to Bits*. Constituting 14 percent of the U.S. gross domestic product, healthcare is the ultimate technology sector.

The second defining characteristic of the healthcare sector is the number of participants in each incident. All the information previously mentioned must be disseminated to various parties, including but not limited to patients, providers, payers (insurance companies), employers, the government, and pharmacies. Providing each of these parties with real-time, accurate, and relevant data will not only improve clinical results and increase patient satisfaction, but will also significantly reduce the cost of care.

Unrelenting pressure to reduce costs is a third major characteristic. Healthcare spending in the United States in 1997 was $1.5 trillion, and it is rising at 5 percent per year. Hospitals are facing increasing cost pressures as managed care penetration reduces reimbursement schedules. In response, insurance companies and hospital administrators are trying to reduce procedural costs as well as the average length of a hospital stay. A greater proportion of medical care is now shifting to clinic settings that are geographically dispersed. The decentralization of care outside the traditional hospital setting will require providers to be more mobile and information to be more accessible over wireless networks.

The first wireless application covered in this healthcare section is wireless local area networks (WLANs). WLANs give caregivers mobile access to a building's central computer system via safe radio frequency transmission from digital devices. Many U.S. hospitals are currently using WLANs to enter and retrieve data in real time, resulting in decreased costs and higher efficiency of treatment and recordkeeping.

With hospitals established as information hubs, additional nodes can be developed outside of healthcare facilities. Consequently, one of the killer apps to emerge is a wireless device used in ambulances. Complemented by the adoption of centralized computer systems within hospitals, wireless technology connects the ambulance crew, or nodes, to the hospital hub. The handheld device will read a smartcard bracelet that contains an individual's medical history and relay it to the central hospital computer system while the patient is en route. Timely access to critical information would save lives and reduce costs.

➤ Wireless LAN in Healthcare

Wireless technology is already making the healthcare industry more efficient through the collection and retrieval of data on a real-time basis from any location in the hospital. Physicians and nurses remotely collect medical and insurance information at the patient's bedside through a PDA device. Entering information directly into a patient's electronic medical record is time-efficient and reduces the chance of errors, such as overdoses or mistaken medication. The days of nurses writing on sticky notes and storing them on their lab coats till the end of the day will soon be gone. Getting nurses' notes into an electronic record immediately will speed up diagnosis and reduce procedural costs such as admitting and scheduling (see Figure 6.1).

Proxim reports that only 10 percent of healthcare enterprises are currently using wireless technology. Installing a wireless network is initially more expensive than installing a wireline network, given the existing wireline infrastructure. However, the cost savings from in-

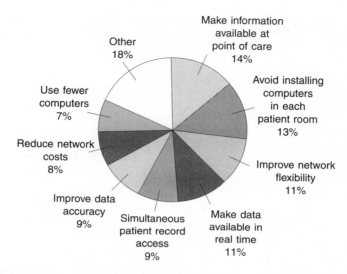

Figure 6.1 Healthcare problems solved with mobile computing.

creased labor efficiencies and incremental upgrades and modifications are tremendous. It is obvious that putting a computer terminal in every patient's room would be not only cost-prohibitive, but also a logistical nightmare. Pulling wire and cable through the ceilings and ducts of typical older hospital buildings would not be practical. This is the beauty of wireless area networks. All you need is a limited number of devices for caregivers and no additional wiring. Hospitals can change computer configurations quickly, in a variety of topologies, at marginal cost.

According to the Wireless LAN Alliance (WLANA), the average time it takes to fully pay back the initial costs of wireless LAN installation is 8.9 months; 48 percent of the total return on investment is manifested through increased labor productivity. Given the demonstrated savings and efficiency of these networks, we should expect continued adoption of WLANs in the healthcare environment. Moreover, satellite facilities, such as nursing homes, hospices, and perhaps even patients' homes, can also be connected via land line or wireless to "hub" hospitals.

As the technology becomes more robust, one can imagine faster transmission of data to mobile nodes even farther out on the network. Ambulance and other emergency medical services are the logical next step. In urgent situations, ambulances are the first points of entry to the healthcare continuum. Wireless technology would offer speed, mobility, and real-time data exchange in a situation where seconds truly count.

➤ Wireless Ambulance

This killer application is best described through a hypothetical situation. Imagine a street in Miami in 2003. A middle-aged woman has chest pains and collapses unconscious on the sidewalk. An ambulance arrives quickly and paramedics diagnose a heart attack. After scanning her "Lifebeat" bracelet/smartcard, the paramedics learn that 58-year-old Mrs. Tanaka (who is visiting from Los Angeles) has asthma and a history of heart problems, including a mild heart attack three years ago. This information is relayed via a WAP handheld device to a centralized computer system (see Figure 6.2). Notification is forwarded to a nearby Miami hospital, where preparations for Ms. Tanaka's arrival commence. En route, paramedics administer asthma medication and begin to treat her heart condition. At the same time, the scan has triggered a number of other communications. The local Miami hospital downloads Mrs. Tanaka's complete medical records from the Lifebeat web site database. Her primary physician in California, Dr. Wells, is automatically alerted, as is her insurance provider and her personal emergency contact, husband Glenn Tanaka. By the time Mrs. Tanaka arrives in the ER, her asthma has been stabilized and a skilled cardiologist is waiting for her. The surgery is a success, thanks to the early information and intervention.

In urgent situations, ambulances are the first points of entry to the healthcare process. Wireless technology offers speed, mobility, and real-time data exchange in an environment where time is crucial. Patients, payers, and providers all benefit from this technology, and should be willing to use and pay for the service. The application would be enabled by smartcard-reading WAP-enabled phones, voice services, and device-to-device communication.

➤ Business Model

Given the application just described, there will be an opportunity for a company to act as an intermediary to facilitate the entire process. This

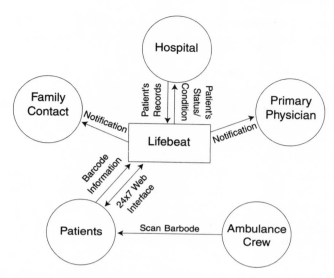

Figure 6.2 Lifebeat information/technology flow.

company will produce barcoded identification bracelets that will allow paramedics or even ER personnel to quickly access a patient's medical history, *regardless of location*. In addition, this company will produce devices for ambulances that can read the barcodes and automatically transfer the medical information from a central host depository of medical records to the hospital to which the patient is being rushed.

The primary sources of revenue for this new company—our hypothetical Lifebeat—will be insurance and pharmaceutical companies. Not only will this new service cut costs for insurance companies, but it may also allow them to charge subscribers *more* for the valuable peace of mind that the Lifebeat network offers. Getting medical professionals the diagnostic information they need on a real-time basis can significantly improve the patient's medical condition and prognosis. This can result in fewer exams and possibly fewer days in the hospital. All this translates into fewer insurance claims.

Lifebeat will be in the business of hosting and updating electronic medical records. The company will develop medical identification cards for all members of a health plan. The health plan will distribute these cards to employers for distribution to employees. The insurance company will also provide members' medical records, which Lifebeat will store, update, and manage in a central database. For these data management services, Lifebeat will receive a per-member, per-month (PMPM) fee.

Lifebeat will also provide ambulances with platform-independent, standard WAP-enabled devices that can read a magnetic strip and instruct Lifebeat's servers to send a particular medical record to a specific hospital in the vicinity. These devices will be provided to the ambulances and hospitals at no cost.

Having a central depository of medical records will improve patient satisfaction as well. Lifebeat will develop a Web site where patients can securely view their medical records, often for the first time. While the patient is online, drug companies can promote literature on drugs that might be pertinent to the patient's condition. This patient interaction with the Web site also allows Lifebeat to receive advertising revenues (see Figure 6.3).

➤ Market Size

Simply put, the healthcare market is enormous. Healthcare information services are a $500 billion business in the United States alone.

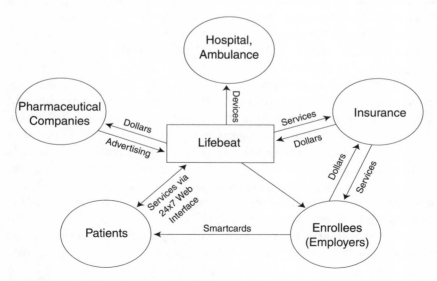

Figure 6.3 Lifebeat revenue model.

Lifebeat would have to capture a mere 0.2 percent to gain $1 billion in revenues. Because of the reduction in costs the service provides, we believe that Lifebeat would actually create and capture value. Moreover, this concept does not require a large critical mass of users to be profitable—perhaps just one small city. At the same time, it is scalable to a national or global basis because it uses the public WAP and Internet Protocol (IP) networks.

The most difficult step will be to reach a critical mass. Visualizing insurance companies as Lifebeat's customers is the key. This will allow the firm to "back-end" thousands of customers at a time, and take advantage of the insurance companies' installed base of users to market its services.

➤ Competitive Landscape

The interest of companies such as Palm Computing and Singapore Network Services in wireless ambulance applications is further validation of the need for the services that Lifebeat is proposing. AMR, the largest privately owned American ambulance company, has replaced its triplicate carbon-copy recordkeeping system with Palm Pilot data entry systems that are hotsynched at the hospital. San Mateo County, California, has realized significant cost savings by cutting data entry time in half. On the other side of the Pacific, Singapore Network Services has pilot-tested a program, in cooperation with the Singapore government, that is even more advanced than Palm's in terms of real-time data entry and two-way exchange. In addition, companies such as Proxim and Symbol (manufacturers of high-speed wireless LANs), and Healtheon/WebMD (which already has access to patient demographic and medical information), are positioned and have the brand equity to move into Lifebeat's space. They could leverage their current competencies to offer a broader, more complete solution for the medical industry.

The Lifebeat concept, however, is several steps ahead of these projects. Lifebeat would offer secure, real-time, two-way data exchange (including the patient's identity) across the public networks from anywhere in the vicinity of the hospital. This application offers speed and true communication to numerous parties in critical situations, rather than simple recordkeeping.

➤ Signposts

Available now:

- Standardized system for accessing and transmitting patient medical records and information
- Barcode reading units, attached to WAP-enabled cellular phones

Available within 12 months:

- Software (middleware) that communicates with WAP protocol
- Barcode or smartcard bracelets worn by the public

Available within 24 months:

- Reliable data transmissions between a hospital and the entire area served by its ambulances
- A standardized system of medical records

We realize that all new applications have their stumbling blocks. Patient privacy rights may be the biggest hurdle regarding this particular application. The amount of information, if any, hard-coded into the bracelets might be a point of contention, as would the degree of interactivity of the transmission. Perhaps the paramedics in the field might only learn the most relevant information about diseases and medical history, without knowing the patient's name or full medical records. These are significant issues that must be addressed. The fundamental value proposition is compelling, however, and one can easily imagine many insurance subscribers eager to improve their chances of recovery after a traumatic incident.

The wireless Lifebeat application has all the aspects of a killer app. It provides mobile, instant data exchange across an independent, scalable platform in a situation in which every second is critical. The field of healthcare has amazing growth potential. The application can be rolled out slowly in one city, yet is ultimately scalable on a worldwide basis. Lifebeat will provide benefits to patients, payers, and providers by containing costs, increasing efficiency, and saving lives.

■ MOBILE ASSET/SUPPLY CHAIN MANAGEMENT

Modern inventory and physical asset management practices have yet to weed out yesterday's error-prone manual data collection methods. Lag time between data collection and information availability results in an absence of real-time accurate data. This severely limits the effectiveness of existing information systems. In addition, the manufacturing sector has not fully embraced the tracking, diagnostic, and technological tools that wireless technology affords.

Our third and final killer app involves relatively inexpensive and innocuous microprocessors embedded within assets that identify, locate, and actually communicate with personnel and other machines through a wireless network. The ability to locate, monitor, and conduct diagnostics of physical assets (see Figure 6.4) from a mobile location will allow tremendous savings in time, personnel, and avoided user error. Imagine the confusion at a loading dock or major construction site. Just by installing a small wireless transmitter on each piece of equipment or valuable cargo, these expensive assets can always be accounted for. This concept has already penetrated the consumer automobile market, because motor vehicle theft is the most frequently committed property crime in the United States, costing consumers and insurance companies $7 billion per year. In fact, one vehicle is stolen

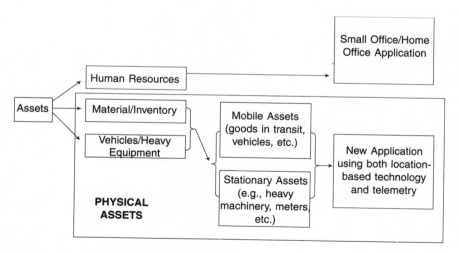

Figure 6.4 Classification of assets.

every 23 seconds in the United States—an incredibly costly act that can be alleviated by tracking companies such as Lojack. Additionally, maintenance and service of static machines and industrial equipment constitute an expensive, labor-intensive, and time-consuming process, especially for those in remote locations. However, if these machines could be monitored and controlled from a distance, it would significantly reduce the need to deploy expensive resources for routine maintenance.

A technology that helps businesses protect and control their products or assets is marketable to virtually any vertical market. Figure 6.5 illustrates the market demand for wireless asset-management technology. By bundling both the real-time location services and the telemetry capabilities, such ASPs will differentiate themselves within the marketplace.

Several vertical markets in particular might benefit from this technology. For example, mobile workers could control machines in their offices; freight and transportation providers (rail, truck, air) could monitor both their fleets and their assets in transit. Although current players in this space cater mostly to heavier equipment tracking and large utility company use, our prediction is that as prices decrease, this

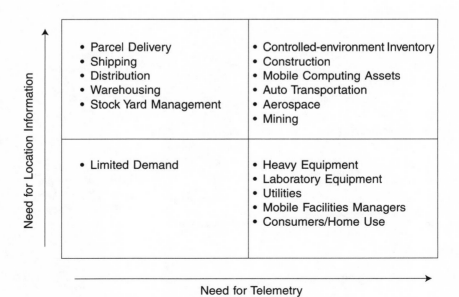

Figure 6.5 Market segmentation strategy.

technology will proliferate in other areas, being used for less valuable inventory and smaller equipment. For example, an industrial supply company like Grainger has a strong need to be able to locate and monitor smaller items within a trailer that contains a variety of disparate items.

Potential cost savings and rapid advances in fundamental technologies translate into tremendous possibilities for this application in many areas. In fact, we eventually see consumers using this technology to monitor their home security systems, appliances, and living environment.

The application will be enabled by technologies that combine location-based services with microprocessors capable of telemetric functionality. The software will be embedded in a silicon-based integrated circuit (IC) housed within a smartcard. The smartcard will reside in a small wireless local transmitter or "locator tag," which will communicate through a wireless network (using SMS or other messaging technologies) to a relational database that stores and relays the information required for diagnostics and location identification.

The application is simple, yet extremely powerful. When a transmitter with a smartcard, embedded with location-based capabilities, is affixed, assets can be tracked and/or monitored via a cellular phone or IP telephony station. In Finland, these applications have been used in the water industry to remotely monitor and control pumping stations via telephone since 1992. In fact, utility companies are already implementing telemetry across the globe. Automatic meter reading is providing a way for energy companies facing deregulation and competition to streamline operations, improve customer relationships, and add new sources of revenue. The technology allows for meter reads in real time, remote diagnosis of power outages and other problems, and the accumulation of important customer data for marketing and customer service.

Field trials conducted by DaimlerChrysler and Volvo have installed GSM chipsets in trucks, both to monitor performance and to provide an early warning system that sends a message to the manufacturer when a problem occurs (e.g., high temperature in the engine, brake problems, or "out of oil" alarm). Similarly, the manufacturer's system will be able to analyze the various data and provide a fix via a software tool to be sent to the truck or by asking the vehicle driver to go to a service station. Thus, developing faults can be found early and the continuous operation of the truck can be ensured, facilitating on-time delivery and lower repair and maintenance costs.

➤ Market Size

Estimating the market potential for this technology is very difficult, but you can see the appeal through the following examples. WhereNet, a supplier of wireless location management systems for use within warehouses and manufacturing facilities, has identified more than 32,000 manufacturing facilities and 10,000 distribution sites (each more than 50,000 square feet in size) in the United States alone, with diverse inventory location, tracking, and reporting requirements. This represents a $10 billion-plus market for WhereNet's $250,000 solution. Nokia's telematics business, called Smart Traffic Products, predicts that every vehicle across the globe will be equipped with at least one IP address in the year 2010. General Motors is beginning this push by committing to making its OnStar telematic system available as a standard option in approximately 2.5 million cars next year. Daimler Chrysler's Mercedes division is taking an even more aggressive approach by making telematics a standard feature on all Mercedes cars in 2001. It is likely that in the future, all cars will be equipped with mobile communication links, starting with the top-of-the-line models first, but quickly moving down the line.

➤ Competition

The number of players entering this industry suggests a bright future. Several companies already have tremendous depth in location-based services and telemetry. For example, WhereNet is deep into the inventory management space, whereas AtRoad markets fleet management, location-based technology. In telemetry, CellNet made significant technological advances while providing automatic meter reading services to utility companies; the auto makers are pushing the envelope in the transportation sector. Though there is competition, the freedom that this technology permits and the different sectors that will benefit indicate that there is room for several players to provide services tailored to specific verticals.

➤ Business Model

Our third killer app has tremendous business potential for heavy machinery users, warehouse management services, and freight forwarders. This proposed technology requires communication hardware that is readily available at a reasonable price, as well as location and telemetry functionality, which are currently being developed. However, we believe that the true value-added service will lie with the software provider who will offer functionality and power through the relational database.

➤ Revenue Model and Partnerships

Cellular airtime is the only component of marginal cost to this technology, so we would look to partner with cellular network providers. By giving away software to these providers, ASPs will be able to bundle their services to their corporate clients into one monthly cellular bill (i.e., voice mail, call waiting, and data with a per-packet rate). The use of the software will encourage higher data network usage, thereby allowing revenue sharing.

Partnering with hardware manufacturers would also be a key component of this application's business model. Our revenue model (see Figure 6.6) shows the ASP buying hardware to bundle services. An alternative approach would be to sell the software to the hardware vendors (the Microsoft model).

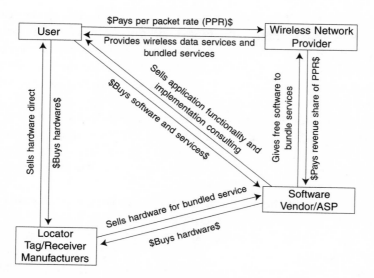

Figure 6.6 Location/telemetry revenue model.

➤ Competitive Landscape

The existing companies that are best positioned to develop a commercially viable version of the application include supply chain-focused players, such as Symbol, which provide many wireless solutions that enhance supply chain processes by incorporating real-time data (such as barcode scanners, WLAN, and portable computing). Epic Data develops data collection systems oriented toward leading enterprise resource planning (ERP) software programs. Players such as these are close to their customers and, therefore, are best positioned to receive information on problems and bottleneck points in inventory management and asset tracking. This will enable them to offer early solutions, as the technology to enable the application becomes feasible, available, and cost effective. Location-based technology firms represent a major portion of the competitive landscape for this application. Although there are many players in the vehicle tracking and fleet management arenas, companies such as WhereNet, which apply radio-frequency identification (RFID) technology to container tracking and yard management, have strong market potential. Telemetry companies are also well positioned to apply their solutions to the asset management application.

➤ Signposts

Telematics will invade our lives in the next five years, as two of the three largest auto makers in the world will push it into the mainstream. This forced adoption will lead to additional demand in both the business and the consumer spaces. Additionally, the continued need for instant access to information will drive the desire to find out where something is instantly.

We already see evidence of the need to integrate real-time information, utilizing wireless technology, into the supply chain. For example, companies like Epic Data are developing automatic data collection specifically for the ERP marketplace by providing data collection products for SAP, Protean, and Baan.

The productivity benefits of using RFID tags over barcodes are being increasingly recognized. Interestingly, a leader in barcode scanning technology, Symbol Technologies, has adopted a technology-neutral position, working with leading RFID technology providers to create RFID-capable product platforms. These platforms will enable Symbol's customers to benefit from integrated technology solutions employing an optimal mix of RFID and barcode technologies. We view this as another sign of the growth of asset management, because Symbol is proposing to focus on strategic applications where RFID is harnessed as a core component to allow retailers to more efficiently track consignments and items through the supply chain from manufacturers. Other opportunities that Symbol and its partners are already pursuing include military logistics, parcel and postal service logistics, transportation fleet management, and corporate asset control.

The size and cost of the "tag" (transmitter/smartcard) in RFID locator technology currently prohibit widespread use of this type of transmitter on smaller, less valuable pieces of equipment. However, just as the personal computer integrated circuit rapidly evolved in functionality and became smaller in both size and price, we believe that the wireless transmitter will grow smaller and become cheaper until it will compete effectively with the barcode in terms of size and cost feasibility. This evolution will be another signpost for a positive inflection point in the location-based market for many new small asset industries. Adoption will consequently be widespread.

Over the long run, the benefits of telemetry bode well for the potential of wireless data solutions in asset management. Improvements in technology, reductions in the cost and size of components, and the increasing standardization of wireless technology will allow asset managers to track, repair, and monitor their mobile assets without having to incur traditional costs of dispatch, recall, and downtime.

■ THE FUTURE

The convergence of wireless communications and the Internet is not simply an extension of—nor a substitute for—land-line infrastructure and communications. Rather, it is technologically disruptive. It signals a paradigm shift in which knowledge of a person's location stimulates the need for targeted content, communications, and commerce. It opens our expectations of personal and business productivity to a new frontier.

The nature of that frontier, however, is amorphous. In the new paradigm, which companies will dominate? Which business models will succeed? What new devices and form factors will engage us in the ultimate mobile Internet experience? What killer applications will emerge to disintegrate existing value chains and reconfigure the face of business? Although we believe that some intriguing opportunities will bring commercial success to those who excel in penetrating the healthcare, asset tracking/management, and field service/dispatch markets, we realize that they are just the beginning.

New technologies and products will continually emerge to substitute for, or complement the current application building blocks. Some of those we view as shaping our future include the following.

1. The growing mobile workforce will serve as the groundswell for a wireless business Internet. Currently, there are 45 million mobile professionals, and the number is growing. Mobile workers comprise not only professionals who travel around the nation or globe, but also those who travel within their communities, or simply between buildings and meeting rooms. All these mobile workers are inconvenienced when they lose access to their primary desktops. As mobile, handheld device penetration increases in the form of wireless PDAs, WAP-enabled phones, and smart phones, more individuals will demand connectivity and access to relevant corporate information on these devices. Corporate IT personnel will heed this movement toward mobile access to business information. Once mobile computing becomes ubiquitous, corporations will pour money into the enterprise application space.

2. Proliferation of third generation (3G) networks will change everything. A central question in the minds of many is who will own the ultimate customer relationship. Will your wireless service provider serve as the gateway to all mobile Internet services, or will a more open architecture emerge? We believe that the answer lies in the proliferation of Internet-protocol-based, 3G networks. Today, much of the power resides in the hands of the wireless carriers, because they own the telephone numbers that get assigned to mobile users. With the proliferation of 3G networks, however, each mobile phone user will be assigned a unique IP address. This fundamental change will shift the balance of power out of the hands of incumbent wireless carriers and into the hands of more nimble wireless Internet service providers who invest in implementing 3G networks. As increasing portions of the wireless spectrum are auctioned off, it is anyone's guess as to who might jump into the fray. Content providers such as Yahoo!, handset manufacturers such as Nokia, and New Economy communications companies such as Qwest could all step in to extend their value propositions to provide mobile Internet access. As a result, we expect consumers and businesses to

benefit from greater choice, lower switching costs, and a higher quality of service.

3. New application-specific devices will emerge to meet the needs of diverse customer segments. As businesses, small and large, seek mobile data connectivity to keep pace with the changing competitive landscape, new opportunities will emerge for enterprises to build advantage through mobility connectivity. We expect new devices to emerge that customize the users' experiences to their business needs. Handspring's design of creating modular handheld devices that are customized to include barcode readers, smartcards, cameras, and the like is, we believe, well positioned to take advantage of the impending revolution. The demand for several different designs, however, may limit how much influence a single operating system, such as the Palm OS or Symbian alliance (between Nokia and Ericsson), might have over this market.

4. In the developing world, where the personal computer is not as pervasive, the mobile Internet will enable the democratization of business information. All businesses, whether small or large, depend on the communication infrastructure to build efficiencies and enable decision making. The emergence of Internet appliances in particular will have a large role in leveling the playing field for small businesses in the developing world. The plain old telephone has integrated itself across almost all strata of age groups, education levels, and income levels. The wireless Internet, therefore, has a strong chance not only of leapfrogging infrastructure roadblocks but also of countering the social constraints of the personal computing revolution. The corner grocery store owner in Mumbai will be willing to invest in a mobile phone that provides him access to a local supply network that alleviates his day-to-day, stock-out problems. The cable television installation person in Thailand will find the mobile Internet device useful to schedule her next appointment across town. In other words, this new communication platform gives small businesses in the developing world a real chance to build efficiencies cost-effectively. If communications were a barrier to entry in the past, the mobile revolution will help overcome this hurdle. Ultimately, we feel that this "democratization" will further spur entrepreneurial spirit in developing countries.

Beyond speculation, one thing seems fairly certain: Generations that follow us will be amused by the use of the term *wireless*. Wireless access to information will be taken for granted. Like "radio with pictures"

and "iron horse," *wireless* may soon disappear from the common vocabulary, remaining only as vestiges in the names of pioneering
companies (just as AT&T and NTT who still acknowledge their origins
in telegraph).

■ REFERENCES

Acuff, A. Marshall Jr. 1999. "Technology and Communications: Growth
Leaders for the New Millennium." *Salomon Smith Barney Report.*

Boehm, Elizabeth. 2000. "Full Service Healthcare Sites Arise." *The Forrester Report* (February).

Cohen, Ethan. 2000. "Back to the Future in AMR: Hope, Hype and Reality." *The Yankee Group: Energy and Internet Strategies Report* (March 7).

Cukier, Kenneth Neil. 2000. "Who owns the customer?" *Red Herring* (April).

"The dawn of mobile commerce." 1999. *Forrester Research* (October).

Essex, David. 1999. "Microsoft opens Windows to smartcards." PC World
(November 19), http://www.cnn.com/TECH/computing/9911/19/
windows.smartcards.idg/index.html.

Evans, Phillip, and Thomas Wurster. 1999. *Blown to Bits.* Harvard Business
School Press.

Gold, Jay. "The Wireless Physician." PDA MD.com (February 2000),
www.pdamd.com.

Hill, G. Christian. "First Voice, Now Data." *Wall Street Journal*, September
20, 1999.

"Killer Apps on Non-PC Devices." *The Forrester Report.* July 1999.

Lash, Alex. 1999. "Phone.com's Great Expectations." *The Industry Standard*
(November 8).

McCarthy, Amanda. 1999. "Is Wireless Replacing Wireline?" *Forrester Brief*
(March).

"Microbrowsers & Mobility: Web Access on the Move." www.smartcom-
puting.com, vol. 8, issue 1 (January 2000).

Muller-Veerse, Falk. 2000. "Mobile Commerce Report." *Durlacher Research.*

"The New World of Wireless: A Service Provider's Guide to Broadband
Fixed Wireless Networks." www.cisco.com.

Nitzke, John. 1998. "Wireless' Digital Destiny." *The Forrester Report* (July).

"Offsite But Connected: Matching Remote Access Hardware, Software with
Company Needs." *PC Today* 12 (no. 6, June 1998).

Paczkowski, John. "Mobile Computing Finds Its Voice." *Red Herring Magazine* (November 1999).

Proxim Healthcare. *1999 Proxim Healthcare Wireless LAN Survey Results.* www.proxim.com, January 2000.

Richards, Bill. 1999. "Watch Closely." *Wall Street Journal*, September 20, 1999.

Rohde, Laura. 2000. "Smartcards to contain biometric data." IDG.net. http://www.cnn.com/2000/TECH/computing/02/09/biometrics.card.idg/ (February 9).

Rutstein, Charles. 1999. "Wireless LANs Finally Matter." *The Forrester Brief* (May).

Sayer, Peter. 2000. "Virgin mobile plays browser smartcard." IDG.net. http://www.idg.net/idgns/2000/02/01/VirginMobilePlays BrowserSmartCard.shtml (February 1).

Schaaf, Jeanne. 1999. "Bandwidth Bottlenecks Burst." *The Forrester Report* (November).

"Selecting and Implementing a Wireless Network in the Healthcare Environment." 1999. Proxim White Paper. www.proxim.com.

Seymour, Jim. 1998. "1998: The Year of the (Un)Wired House." *PC Magazine* (April).

"WinWap—WAP Browser for WML Pages." 2000. www.slobtrot.com.

"The Wireless Application Protocol: The Wireless Internet Today." 1999. Phone.com white paper (February).

"Wireless Barriers." 2000. *Upside* (March).

"Wireless Phones Will Stay Small and Simple." 1999. *Forrester Brief* (October).

Wolk, Marianne, and Bryan Candace. 2000. "Wireless Data—The Next Internet Frontier." *Robertson Stephens Technology Research* (January 25).

"Your wireless future." 1999. *Business 2.0* (August).

Zachary, G. Pascal. 1999. "Beyond Credit and Debit." *Wall Street Journal*, September 20, 1999.

Zeichick, Alan. 1999. "Cell Networks Explained." *Red Herring Magazine* (August).

Zerega, Blaise. 1999. "Business to Business E-Commerce: Quality of Service Closes the Deal." *Red Herring Magazine* (February).

———. 1999. "Crank Up the Broadband." *Red Herring Magazine* (August).

Zohar, Mark. 1999. "The Dawn of Mobile E-Commerce." *The Forrester Report* (October).

Chapter

Customer Competencies

Data Mining and Customer Relationship Management

■ INTRODUCTION

Data mining refers to the process of extracting trends and predicting future patterns by applying mathematical algorithms to data. Businesses have just begun to realize the potential of this process, but the ability to harness the power of information within an organization is fast becoming a competitive necessity. Data mining enables users to distill complex situations into manageable projects by translating available data into valuable, actionable information. Customer resource management (CRM) methods use data-mining tools to tap into a company's current and potential customer base to market products more effectively.

➤ Emergence of Data Mining

So much data is collected today that many databases are quantified in terabytes (trillions of bytes). They contain valuable information on customers, suppliers, employees, the competition, and general economic conditions. Extracting meaning from these trillions of bytes may be the difference between success and failure for many businesses. The need to understand and interpret the data, as daunting a task as it sounds, places an ever-increasing burden on business analysts and managers. Without data-mining techniques, as the amount and complexity of data in corporate databases grow at unprecedented rates, the ability of analysts and managers to act and make strategic decisions is severely limited.

Data-mining tools attempt to alleviate this data overload problem by synthesizing succinct insights from the seemingly disparate information contained within these vast databases. Companies have turned to data-mining techniques to do three primary things:

1. Find patterns and trends embedded within the information
2. Extract hidden predictive information
3. Locate and differentiate anomalies and irregularities that do not fit the other data.

Fortune 1000 companies are beginning to notice data mining's ability to unearth the rich content held within massive databases. Although powerful computers have long had the ability to sift through vast volumes of data to find key information required by the user, only recently—with the advent of cheaper disk storage, the dramatic drop in prices of processing, increased processing speeds, and the advances in parallel computing architectures—has data-mining performance matched the cost of investment. This once-nascent industry technique is being touted as a key source of value for many companies. In a recent industry poll, 28 percent of 50 information technology (IT) executives said that they actively mined data, and the rest said that it was a strategic imperative to do so by the year 2001.

In fact, many diverse and wide-ranging forms of data mining are used today. For example, data-mining systems can sift through vast quantities of data collected during the semiconductor fabrication process to identify conditions that are causing yield problems. A market-share prediction system allows television programming executives to arrange show schedules to maximize market share and increase advertising revenues. By more accurately predicting the effectiveness of expensive medical procedures, healthcare costs can be reduced without affecting quality of care. An offshore oil well may cost tens of millions of dollars, but advanced data-mining technology can increase the probability that this investment will pay off.

A common theme in these examples is the use of data mining to increase the bottom line of each company. Whether by increasing revenues or decreasing costs, the ultimate goal of data-mining applications used in a business is to increase the company's profitability.

This chapter discusses the goals of data mining, the value it brings to business, the benefits promised, and some of the companies at the forefront of data-mining business applications. The chapter closes with a look at the state of customer resource management (CRM), an approach that pioneered the use of data-mining tools.

■ THE HISTORY OF DATA MINING

The core components of data-mining technology have been under development for decades in research areas such as statistics, artificial intelligence, and machine learning. More recent developments, in the form of ability to collect a massive amount of data in an extremely short time, powerful multiprocessor computers, and the advent of data-mining algorithms, have hastened the spread of the need for and adaptation of data-mining techniques.

Currently, data mining exists in three forms (see Figure 7.1). The first form of data mining is the automated discovery of trends and patterns that were previously unknown or thought to be inconsequential. Data mining *discovery* is the process of identifying new patterns without specific direction as to the exact determining factors. This is a time-consuming process requiring multiple iterations, as the search for patterns is not focused and may bring up spurious relationships. However, it is a very powerful method for identifying current relationships. Discovery mining has been especially useful in decoding human gene sequences.

The second form is the automated prediction of trends and behaviors. In *predictive modeling*, the data-mining tool identifies patterns and uses that information to predict the future. This data-mining application is particularly popular in customer retention programs, which use data mining to segment the customer base, determine the most profitable category of customer, and predict the ability to retain that customer. Using this data, these retention programs can decide to implement a targeted program to retain the most profitable customers.

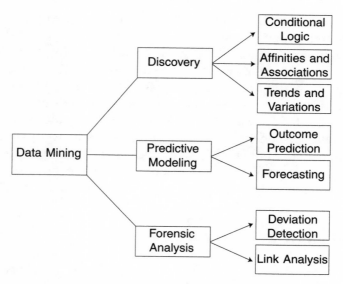

Figure 7.1   Data mining applications and algorithms.

The third form of data mining, known as *forensic analysis*, entails applying a pattern to the data (which may have been determined through a previous data-mining exercise) to identify data anomalies. This application of data mining is primarily used today by quality assurance and credit card fraud systems.

■ THE PROCESS OF DATA MINING

To find trends and patterns, predict behavior, or find anomalies in a series of data, data mining follows a process involving several steps. These steps are shown in Figure 7.2.

➤ Acquire Data from Disparate Systems

The first step in the data-mining process is the acquisition of data. The repositories of required data are usually disparate systems that include legacy databases, nonlegacy databases, third-party data sources (i.e., supplier databases), and even real-time transactions not currently stored, such as user Web page surfing that may be used to illuminate

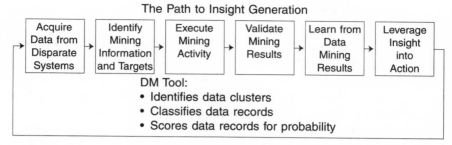

Figure 7.2   Data mining and supporting processes.

potential consumers' interests and behavioral patterns. This data is then passed along to a central information repository called a *data warehouse*. At the data warehouse, the data is:

- "Translated" to a format that the data warehouse comprehends
- "Cleansed" to correct blank or invalid fields (this is done through a set of business rules, which, for instance, might correct a missing age by using the overall data set average or modal, or perhaps by marking that the attribute is "blank")
- "Transformed" to a standardized format (for instance, a system might translate gender data from one source, in the form "F," to the standardized format of "female").

Once the data is processed, it is entered into the data warehouse and other respective data repositories.

➤ Identify Mining Target and Parameters

The second step is the identification of a specific hypothesis for which to mine and identify or apply data patterns. A business analyst or an automated system (in adaptive or learning systems) accomplishes this by supplying the data-mining tool with the appropriate data set and desired algorithm type (ranging from simple linear regression to genetic algorithms, such as "selective breeding" data patterns). Depending on the particular data-mining tool, it is also possible to indicate certain parameters by which to constrain and control the data-mining activity (e.g., the number of distinct data categories or clusters and accuracy thresholds).

➤ Execute Data Mining Activity

Supplied with the target data set, algorithm type, and appropriate constraints, the data-mining tool will begin its work of clustering, classifying, and scoring records. In *clustering*, the data-mining tool identifies distinct clusters or groupings of similar data records, using the defined parameters. Using these clusters, the data-mining tool then classifies or categorizes each record into a cluster and assigns a score indicating the probability of the record truly fitting into and exhibiting the behavior of the identified cluster.

➤ Validate Data Mining Results

Upon completion of the data-mining activity, the initiator (either the business analyst or the automated system) must validate the analysis to ensure that the results are not spurious. The initiator may use one of several common validation tests:

- Check against common business sense and rationality (applicable if the initiator is a business analyst), because some random relationships may exist but lack value.
- Compare to spot sample data using online analytical processing (OLAP) tools.
- Apply the generated model against a segregated, controlled sample data set to see if similar results are generated.

■ LEARNING FROM DATA MINING RESULTS

If the data-mining results pass these tests, the initiator must translate the findings into meaningful action. In the case of a learning system (a hybrid system that combines artificial intelligence with data mining to "learn"), the system incorporates findings into the data warehouse to be used for future mining and prediction activities. In the case of an automated process, such as an e-commerce site, the findings may be used to present a specific product offering or discount to a current site visitor and potential customer. Similarly, if a degradation pattern is identified in an automated production quality monitoring and prediction system, the system will auto-alert the responsible production manager via e-mail or a page. If, however, the initiator is a business analyst, it is his or her responsibility to translate the discovered insight into meaningful action. Arguably, the resulting patterns themselves add no value to the business or organization. Only changes enacted as a result of identifying and interpreting these data patterns and relationships add such value.

■ INVESTING IN DATA MINING

A key reason why more companies are not aggressively participating in data mining is a lack of understanding of the value derived from investing in such capabilities. The fact that traditional return-on-investment analysis is difficult to measure from stand-alone analysis only complicates the issue. For example, Wal-Mart, a leader in the implementation of sophisticated data-mining software, must coordinate knowledge gained from its databases with implementation of practices that use this knowledge. Determining whether resulting gains in profitability are due to data mining or to the practice implemented as a result of the knowledge gained from mining is extremely difficult.

To remain competitive, companies must recognize the strategic importance and role of data mining in the overall scheme of the company's corporate strategy. For example, retailers who compete for customers and understand the importance of customer service may wish to use data-mining techniques to learn which services receive greater response rates and which customers are most valuable, so that they can use that information to improve and optimize their level of customer service. Neither the customer service nor the associated improvements are easy to measure in terms of a bottom-line number, yet companies that understand the importance of the underlying data mining will be in a far better competitive position. Data mining, in the short term, can actually be a source of competitive advantage for many firms. At the very minimum, employing the power of data mining can keep companies on a par with the competition.

The as-yet-unfulfilled promise of data mining lies in the power and effectiveness of the business decisions and plans that result from having knowledge of an entire institution. Data mining has the potential to turn mountains of data into meaningful and insightful information— information that could make the difference between being a market leader or market laggard.

➤ When to Invest?

As current technical trends lead to increased utilization of IT resources, it is no longer a question of whether the IT department is valuable. Rather, the question is how a company can turn its IT department into a competitive weapon. If each player sees the value of data mining and is equally capable of acting upon its abilities, the best-case scenario is that each company will be on equal footing with its competition. If, however, a company chooses not to take advantage of the opportunity to acquire and find predictive trends, the competition will move faster and more effectively. Competition against foes that are armed with more powerful, expandable knowledge is really not competition at all.

The real options approach to investment decisions might further illustrate the value proposition of investing in data-mining technologies. The incredible rate of technological innovation, combined with the ever-present question of which technologies will win or become the industry standard, creates tremendous uncertainty. In an uncertain environment, the ability to wait until better information is available is extremely valuable. To have that option, however, certain incremental investments must be made to ensure that the option to take full advantage of a technology remains available. That option is known as a *real option*. The value of a real option is best expressed by the Black-Scholes model of option analysis, which states that as volatility increases, the value of the option increases (see Chapter 4). Black-Scholes also says that the best path turns out to be the one that assumes the most risk. Without sufficient risk or investment, it is impossible to realize greater financial returns.

➤ Financial Benefits

Although a specific return on investment in data-mining capabilities is difficult to measure financially, sources of improvements to the bottom line from such investments are easy to distinguish. The ability to find patterns and predict trends can have tremendous value by increasing revenues, maximizing operating efficiency, cutting costs, or improving customer satisfaction. Thorough and thoughtful examination of data can lead to better estimates of the elasticity of consumer demand, indifference curves, supplier price points, and general forecasting ability. With better knowledge, companies can increase the competitiveness and effectiveness of their strategic actions, for example:

- Credit card and telecommunications companies use data mining to detect fraud by monitoring hundreds of millions of transactions for unusual purchasing behavior.

- Companies can use their vast warehouses of transaction data to identify customers who would be interested in new programs, and to compile those names in a targeted database. If it understands why certain customers make better candidates than others, a company can realize huge cost savings by increasing the efficiency and yield on its marketing efforts and by retaining key customers. Also, the company can increase revenues by bringing in appropriate new customers.

- Companies can analyze sales trends and compare them to the results of marketing and sales force activities to determine which of those activities works best. A thorough analysis of competitive environment and customer sentiment can yield valuable information for sales representatives and increase their ability to competitively position products.

- Data mining can give companies the ability to segment their customers. By creating classes or categories of customers based on lifetime profitability, companies can devote more energy and resources to satisfying the "heavy users" while spending much less (or nothing) on less profitable customers. In this manner, companies can create priority lists, which in turn increase efficiency and returns.

- Companies can access multiple channels of information, then turn to data mining to interpret trends that would otherwise be nearly impossible to digest. Information about competition, economic environment, suppliers, and prior sales can come from many disparate parts of a company. Making sense of all the data would require a sophisticated and coordinated effort. By forming coherent analyses of the information, the company can better understand its strategic and competitive position.

- Business line managers can incorporate trend analysis and predictions into their day-to-day tasks, such as spreadsheet modeling, to facilitate and speed up decision making. Also, the line staff, such as call center representatives or clerks, will have ready access to sophisticated data already embedded in their applications. By having the ability to access this valuable data, the line staff can create personalized offerings in real time, quickly and effortlessly.

■ DATA MINING APPLICATIONS

Probably the most common, and best developed, use of data mining in business is in the attraction, retention, and drive to increase the profitability of customers. In a business context, most data-mining campaigns begin with the creation of a list of prospective customers, culled either from lists of previous customers or from lists purchased from outside consumer information vendors. Existing customer lists provide a wealth of historical information about responses to previous offerings; mining this information is critical to understanding one's customers. However, to acquire new customers, certain hypotheses must be developed around available information that will predict customers' responses to marketing campaigns or new products. These hypotheses can be created by overlaying information about purchase and response behaviors collected and refined by information vendors. These data come from a "variety of sources including retailers, state and local governments (e.g., make of car from the DMV), and the customers themselves."[1] This section discusses how these marketing campaigns are pursued, the strategic options available to businesses with extensive customer information, and some of the factors that enable companies to mine their data.

➤ Applications in Financial Services

Mining customer data can be a significant source of competitive advantage for numerous industries; however, the correlation between predictive ability and increased profitability is perhaps strongest in the financial services industry. With access to consumers' buying patterns and purchase histories, credit card companies have mountains of demographic and psychographic information embedded in the records of individual customer purchases. Analysis of the patterns and trends that emerge from the aggregation of such information gives unparalleled insight into factors that improve customer acquisition, retention, and sales opportunities throughout that customer's lifetime. These insights enable credit card issuers to predict such things as customers' reactions to rate increases and new product offerings, as well as the value of the customers to the company. One of the primary strategic uses of data mining is to provide a form of mass-customized product tailored to customers' needs. Two types of marketing organizations use data mining to achieve strategic advantages:

- *Collaborative customizers* engage customers in an ongoing dialogue regarding their needs, in the pursuit of a product that is as individualized as possible. Instead of confronting consumers with a confusing array of options, data mining can help the mass customizer isolate the options that will be most attractive to a particular user.

- *Transparent customizers* provide individual customers with unique goods or services without letting them know explicitly that those products and services have in fact been customized. As a result, the company pursuing a transparent customization of its products can use its data to appeal very directly to the preferences of individual consumers, even if the product is largely the same as the ones offered to other customers.

In both cases, the ability to tailor a product to specific customer needs is inexorably tied to the development of a company's strategy. Tailoring a product "permeates everything [a company] does—pricing, promotion and product development," says Russel Herz, senior vice president in charge of liability product management at the Chase Manhattan Bank in New York.[2] As Mr. Herz suggests, data mining is quickly becoming less of a luxury and more of a key marketing tool.

> ### ➤ Sell to Thy Customer

Capital One (CapOne) pioneered the use of data mining in the financial services industry in 1988, when it began analyzing its customer data in a quest for commonalities among "perfect customers" (those who carry a balance but pay regularly). By recognizing such patterns, CapOne was able to eliminate these customers' annual fee and offer them other attractive, profitable programs while seeking new customers who fit similar profiles. Interest rates, balance transfers, and a card with a picture of the customer's choice can be targeted to those profiles. Do you have a lot of cat food and kitty litter on your card statement? CapOne can send you a credit card emblazoned with a picture of kittens, appealing to your emotions and forging a relationship that makes it difficult to cancel and cut up the "kitten card." CapOne's competencies in data mining have improved to the point where it implements real-time mass customization, offering more than 3,000 different credit card products that address the individual needs of 8.2 million customers.

Similarly, Chase Manhattan Bank mined its customer data to determine whether the customers who complained about minimum checking balances were actually profitable customers, or whether Chase should allow those customers to defect to another bank with lower minimum balances. In so doing, Chase was able to implement changes to its product offerings based on predictive models about its customers' behavior. Real-time data mining is clearly an invaluable tool in providing effective customer service, as it allows companies to interact with their customers and anticipate customer needs in ways previously only imagined.

➤ What Business Are We in Anyway?

Having voluminous amounts of customer data provides a path to competitive advantage in the financial services industry. But if financial services companies are armed with the buying habits of millions of customers, why should they limit their business to credit cards? CapOne asked itself this classic strategy question when it began its data-mining program. Faced with increasing amounts of data, previously known as "information exhaust"—leftover customer and transactional records that were seemingly worthless—the visionaries behind CapOne realized that "the credit card business was not just a finance activity but an information-based activity about customers."[3] The breakthrough idea was that financial services was merely the venue through which CapOne could market additional products and services to its customers. Using its knowledge base of consumer behavior as a foundation, CapOne has consequently extended its reach into other markets as well, including mobile phone service from a subsidiary, America One. Although there are numerous mobile phone companies providing service and a multitude of product choices, CapOne tries to differentiate itself by simplifying consumer choices through the use of its existing data to predict the rate plans and features they will want. Similarly, MasterCard, another aggregator of consumer information, recognized the market value of its data to others who were seeking to mine new opportunities. Instead of pursuing CapOne's path of extending its own product offerings, MasterCard uses its data to help its member banks understand the habits of particular consumer segments.

Like CapOne and MasterCard in financial services, Amazon.com is clearly a leader in the field of e-retailing. Among the company's many strengths is an unerring focus on providing a best-in-class customer shopping experience. Amazon is able to do this by actively mining its data to cross-sell products and provide personalized customer service. Suggesting products that readers might enjoy based on previous purchases; cross-indexing toys to help parents find items that their kids might really like; and maintaining a real-time list of best sellers are only a few of the data-mining applications that Amazon employs to better target its products and services. Even the passive information about what item is deleted from a person's shopping cart is mined to prompt questions about what went wrong with a particular product's price, placement, or promotion. The benefit is not only that Amazon not only provides the right product for the right customer at the right time, but that it also helps the consumer find products much more easily.

➤ An E.piphany for Customer Relationship Management

The ability of data mining to improve customer profitability does not end with a more effective sales process. Actively managing the entire customer relationship is key to the vitality of most companies. One of the leaders in the use of data mining in customer relationship management software, and more specifically marketing automation, is E.piphany.

E.piphany provides a solution to one of the most common complaints about warehousing and data mining: the difficulty of accessing data on legacy systems. As incompatible database technologies proliferated during the past few decades, companies found themselves with a wealth of data stored in a variety of incompatible databases and mainframes throughout the company. Because the company's data was dispersed across incompatible systems, it was often difficult to retrieve. If a marketing manager wanted to determine the characteristics of a certain product's customers, it was not uncommon for the manager to have to submit a request to the company's IT department to write code that could extract the information from a particular database. Such a request could take days or weeks to fulfill, and the manager often received information that made little sense or otherwise needed extensive modifications and rework. E.piphany's data-extraction technology, however, allows companies to pull data from previously incompatible legacy systems with the punch of a button, allowing companies to aggregate all their data without having to dump the legacy systems they spent millions to install.

After extracting customer data, E.piphany software can use data mining to differentiate and analyze customers based upon demonstrated and predicted preferences (such as product preferences and thank-you mailing response rates), as well as to predict the lifetime value of the customer to the company. With such information, companies can enhance and personalize direct customer interaction at all touchpoints in the company's system. Whether the contact is through the Web, e-mail, call centers, direct mail, or other point of sale, E.piphany's solutions allow companies to better serve their customers and to target personalized offers, promotions, and marketing materials to the consumers most likely to buy the company's products, in a manner consistent with the information gathered. For example, Sallie Mae tracks its borrowers' profiles and has the ability to cross-sell financial products and services based on borrowers' respective changes in financial status.

E.piphany also distributes and manages this customer knowledge throughout the entire organization. Instead of each division having its own data in its own database, E.piphany allows any person in the organization to access and use customer knowledge hiding in data dispersed throughout the whole organization. Salespeople can learn about customer histories and preferences; service people can diagnose problems and implement appropriate solutions; R&D can predict desired product features; financial people can use knowledge about marketing campaigns for planning purposes; and so forth. What is more, E.piphany's easy-to-use interface removes knowledge acquisition from the IT department and puts it in the hands of the nontechnical employees who need and can actually use the knowledge for practical business purposes. Prebuilt templates allow information to be disseminated throughout the organization in user-friendly Web browsers.

➤ DoubleClick: Goal of One-to-One Marketing

Perhaps the most poignant example of the impact of data mining on e-commerce is its use in advertising on the Web. At the time this book was written, DoubleClick emerged as an industry leader in managing and serving Web advertisements. If you have done even the most minimal Web surfing, DoubleClick, more likely than not, is already lurking on your hard drive, ready to leap into action the next time you happen upon one of the 1,500-plus sites that uses its technology. By placing seemingly innocuous little files called "cookies" on your hard drive the first time you visit a DoubleClick-affiliated site, DoubleClick is able to record and store in a database an astounding amount of information about your behavior on these sites. When you next visit an affiliated site, DoubleClick will use the data it has collected on you to pick an advertisement that is likely to appeal to a customer with a behavior profile similar to the one your data suggests. Over time, as DoubleClick collects more information about you and your surfing patterns, your profile will come into sharper focus, enabling DoubleClick's clients to better understand you as a customer. As these profiles are being refined, DoubleClick uses data-mining tools to help advertisers gauge the success of their advertising campaigns and learn more about who is buying their products, who is not buying, and even who considered buying but passed.

DoubleClick's value to Web publishers and advertisers, however, does not lie solely in its ability to manage and assess advertisements. DoubleClick provides several benefits to publishers, advertisers, and, at least arguably, the Web surfer. DoubleClick allows advertisers to precisely target ads at the individuals most likely to buy the product and to retarget past customers even though those customers are on a different site. It provides marketers with data on the success of their campaigns and allows them to find patterns and correlations between their advertising campaigns and customer behavior. Visitors also benefit when they receive advertising information tailored to them rather than randomly generated ads in which they are unlikely to have any interest.

In contrast to an advertiser that simply places ads on sites that the advertiser thinks attracts people with its desired customer demographic, DoubleClick enables the advertiser to send its advertisements directly to Web users who have actually demonstrated behavior suggesting that they would be interested in the advertiser's product. No longer does the advertiser have to buy ad impressions on hundreds of sites to reach these customers (as well as many more who would never be interested in the advertiser's product); the advertiser can send the ads only to the specific customers it wants to reach across the entire network of DoubleClick sites. With such targeting, advertisers greatly improve their response rate and return on investment in the impressions. By providing higher return on the advertising dollar, DoubleClick and its publishers can charge higher cost-per-click rates.

DoubleClick has benefited from the network relationships or externalities generated by its affiliates. The company serves ads to (and gathers user data from) thousands of Web sites and stores the data in one place. This provides DoubleClick with possibly the largest existing database of visitor information, allowing it to achieve the most precise targeting of its ads. In turn, DoubleClick can provide its advertisers with a wider population from which to pick suitable ad recipients. As DoubleClick's targeting abilities and network of sites grow, more advertisers will become interested in participating. As more advertisers participate, more Web sites will wish to participate, further increasing the effect of network externalities. The benefits of these externalities are reflected in the drastic increase in ads served by DoubleClick. In fact, DoubleClick's executive vice president, Jeffrey Epstein, projects that in the near future DoubleClick will be serving 80 billion ads per month.

DoubleClick also allows advertisers to retarget past customers through its boomerang technology. For instance, if a visitor clicks through to an online CD store and buys a Foo Fighters' CD, the advertiser could later have DoubleClick retarget that customer when he or she visits another DoubleClick-affiliated Web site with a banner ad promoting a special on other similar CDs, thus driving the visitor back to the advertiser's Web site and generating more repeat business.

More impressive is DoubleClick's ability to record exactly who viewed an ad, who clicked through, and who bought from (or registered with) the advertiser. DoubleClick is thus able to provide its advertisers' marketing managers with real-time statistics on the success of their campaigns. The marketers can view the demographic of who is clicking through, who is not clicking through, and who is clicking through but not buying . . . yet. In contrast to direct mail or traditional advertising campaigns, where response rates and demographic information are lagging indicators that provide sketchy data, DoubleClick's reporting enables marketers to adjust content or their target customer profile in mid-campaign. Being able to respond immediately and with relevant information maximizes the campaign response rate and the return on investment.

Finally, DoubleClick arguably provides a benefit to Web surfers by targeting ads to them that they are more likely to care about. The visitor receives a more personalized experience; however, some visitors are offended by overpersonalized targeting and the actual or perceived invasion of privacy that accompanies such targeting.

From CapOne to DoubleClick, companies are using their data to make their businesses customer-centric. When appropriately analyzed, these data allow companies to achieve levels of customer segmentation and product personalization only dreamed of by those who do not mine data.

■ WHY DATA MINING?

The fundamental question that all managers must ask themselves when considering investing in data mining is: "What do I want data-mining applications to accomplish and why?" Without having the answers to these seemingly simple questions, companies will miss out on data mining's key benefits. Managers should think about these questions as they relate to four potential problem areas:

- A company's understanding of key strategic and marketplace issues, such as consumer privacy concerns, could become clouded by the allure of data mining's capabilities.
- Companies may start relying on data mining to make decisions for them, instead of recognizing that the information produced by data mining is only as good as the person who interprets it.
- As data-mining expectations align with capabilities, companies will often need to make organizational changes to optimize the benefits of data mining and to address the scalability issues inherent in the interpretation of data.
- Concurrent with the organizational issues, data-mining usage will not alleviate management's responsibility to formulate and pursue strategies, because data mining by itself will not create sustainable competitive advantages.

Ultimately, companies' choices with regard to these issues will drive the data-mining industry toward consolidation. The need for standard solutions to data-mining needs will increase as companies spend greater amounts of thought and preparation in determining how they will use the applications, considering data-mining's value proposition, and deciding what types of systems they will require.

➤ Exactly How Well Should You Get to Know Your Customers?

A current example of the inability to relate data-mining capabilities to marketplace dynamics is in the area of consumer privacy. Caught up in the ability to create massive databases filled with consumer profiles, companies such as DoubleClick have failed to recognize the strategic implications of encroaching on consumer privacy. After spending $1.7 billion to acquire Abacus Direct, in an effort to link the names and addresses of 88 million U.S. households from Abacus's offline database with DoubleClick's online database of clickstream behavior, DoubleClick was forced to scrap its plans to use the merged data. In response to the mounting pressure from privacy groups and government agencies, on March 2, 2000, DoubleClick announced a moratorium on tracking by name. CEO Kevin O'Connor stated, "Until there is an agreement between the government and industry on privacy standards, we will not link" the personal data with anonymous Internet activity.[4] The technology and capability mesmerized DoubleClick into believing that this powerful new identification tool created out of data-mining techniques would be able to generate an entirely new market for direct consumer advertising. In fact, DoubleClick's inability to foresee the consumer backlash may cost it dearly in the long run. The implications are clear: Companies must establish rules that will allow them to utilize data mining while not crossing the line of consumer privacy invasion—or else the government will do it for them, as has occurred in other countries.

➤ The Future for the Final Consumer

Besides privacy concerns, customers also need to be aware that companies will rank them based on the value they provide to these businesses. Currently, First Union Bank customer service personnel use data-mining tools that rank the customers they are serving. The rank tells the employee what level of service the customer should receive. If the customer has a poor ranking, the bank has little concern about giving the customer superior service, because the bank may actually be better off if the customer takes his or her business elsewhere. So, for example, although current credit card users who consistently pay their balances in full each month might think of themselves as "good" customers, VISA may think of them as "unprofitable" customers and decide to give them a low ranking. This example represents ranking based on previous behavior. As predictive data-mining tools evolve, however, it is possible that customers will be unfavorably ranked based solely on factors indicating that the customer will be a low-value customer. In a worst-case scenario, customers could be blacklisted based on their demographics (e.g., race, gender, geographic abode) instead of on the basis of their actual profitability. This profitability discrimination could potentially cause customer outrage. The solution may be competing business models that promise anonymity to customers. Currently, several Web sites offer anonymous browsing so that companies will not be able to track consumer behavior. Consumers like personalization, but they do not like customer rankings.

➤ Unrealistic Expectations of Data Mining

As hype regarding the promise of data mining grows in the business community, it is important to manage the expectations surrounding its immediate results. Companies must educate their consumers to realize that data mining deals with human behavior and human interpretation of results. Faultless prediction of behavioral responses to complex stimuli is extremely difficult, if not impossible. Emotions sway consumers' opinions beyond the predicted model and then prompt them to change their minds moments later. The data-mining decision process facilitates only the most basic steps of the human decision-making process. With this caution, companies must remember that although data mining can help guide in terms of the type and timing of options, even the best data mining is susceptible to human fallibility.

There is a flip side to this argument: backing into a conclusion. If the data mining produces a particular rule that is counterintuitive, a common response is to explain away the discrepancy using intuition and background knowledge. The analysts are likely to develop an explanation, even if it is wrong. It is important to keep in mind that data mining is one tool of many with which to solve a problem. It is not perfect and will, at times, detect trends or patterns that are either misleading or otherwise useless.

Finally, customers also need to be aware that companies will be at various levels of data-mining expertise. This will correlate to different levels of value. Though data mining will not find a needle in a haystack, it should be able to reduce the haystack to a manageable size. For example, targeted advertising may become more relevant, but it does not guarantee a 100 percent response rate or even 100 percent precision targeting. The personalization that results from data mining will be one company's interpretation of statistical patterns.

Ultimately, data mining is neither a silver bullet nor a golden goose for business management decision making. Despite more powerful computers, the refinement of human prediction software algorithms, and the global proliferation of the Internet, technology still lacks the fundamental ability to think for its user. Data mining cannot replace institutional thinking and knowledge; rather, it is an enhancing tool to assist management in making key decisions. It will be crucial to overcome managers' cultural biases so that they understand what data mining can and cannot do. Data mining should not be used as a replacement for understanding the fundamentals of a company's business.

➤ Does Your Data Scale?

Scalability will be a growing concern to decision makers in the coming years. Processing speeds are increasing, servers and data warehouses are growing, call centers are becoming more efficient, and Web sites are gathering new information—all in real time. The bottleneck will not be the ability to process the data, but the ability to make executive decisions based on the data. One way this problem could be ameliorated would be to build cross-functional teams that include both data-mining experts and strategic managers to understand business goals and support decision makers. That solution, however, will be short-lived because of companies' needs for ever-faster decision making. A longer-term solution is to distribute decision-making power down the chain of command to end users, as seen in such user-friendly tools as VirtualMiner™. But such decentralized decision making creates its own set of organizational issues.

■ ORGANIZATIONAL IMPACTS OF DATA MINING

Data mining's value is not limited to external factors alone. For businesses, the most immediate impact of data mining will be an increase in productivity and reaction time. As these tools become increasingly accurate and able to facilitate quick and accurate market reactions, the people running the daily aspects of the business will have the freedom to focus their efforts on other, forward-looking activities. Naturally, this will allow the organization to shift its resources and operations in other competitively advantageous ways.

The organizational effects of data mining also include cultural changes associated with pushing data to the company's front lines. With such a wealth of information about customers, sales personnel and customer service representatives will be even more effective in their interactions with customers. These individuals will have a greater degree of decision-making accountability, and at lower levels. A greater amount of trust and responsibility will be necessary for these employees, and they will have to have greater latitude in interacting with customers because of the information they have at hand. Opportunities for reengineering processes can be uncovered by mining one's internal workflow data.

Conversely, a focus on mining data that deemphasizes intuition could foster overreliance on this technology, increase the impact of (information) availability bias, and, most importantly, inhibit the emergence of paradigm-shifting ideas. Overreliance on any software application is inherently dangerous, as market anomalies will occur. Data-mining models that have not adjusted to such anomalies will arrive at in-correct conclusions. For instance, a strange market event in the data-mining model might indicate that a 110 percent discount coupon should be sent to all customers—but such an action could be disastrous for the entire organization.

■ THE STRATEGIC IMPLICATIONS OF DATA MINING

Businesses are just beginning to scratch the surface of data mining and the value it offers. Those that have chosen to pioneer its usage have been rewarded with a certain level of competitive advantage. However, data mining, like most technological advances, will soon cease to provide a sustainable advantage and will emerge as a competitive necessity as more businesses begin to understand its value and implement their own data-mining programs. This trend is best illustrated by the fact that 23 percent of businesses in 1999 used data-mining tools to segment their customers, and an estimated 60 percent used them in early 2000.

Perhaps the most surprising strategic implication for the future of data mining is that its use will not be a strategic decision at all. Data mining by itself will not lead to sustained profitability, because it will essentially be a tool to improve operational effectiveness rather than a means of establishing a competitive advantage. As Michael Porter observed, the pursuit of operational effectiveness is not in itself a strategy, because any advantage created by operational effectiveness is inherently unsustainable. Porter recognized that there is a productivity frontier consisting of the sum of the existing best practices at any given time. The frontier represents the maximum amount of value that a company can create at a given cost.

Data mining falls squarely under the operational effectiveness umbrella. For example, customer relationship management (CRM) data-mining applications allow companies to market and design their products more effectively. However, as is demonstrated by the onslaught of CRM data-mining applications, best practices are already being widely disseminated. CRM data-mining first movers have been reaping the benefits thus far, but now competitors are catching up. If these early adopters do not focus their attention on their overall business strategy, competitors will achieve the same level of marketing efficiency and effectiveness. These competitors may even make quantum leaps if the early movers do not evolve their data-mining techniques or move on to new tools. The state of CRM is discussed in the following sections.

■ CUSTOMER RELATIONSHIP MANAGEMENT

CRM is one of the fastest software growth segments in high-tech today, with projected revenues of $3 billion by this year. CRM systems offer companies new ways to centrally manage all their customer interactions, with a heavy focus on increasing the revenue side of the profitability equation. According to a 1999 Gartner Group study, sales of CRM systems were $600 million in 1997 and are on track to top $3 billion this year (a 50 percent annually compounded growth rate over four years).

The idea of intimate customer management relations is not new, so why has the CRM system marketplace seen such explosive growth? The answer is twofold: technology and globalization. The emergence of powerful relational database technology and the one-click immediacy of the Internet have made CRM systems not merely viable, but a necessity. Additionally, the pressures of global competition on firms have driven up the stakes for profitability. Although implementing a CRM system entails many of the same challenges as implementing an enterprise resource planning (ERP) system, firms that are successful can attain a unique competitive advantage. As with ERP, CRM is another step toward fully-integrated information systems.

Initially, when software firms focused on producing customer-centric systems, the emphasis was entirely on sales force automation. However, as producers realized the value of shifting to outward-looking enterprise systems, they saw the value of applying this notion to other customer-focused sectors as well. Existing call-center software firms repositioned themselves as customer relationship enhancement systems. More recently, firms have introduced tools to help marketing departments better manage their customer interactions. As consumer acceptance and demand grew, producers turned their attention to the overall view of the customer relationship experience. They recognized the value of offering a suite that encompassed all aspects of the customer interaction experience. Recently, the marketplace has seen the emergence of acquisitions and supplementary system offerings from some of the larger CRM firms.

■ CUSTOMER RELATIONSHIP MANAGEMENT GOALS

It is important to understand the motivations of firms that seek to implement customer-focused systems. Of course, the most rudimentary explanation for instituting such a system is to increase firm profits through top-line growth. However, to grasp the evolution of the CRM business one must look at the root drivers of this basic goal. CRM proponents suggest that these systems help the firm present a single face to the customer. Although this customer-engagement goal is noble, there are also internal revenue-seeking goals that drive the purchasing decision process. To enhance revenues, firms must incorporate all aspects of customer data, not just interactional data. The true ideal for a customer-focused system will be to use customer descriptive, transactional, and interactional data in a meaningful way to best mobilize a firm's internal resources to meet the customer's needs. It is this integration of information that, theoretically, will lead to top-line growth. Firms competing in this space have taken note of this customer ideal, and are racing to understand how best to achieve it. In fact, conversations with market players reveal that CRM is moving to a more universal e-business classification. With these goals and trends in mind, we will turn our focus to the current offerings of the CRM producers.

➤ Horizontal Applications

CRM software is a loosely-defined broad category that encompasses any customer-facing or front-office applications. Within the CRM market there are three major product segments: sales force automation, customer service and support, and marketing.

Sales Force Automation

The primary goals of sales force automation (SFA) software are to shrink the sales cycle, increase the efficiency of the sales force, increase revenue, and enhance the customer's buying experience. SFA applications can be further broken down into configurators, collaborative selling solutions, and sales force empowerment tools.

Configurators are software programs that provide a straightforward, customized, graphic interface linked to a complex database that keeps track of the multiple components, features, options, interoperability, and pricing of a broad set of products. These programs can be used to assist salespeople in the field, telephone order takers, or Internet customers. By using this software, companies can offer real-time, accurate product and pricing configuration to their customers. Benefits include: reduction in time to market, reduction in time spent configuring quotations and products, improved use of the sales force, reduction in product returns, and an improved customer experience.

Collaborative selling products enable a company to monitor all sales activity so that disconnects are stamped out and all sales activity information flows easily through the sales pipeline. By linking disparate information systems across the value chain, collaborative selling enables companies to turn their disparate sales forces into an efficient and homogenous team.

On average, salespeople spend the majority of their time in the first two stages of the sales cycle: prospecting and information gathering. Yet their value is realized only in the closing stage. *Sales force empowerment* tools assist sales agents by increasing their efficiency, shortening the sales cycle, and increasing the probability of closing each deal. In reality, many salespeople spend a significant amount of time working on activities unrelated to the sales cycle. Paperwork, administrative tasks, call reports, expense reimbursement forms, forecasts, and periodic marketing surveys cut deeply into their *selling* time. Sales force empowerment tools minimize these tasks through standardization and in some cases automation.

The Charles Schwab Corporation illustrates the impact that collaborative selling and sales force empowerment tools can have. With assets greater than $200 billion, and more than 3.5 million active customers and prospects, Schwab is one of the fastest growing financial service firms in the world. However, because of rapid growth, a diverse customer base, broad geographical scope, and diversified product and service offerings, Schwab was struggling to meet customer requirements and get the most out of its sales force. Schwab installed Siebel System's Sales Enterprise package, a closed-loop sales information system that enables sales professionals to collect, share, and manage customer and lead information. Schwab was able to use the application to increase the efficiency of its team's sales model by sharing customer and lead information across the company, and to improve the probability of closure by increasing the productivity of each salesperson.

Customer Service and Support

Over time, customer service and support applications have evolved from ancillary cost-cutting tools into the principal tools used to meet customer expectations and increase profitability. One of the key functions of customer service and support applications is to synchronize all customer touchpoints so that all interactions are recorded in one shared repository. Customers today want recognition and personalized service, which demands cross-channel coordination. Even if a customer calls the help desk one day, faxes a request in the next day, uses the online help desk on the third day, and visits with a direct sales representative the following day, all transactions will be recorded in a common database. By assimilating this information, companies can improve their understanding of their customers and meet their customers' increasingly high expectations.

CRM customer service and support applications can be divided into two separate functions: call center management and online support. *Call center applications* manage the customer interactions from beginning to end with the primary goal of delivering a positive customer experience. Many such programs also provide customized scripts that guide service agents through calls. As companies move toward a customer-centric business model, it will be necessary for them to provide the customer with this level of one-stop customer service. Call center applications can also stimulate additional revenue by informing the customer service representative of additional sales opportunities, including upgrades, complementary products, and add-ons.

Online support desk applications enable customers to resolve many issues without having to speak with a service representative. These applications allow companies to reduce the number of customer service agents required and to offer 24-hour assistance to their customers. Examples of content for online support include frequently asked questions, product or service information, order and delivery status, order confirmation, return information, rebate information, technical support, and an outlet for complaints or suggestions.

Marketing

The marketing functions of CRM software can be divided into marketing information applications and strategic decision support tools. The underlying premise of both marketing applications is that by linking all sources of customer interaction, marketing professionals will be able to reduce their information-gathering costs and increase the reliability of their information, thereby increasing the overall effectiveness of their marketing efforts and decision making.

Most companies have a plethora of information: data on their products, customers, processes, markets, and so forth. The problem is that they are unable to tap into this information in a meaningful way, because it resides on disconnected servers with no way to correlate the information or make sense of it. By assimilating all the information generated through the various customer touchpoints, companies can get the most out of the marketing process, easily identifying the target markets and customers with the greatest potential value. CRM marketing applications can also help companies realize their one-to-one personalized promotion goals by tracking customer interactions, customer history, promotional campaigns, sales force effectiveness, and the impact of pricing changes, and by creating uniquely tailored marketing and promotional campaigns.

By tightly integrating all customer touchpoints into one connected repository, managers will have more confidence and consistent information upon which to base their decisions. CRM marketing applications typically include data-mining programs and business decision models that assist companies in making well-informed strategic decisions. Many of these applications are easily customized, so that a manager, for example, could design a model to optimize the deployment of the field sales force.

Because of the complex nature of the required analyses, and because of the large differences in firms' expectations for these applications, strategic decision support tools are often the weakest link within a CRM suite. For the most part, these applications are too topical and general to meet the needs of the entire market. CRM vendors' efforts are more focused on bridging communication channels and customer-facing functions than on providing inward-focused, analytical horsepower.

➤ CRM Limitations

Although CRM systems have brought enormous value to their current clients, many firms are still waiting on the fence because of the limitations inherent in today's applications. As CRM systems evolved, they placed primary importance on the tactical aspects of customer relationships. However, two principal limitations persist: analytical resources and depth of functionality.

In an ideal world, a CRM system would allow firms to recognize customer profitability and optimize the internal resources needed to meet customers' needs. The greatest limitation of current systems to do so is the analytical functionality of the product offerings. Although some vendors, such as Siebel and Clarify, offer entry-level profitability analysis tools, the vast majority focus entirely on the static internal customer interaction data and overlook other key strategic indicators, such as share of the customer's wallet. The limits of current CRM systems are no secret to vendors. Conversations with several firms indicate strategic plans either to build on this functionality, or to obtain the capability through mergers and acquisitions. Meantime, in the absence of internally-incorporated analytical tools, firms are forced to turn to ancillary vendors.

Consulting companies such as NCR and eLoyalty have seen their businesses boom in support of CRM installations. Additionally, software producers such as E.piphany and Knowledge Stream Partners offer shrinkwrap (prepackaged) programs to aid in profitability analysis. However, most of these systems require extensive (and expensive) consulting services to effectively implement their core products.

The depth of functionality is also seen as a limit to CRM applications. There are two dimensions to these limitations: horizontal and vertical. From a horizontal perspective, firms bemoan the limitations or lack of functionality in such critical relationship optimization areas as customer-rules authoring and maintenance, customer value by activity, and campaign simulation. Vertical gaps present even greater challenges to CRM vendors. Although great value is attained from CRM systems across industry verticals, the somewhat generic nature of the applications fails to meet certain industry-specific needs. To meet these needs, CRM vendors will either have to expand the core functionality of the product (possibly rendering it more cumbersome), or develop one-off systems to attack each vertical industry (thus drastically increasing the development/support requirements for vendors). In response to these vertical challenges, small niche vendors have arisen, adding to the application integration issues faced by purchasing firms.

These niche software firms have sprung up to fill the gap around the myriad of features that corporations demand. Along with major players (Siebel and Oracle) offering additional Web-based features, up-and-coming firms that manage e-mail marketing (Kana, Interactive), telephony (Clarify), online sales (Vignette), and closed-loop marketing solutions are seeing strong market capitalization values. According to AMR Research, this market is expected to grow from $4.45 billion in 1999 to $21.8 billion in 2003—a growth rate nearly five times that of the overall software market.

➤ Ancillary Support Systems

To work around the limitations of CRM, several ancillary industries and trends have developed. These ancillary industries have been delivering products and services that fill the connection gaps across information systems where CRM software falls short. These firms and applications include:

- External service providers (ESPs), who are typically called in on a CRM project to help design the strategy and select vendors and applications.
- Enterprise application integration (EAI) software, which automates key legacy systems with new application packages using four main approaches (data warehousing technologies, middleware, fast application switching and repository-based transformation, and data routing between applications).
- Application service providers (ASPs), who provide IT capabilities on an integrated platform that includes Web hosting, front- and back-end business software, expandable hardware, legacy system integration, and telecommunications wiring.

■ E-BUSINESS AND CRM

E-business has revolutionized CRM approaches and tools, enabling enterprises to offer personalized e-commerce solutions to their customers. The competitive advantage will shift to those with the ability to analyze information and effectively apply business rules. Connecting one-to-one with customers through the Web, and capturing vital information about customer requirements, preferences, and problems, will be the areas of business advantage. The ease of use allowed by the Web is creating explosive growth in electronic dialogue. Firms will create customer solutions that offer more value and keep customers connected for life. This is ultimately the value and goal of e-business. Customers do not care whether you have channels or not. When a company sells through 256 resellers, a telesales force, and a small direct-sales force, for instance, one hand needs to know what the other hand is doing. Delivery of specific B2B capabilities is crucial to early adoption and long-term sustainability of e-business systems. E-business systems must be capable of:

- Sharing all customer information across the entire enterprise.
- Interacting with customers directly through multiple channels, including the Internet, WWW, e-mail, fax, direct mail, interactive voice response, call centers, and mobile agents.

- Enabling e-commerce transactions by using any channel and self-service platforms that interact with the enterprise.
- Providing an open, extendable architectural platform to enable enterprises to respond quickly as business requirements evolve.
- Applying analytical power to collected data.
- Developing rules-based logic into applications.

Organizations are starting to realize that an all-encompassing approach is required to create a sustainable, competitive advantage in today's Internet-driven marketplace. This approach must address the communication needs of the internal organization, the extended organization, and the organization's business partners.

E-business models have to be backed with CRM implementation and capabilities, which will lead to full service e-business packages that drive increased customer retention. The dynamics of the customer–business model are changing too rapidly for old systems to keep up in the current unforgiving market. E-business systems will leverage the unique and still undiscovered capabilities of the Web and other technologies to capture and send a single message to each consumer.

■ E-BUSINESS MODELS

For those who have worked in the technology field or been in a position to apply technologies to their business models, it is understood that technology is an enabling device, not an end in itself. So what is the true goal of systems such as e-business solutions? Obviously, increased profits are the goal, but just applying systems does not achieve this goal. The true value that e-business applications provide is the increase in corporate knowledge about the firm and its customers.

The evolution of e-business systems has been and will continue to be a natural progression based on the emergence of enabling/disruptive technologies. Powerful databases and networked environments allowed ERP applications to emerge. They provided an aggregation of data about the firm itself, which yielded increased efficiencies and reduced costs. CRM systems took the same underlying technologies and allowed firms to aggregate data about their customer interactions. Firms employing these two systems now have a wealth of data collected. The novelty and competitive advantage of having such data will soon wear off as these systems mature and move to the commodity stage of their life cycle.

The future value of e-business systems must evolve from data aggregation to data interpretation and beyond. This poses a real threat to the viability of current enterprise system vendors. To date, these ISVs have relied on their core competencies in data collection, storage, and networking. In contrast, firms that become experts at data analysis and interpretation will provide the future value for enterprise customers. If current vendors are to remain competitive, they must either develop or acquire these new skills.

However, the value chain in enhancing corporate knowledge cannot end there. Data analysis and interpretation technologies, as all other technologies before them, will become a commodity, yet they will become a stepping stone to the next technology plateau. Now that all this data has been aggregated and interpreted, technologies should emerge to direct firms on how to deploy their resources optimally, to best serve their profit-maximizing customers. The climb to the efficient use of corporate knowledge will not end here. All the stepping stones of enabling technologies will pave the way for the re-emergence of artificial intelligence.

The collection and interpretation of this corporate data can be used to establish rule-based logic in enterprise systems that will optimize the interactions of the firm and the customer. This technology is not much different from existing configurator software used, for example, by companies such as Dell to allow customers and salespeople to accurately configure a system based on compatibility rules and performance needs.

Imagine a current customer calling into Sun with a technical question about server reliability. By the time the call reaches an agent, the customer's entire descriptive, interactive, and transactional data will be showing on the agent's screen. Behind the scenes, logic in the systems will have evaluated the customer's buying cycle, support level characteristics, and independent financial performance. Based on this information, the agent will be prompted to offer new products or services, as well as the answer to the customer's question based on the previous purchase information. In the background, the system will determine the appropriate sales channels and notify them of this customer inquiry. At the same time, this contact information might be sent to a partner company providing backup systems. In this ideal scenario, the customer's experience, the firm's resources, and the revenue-generating opportunities have been maximized.

Our analysis is similar to the analogy of the Phoenix rising from the fire. As enabling technologies emerge, they experience a period of competitive dominance and value positioning. As these technologies mature, they become mere commodities, and are soon overtaken by emergent technologies. However, the foundations of the enabling technology are critical for the next generation of enabling systems.

It is unlikely that any one step in this genesis should be or will be skipped. The key take-away for vendors competing in this enterprise system space is that if they are to remain competitive, they must continually redefine themselves to stay ahead of the next wave in the evolution of e-business applications.

---

e-CRM: The Future in Customer Relationship Management

E-CRM extends the business relationship to an online platform. It is not B2B or B2C; e-CRM is independent of channel, method of access, and customer type. Enabling CRM solutions online is a viable alternative to traditional call centers, and customers have expressed enthusiasm over this type of service for several reasons: the accessibility and convenience of the Internet, the perception that there is a shortage of skilled service people manning customer calling centers, and increased confidence in a self-directed process.

E-CRM applications work to extend the customer service and marketing capabilities of the business that uses them, providing more accurate market information than has been previously available and delivering it in real time. Companies can track customers' Web interactions minute-by-minute and build a customer profile with incredible accuracy. In the new world of the customer-driven company, this capability is critical. E-CRM tools allow firms to gain more insight into customers, as companies can now monitor customer/Web interactions and

(continued)

use this information to capitalize on selling, service, and product development opportunities.

By the close of the year 2000, the e-CRM market was estimated to be at $6.1 billion, with projections that it will reach $34.7 billion by 2005. These projections, and the fact that e-CRM is a fairly new market sector with extraordinary growth potential, make it an attractive investment opportunity. In addition, the potential for companies to realize hard-dollar benefits as the sector matures has increased investor interest in this sector.

Analysts have cited Art Technologies, BroadVision, and Vignette as the leading platform companies in this sector. All have posted strong revenue and customer growth over the past year and we expect these companies to achieve sustainable leadership positions in this sector by the close of 2001. Currently, no company claims more than 5 percent of the e-CRM market, so the playing field is wide open.

■ NOTES

1. Alex Berson, Stephen Smith, and Kurt Thearling, *Building Data Mining Applications for CRM* ch. 10 (McGraw-Hill Professional Publishing, 1999).
2. Peter Fabris, "Data Mining—Advanced Navigation," *CIO Magazine* (May 15, 1998).
3. Derek Slater, "The Data Game: Companies Are Learning How to Turn Customer Information into Product—and Profit," *CIO Magazine* (May 1, 1997).
4. Will Rodger, "Activists Charge DoubleClick Double Cross," *USA Today*, January 31, 2000.

■ REFERENCES

Alaniz, Scott, and Robin Roberts. "E-Procurement: A Guide to Buy-Side Applications." Stephens Inc. (December 21, 1999).

Arunasalem, Mark. "Datamining." Doctoral dissertation, Rensselaer Polytechnic Institute, 1996.

Barnett, Megan. "Foiling Fraudsters." *The Industry Standard* (November 15, 1999).

Berson, Alex, Stephen Smith, and Kurt Thearling. *Building Data Mining Applications for CRM* ch. 10. McGraw-Hill Professional Publishing, 1999.

Bhatia, Anil. "A Roadmap to Implementation of Customer Relationship Management. CRM." IT Toolbox Portal for CRM, 1999.

Brown, Eric G. "Internet Middleware." *Forrester Report* (July 1999).

Brown, Eric G., et al. "Personalize or Perish?" *Forrester Report* (May 1997).

Burwen, Michael P. "Database Solutions." Palo Alto Management Group, Inc. (July 1998).

Calico Commerce Inc. "Customer Profile: Kodak." February 8, 2000.

Cavoukian, Ann. "Data Mining: Staking a Claim on Your Privacy." *Ontario Report* (January 1998).

Chatham, Bob. "Kana Buys Silknet: That Was the Easy Part." *Forrester Report* (February 17, 2000).

———. "Managing Customer Profitability." *Forrester Report* (February 2000).

———. "Nortel Misreads eRM with Clarify Acquisition." *Forrester Report* (October 25, 1999).

Cherry Street & Co. "Extending Enterprise Applications." *Framing the IT Services Industry* (January 2000).

Close, W., and C. Claps. "Which Vendors Will Thrive, Survive or Dive in the CRM Software Application Market?" *Gartner Group Strategic Analysis Report* (September 1999).

Cole, Stephen J. "The Apps Market: 1998–2003." *Forrester Report* (April 1999).

Epstein, Jeffrey E. "DoubleClick, Inc. Executive Vice President Talks About His Firm's Future." *Wall Street Transcript* (June 4, 1999).

Fabris, Peter. "Data Mining—Advanced Navigation." *CIO Magazine* (May 15, 1998).

———. "A New Lease." *CIO Magazine* (May 1, 1999).

Fischer, Lawrence. "Here Comes Front-Office Automation." *Technology* 13 (fourth quarter 1998), 1–9.

Fishman, Charles. "This Is a Marketing Revolution." *Fast Company* (May 1999).

Fitzgerald, Michael. "Feeding Frenzy: Reach Out and Buy Someone." *Red Herring* (February 8, 2000).

Gillet, Frank. "Business-Centered Data Mining." *Forrester Report* (February 1999).

————. "The Data Tools Market Will Consolidate." *Forrester Report* (March 1999).

————. "Stand-alone Data Mining is Dead." *Forrester Report* (June 1999).

Gilmore, James H., and B. Joseph Pine II. "The Four Faces of Mass Customization." *Harvard Business Review* (January-February 1997).

Gormley, J. Thomas III. "The Demise of CRM." *Forrester Report* (June 1999).

Gupta, Vivek R. "An Introduction to Data Warehousing." *System Services Corporation* (August 1997).

Hagan, Paul R. "Smart Personalization." *Forrester Report* (July 1999).

Hamn, Steve, and Robert Hof. "An Eagle Eye on Customers." *Business Week*, February 21, 2000.

Hildebrand, Carol. "One to a Customer." *CIO Magazine* (October 15, 1999).

i2 Technologies, Inc. "i2 and Siebel Systems Partner to Offer End-to-End Intelligent eBusiness." Reuters, Corporate Press Release, February 3, 2000.

Information Discovery, Incorporated. *A Characterization of Data Mining Technologies and Processes.* 1997

Intelligent Data Analysis Group. "As Number of Vendors Offering Web Personalization Software Grows, So Do Privacy Concerns." *Data Mining News* (Fall 1999).

Jacobs, Peter. "Data Mining: What General Managers Need to Know." *Harvard Business Review Management Update* (October 1999).

John, George H. "Behind-the-Scenes Data Mining: A Report on the KDD-98 Panel." *SIGKDD Explorations* (June 1999).

Kaneshige, Tom. "Eye on the Customer." *CIO Magazine* (February 1, 2000).

Kelly, Jason. "The Play for On-Click Support." *UpsideToday: The Tech Insider* (January 21, 2000).

Kimball, Ralph, and Richard Merz. *The Webhouse Toolkit: Building the Web-enabled Data Warehouse*, ch. 4. New York: John Wiley & Sons, 2000.

Koch, Christopher. "Can You Do the WWW?" *CIO Magazine* (October 15, 1999).

Lenatti, Chuck. "Enterprise Software's Oracle: Chuck Phillips." *Upside Magazine* (December 29, 1999).

Leon, Mark. "Enterprise Application Integration—Tools to Get ERP Systems to Work Together." www.erp.org, September 2000.

Macavinta, Courtney. "Privacy Fears Raised by DoubleClick Database Plans." *CNET News.com* (January 25, 2000).

Madden, Andrew P. "Paradise Lost: How the ERP Market Lost Its Way and What Path It Must Follow to Recover." *Red Herring Magazine* (July 1999).

————. "Scratching the Surface: Untapped Vertical Markets Create New Opportunities for ERP Vendors Large and Small." *Red Herring Magazine* (August 1998).

Mayer, Caroline. "DoubleClick Is Probed On Data Collection." *Washington Post* (February 17, 2000).

Mena, Jesus. "E-mining Customer Behavior." *DB2 Magazine* (Winter 1999).

META Group. "Data Mining, Trends, Technology, and Implementation Imperatives." 1997.

Moore, Geoffrey A. "Inside the Tornado." New York: Harper Collins, 1995.

Nail, Jim. "The Email Marketing Dialogue." *Forrester Report* (January 2000).

Norfolk, David. "Systems Link Up with EAI." www.zdnet.co.uk, 2000.

Official Journal of the European Communities. No L. 281 (November 23, 1995).

Orlov, Laurie M. "ERP eCommerce Realities." *Forrester Report* (April 1999).

————. "PeopleSoft Targets eRM with Vantive Purchase." *Forrester Report* (October 12, 1999).

Parsaye, K. "OLAP and Data Mining: Bridging the Gap." *Database Programming & Design* (February 1997).

Petersen, Andrea. "DoubleClick Reverses Course After Privacy Outcry." *Wall Street Journal,* March 3, 2000.

————. "A Privacy Firestorm at DoubleClick." *Wall Street Journal,* February 12, 2000.

Pilot Software, Incorporated. "Finding Hidden Value in Your Data Warehouse." 1999.

Pitta, Julie. "Garbage in, Gold out." *Forbes* (April 5, 1999).

Pivotal Corporation. "Pivotal eBusiness Relationship." October 6, 1999.

Porter, Michael E. "What Is Strategy?" *Harvard Business Review* (November-December 1996).

PR Newswire. "Emerging ASP Market Is Likely to Reshape the Information Technology Landscape; Demand is Building for Integrated Service Offerings, According to Bank of America Securities Analyst" (February 7, 2000).

Red Brick Systems, Inc. "Data Mining: The Power of Integration." 1996.

Rodger, Will. "Activists Charge DoubleClick Double Cross." *USA Today,* January 31, 2000.

————. "DoubleClick Backs Off Web-tracking Plan." *USA Today,* March 3, 2000.

Rodin, Robert. *Free, Perfect, Now: Connecting to the Three Insatiable Customer Demands.* Simon & Schuster, 1999.

Sawhney, Mohan. "How It Works." *Business 2.0* (February 2000): 112–40.

Shevlin, Ron, and Waverly Duetsch. "Knowledge Management's Half-life." *Forrester Report* (October 1998).

Siebel Corporation. "Siebel Customers: Siebel@Work with Charles Schwab." www.siebel.com.

Slater, Derek. "The Data Game: Companies Are Learning How to Turn Customer Information into Product—and Profit." *CIO Magazine* (May 1, 1997).

Sokol, Lisa. "Data Mining and Knowledge Discovery: Theory, Tools, and Technology." *Proceedings of the International Society for Optical Engineering—Volume 3695* (April 1999).

———. "Data Mining in the Real World." *Proceedings of the International Society for Optical Engineering—Volume 3695* (April 1999).

Stauffer, David. "The Art of Delivering Great Customer Service." *Harvard Management Update* (September 1, 1999).

Stepanek, Marcia. "Commentary: Washington Must Step in to Protect E-Privacy." *BusinessWeek,* January 26, 1999.

Sweat, Jeff. "Know Your Customers." *InformationWeek,* November 11, 1998

Thearling, Kurt. "Data Mining and Privacy: A Conflict in the Making?" *DSstar* (March 17, 1998).

Trilogy Software, Inc. "Case Study: The Boeing Company." www.trilogy.com.

Two Crows Corporation. *Introduction to Data Mining and Knowledge Discovery, Third Edition.* 1999.

UBS Warburg, "eCRM: Stop the Insanity," 10/16/2000.

Williams, Seema. "Post-Web Retail." *Forrester Report* (September 1999).

Williamson, Debra Aho. "Getting Your Clicks." *Industry Standard* (July 12, 1999).

———. "The Information Exchange Economy." *Industry Standard* (April 23, 1999).

Wisner, Scott. "The Realities of Datamining." *Catalog Age* (January 1999).

Zerega, Blaise. "Making the Enterprise Whole." *Red Herring Magazine* (July 1999).

Chapter

Electronic Payment Systems

New Opportunities for Value Exchange

■ INTRODUCTION

Each day, a staggering amount of virtual money circles the globe. The Federal Reserve's Fedwire and the New York-based Clearing House Interbank Payment System (CHIPS) alone electronically send out well over $2 trillion daily. Retail systems such as credit and debit cards deliver several hundred billion more. In fact, the combined electronic dollar flow in one day equals more than one-third of the U.S. gross domestic product for the entire year. What is more, these numbers should only continue to grow given the recent dramatic growth in the Internet and related technologies.

In the year 2000, more than 200 million users were connected to the Internet. From 1998 to 1999, the number of Web users worldwide increased by 55 percent, the number of Internet hosts rose by 46 percent, the number of Web servers increased by 128 percent, and the number of new Web address registrations rose by 137 percent. This phenomenon has already affected many facets of our lifestyles and work styles, yet most indications point to a revolution that is still in its infancy (see Figure 8.1). Optimistic predictions from only a year ago are already

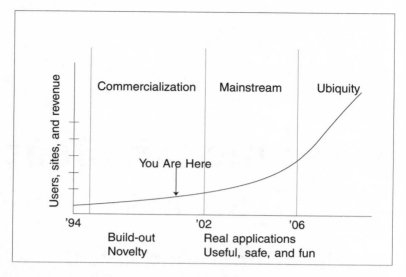

Figure 8.1   Stages of Internet growth.
Source: Deloitte Research.

being revised dramatically upward. Recently, Forrester Research doubled its B2B Internet commerce forecast for the United States to $842 billion by the year 2002 and $2.7 trillion by 2004. With the addition of U.S. retail Internet transactions and non-U.S. Internet commerce, e-business is predicted to generate revenue of more than $1.1 trillion in 2002 (see Figure 8.2).

The dramatic growth in the use of the Internet as a medium for commerce is, in large part, a result of the increased benefits gained by both businesses and consumers. Businesses in virtually every sector of the economy are beginning to use the Internet as a means to cut the cost of purchasing, manage supplier relationships, streamline logistics and inventory, plan production, and reach new and existing customers more effectively. Consumers benefit from improved choice, increased convenience, better information, increased customization, and lower prices. The significant benefits and increasing interest of consumers and businesses in the Internet provide strong evidence that the Internet will continue to grow as a means for conducting commerce online.

A natural outcome of the interest in e-commerce has been an increase in demand for electronic payment systems. The Internet provides the infrastructure and potential for creating a highly cost-effective payment system. In theory, it provides the capability to

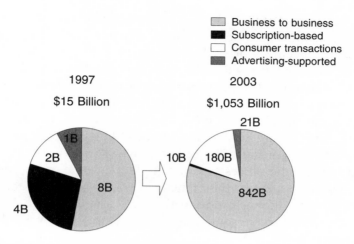

Figure 8.2 Composition of Internet commerce.

Source: Deloitte Research.

affordably handle almost instantaneous payment and settlement of transactions. The potential savings attributed to online bill presentment and payment are huge. In the United States alone, some 15 billion invoices are sent each year, at a current cost to the billers of about $1.25 per invoice. Reports from such leading consulting firms as Deloitte & Touche indicate that various online approaches cost the biller about 35 cents per invoice. At the same time, the bill payer saves the cost of postage back to the bill sender, adding even more to the potential savings. In addition, a typical trade transaction may involve several different parties and different documents, which have to be checked, transmitted, reentered into various information systems, processed, and filed. The United Nations Conference on Trade and Development (UNCTAD) believes that unnecessary transaction costs amount to more than $400 billion in U.S. dollars per year, which could be reduced by 25 percent or more by streamlining procedures and extending the use of paperless trading.

Although the benefits of and demand for electronic payment systems are substantial, considerable challenges must still be addressed before new and emerging payment technologies will be adopted. These issues include concerns about security and privacy, lack of common standards and infrastructure, and unresolved legal and regulatory policies.

Low consumer and business acceptance of e-payment technologies are primary factors underlying these obstacles. Individuals require an emotional relationship with their money; acceptance is not a simple matter. Consumers require low cost, convenience, and the confidence that the product or service will do what it promises. They will not simply take leaps of faith with their money, as evidenced by the fact that close to 94 percent of all payments in the United States are still cash or check transactions. Many consumers, for example, are uncomfortable with the idea of submitting credit card information over the Internet. Many consumers are frustrated with the online purchase process; approximately 27 percent of all online purchase transactions are abandoned because the process is too complex. In some cases, businesses have chosen not to invest their time and dollars in electronic commerce methods, preferring instead to focus on automating internal administrative processes and in some cases capitalizing on other benefits such as monetary float.

It seems contradictory, given all the dramatic advances in technology and promises about the potential for e-commerce, that firms still use traditional forms of payment—including cash and checks as the primary payment media. This paradox results from two very important but nonobvious economic forces (see Figure 8.3).

These two primary forces are path dependencies and network externalities. *Path dependency* means that decisions made in the past will often determine current decisions, because they are based on condi-

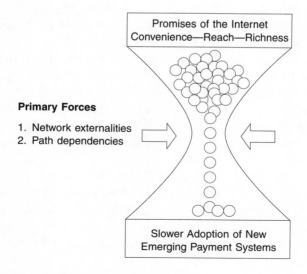

Figure 8.3   The payment paradox.

tioned behavior. In other words, the path that an economy initially follows may depend on seemingly trivial considerations, or on technical details that might have been very important at the time of the choice but subsequently became unimportant. Once the path is chosen, it is very difficult to change, even when other considerations make the choice less desirable relative to other available alternatives. Path dependency is thought to be most endemic where there are networks of participants. These positive effects are an externality—where the benefits of a person's actions do not go to the individual alone but also benefit other participants in the network. The required infrastructure must be developed to create network externalities. Many of the emerging online value transfer systems have been slow to develop because the proper infrastructure is not in place.

How have these two forces shaped the current landscape of the payment market space? Take smartcards as an example: Path dependencies and network externalities are likely to cause the failure of this new payment medium in the United States, at least for the foreseeable future. Smartcards look a lot like credit cards, but they are distinguishable in several important ways. Microchips embedded onto smartcards enable them to retain and update account information, so debits from the purchaser's account are made immediately. Credit cards require credit card providers to act as intermediaries, billing the buyer and paying the merchant. Of course, credit card providers charge a relatively high transaction fee to handle the exchange.

Smartcards are actually more similar to cash than to credit cards. Although smartcards are backed by demand deposits just like checks, they offer many advantages over cash or checks. Bookkeeping is much simpler because each smartcard transaction creates an entry in magnetic form for both the purchaser and the seller. Carrying a smartcard, even with a huge balance, is much safer than carrying large amounts of cash (because smartcard microchips provide a level of security that reduces the risk of armed robbery and fraud). Nevertheless, even given these advantages, people in the United States continue to use other exchange media. Experiments introducing smartcards in Atlanta, St. Louis, and other metropolitan cities have been largely unsuccessful. In the Atlanta trial, people were reluctant to use smartcards even when given a free balance to spend! The problem is related to network economies, in that no purchaser benefits from using a smartcard until enough shops accept them, and no shop is willing to invest in a machine that will read smartcards until it attracts enough sales from potential purchasers. This contrasts with the situation in France, where smartcards are rapidly gaining acceptance. Interestingly, this may be because other exchange media have not penetrated the French markets, creating path dependencies. In the United States, credit cards are widely used and widely accepted, whereas in France this is not the case. Thus, in France a shop may invest in a smartcard reader knowing that smartcards are more likely to be used by its customers, who do not carry credit cards. France, which has a poorer exchange technology because of its different historical path, is more likely to adopt the newer technology (a path dependency) than is the United States.

The greatest threat to understanding the present and to predicting the future is ignoring the past. Accordingly, we spent the last few paragraphs building an understanding of two critical forces, path dependencies and network externalities, which are likely to significantly affect the ultimate success of emerging e-payment systems. The first section of this chapter focuses on the current payment system landscape and the underlying mechanics of the industry today. The payment system space is extremely broad. For the purpose of our discussion, we have identified five major "hot spots:" e-credit, electronic bill presentment and payment, e-bartering, digital currency, and micropayments. Although seemingly disparate, these are, in the opinion of the popular press, the systems with the most potential.

■ CURRENT PAYMENT SPACE DEFINED

According to the United States General Accounting Office, the general term *payment system* refers to a mechanism for the transfer of monetary value and related information. Payment systems, which generally consist of payment, clearance, and settlement processes, are vital to the smooth functioning of our nation's economy and the free flow of economic activity worldwide. Let us pause to define these payment system components. *Clearance* is the process of transmitting, reconciling, and (in some cases) confirming payment orders or securities transfer instructions before settlement takes place. *Settlement* is the final step in the transfer of ownership. In a banking transaction, *settlement* is the process of recording the debit and credit positions of the parties involved in a transfer of funds.

The United States has a wide variety of payment, clearance, and settlement systems. Some systems are used primarily for large-dollar payments, such as Fedwire (the electronic funds transfer system operated by the Federal Reserve) and the Clearing House Interbank Payment System (a private-sector electronic funds transfer system run by the New York Clearing House Association). Others are used for the clearance and settlement of financial products, such as securities, futures, and options. These systems are used mainly by major financial entities, such as banks and other corporations, and are generally referred to as *wholesale systems*. Other systems are used for the smaller transactions with which most consumers are familiar (checks, credit cards, and automated clearing house payments such as electronic deposits of paychecks or Social Security payments). Generally, these small-dollar systems are referred to as *retail systems*.

Wholesale payments have been processed through electronically-based systems since the 1960s. These transactions, however, are handled over closed proprietary networks, creating incompatibilities among different systems. The average value of a wholesale payment in 1996 was $4.3 million. Retail payments, which are largely paper-based, include consumer-to-business and business-to-business payments. The average value of a retail transaction varies by medium. In 1996, the average check transaction was $1,158; the average credit card purchase was $61; and the average debit card transaction was $37. Although wholesale payments represent a large dollar amount, they account for less than 1 percent of the *number* of payments in the United States. Given the large number of retail transactions, this chapter focuses on retail payments, with the Internet serving as the underlying infrastructure.

➤ Current Payment Media

Although the U.S. economy, according to some analysts, is in the process of entering an even newer digital age, the U.S. payment system continues to rely heavily on paper-based methods for conducting transactions. New instruments are beginning to emerge, but it is currently the traditional e-payment methods, such as credit cards, debit cards, and automated clearing house (ACH) transactions, that are steadily gaining a greater presence and driving advances in U.S. payment systems.

Cash and checks remain the dominant forms of payment in the United States. Recent data from the Bank for International Settlements (BIS) and the National Automated Clearing House Association

(NACHA) shows that approximately 94 percent of retail payments in the United States are made with either cash or checks, with less than 6 percent of retail payments being made electronically. Although it is difficult to estimate precisely the use of cash in an economy, it is clear that cash is the overwhelming choice for conducting small-value transactions.

The other principal paper-based method, the check, also remains deeply embedded in the U.S. payment system. The United States uses checks more than any other industrialized country. In particular, 66 billion checks were written in the United States in 1997, accounting for 72 percent of the total number of noncash transactions. Still, although check usage remains at an extremely high level, its share is trending downward as the growth in check use trails the growth of other electronic payment types. Credit cards, debit cards, ACH transactions, and wire transfers are all experiencing faster growth than checks, with the result that the sum of their transaction shares rose from 21 percent in 1993 to 28 percent in 1997. Thus, e-payments are on the rise in the United States.

The first major category of electronic payment methods is credit cards and debit cards. Together they account for nearly a quarter of noncash transactions in the U.S. economy. Credit cards are the most common and most familiar e-payment type in the United States. Credit card transactions are conducted over large networks that typically link cardholders, merchants, card-issuing banks, merchants' banks, and the credit card companies. Roughly half-a-billion general-purpose cards are in circulation, with 85 percent of those being bank-issued MasterCard or Visa cards.

Sampling of Traditional and Emerging Payment Methods

- **Traditional Checks**—The paper check is the most frequently used and oldest noncash payment instrument in the United States.

- **Electronic Funds Transfer (EFT)**—EFT refers to the transfer of funds from one account to another by electronic rather than paper-based instructions. The U.S. Treasury estimates that it costs the government 42 cents to issue and mail a paper check, but only 2 cents to process an electronic payment.

- **Automated Clearing House (ACH)**—An automated clearing house network is an electronic batch processing system by which payment orders are exchanged among financial institutions. It is designed for high-volume, predominantly small-dollar recurring payments, such as payroll, mortgage, car loan, or Social Security payments.

- **Wire Transfer**—Wire transfer transactions are high-value, "wholesale" payments made among banks and other financial institutions.

- **Digital Wallet**—Software that permits the cardholder to store credit card, billing, and shipping information on the consumer's computer, which can be transmitted with a single click of the mouse when ready to make an online purchase.

- **Check Conversion**—A process by which a paper check is converted at the point of sale (POS) into an ACH transaction. POS check conversion is being tested at 1,700 pilot locations and is beginning to be offered by some major retailers.

- **Stored Value Cards**—A credit-card-sized device in which money value is stored digitally. Although these cards resemble credit or debit cards, transactions made with stored value cards resemble transactions made with currency.

- **e-Cash**—E-cash products are typically multipurpose in design. Such products may entail installing software on consumer and merchant computers that allows some type of "digital coin" to be exchanged.

- **e-Checks**—A payment instrument developed by the Financial Services Technology Consortium (FSTC). Each step of the process—writing, delivering, depositing, clearing, and settling the check—is done electronically.

Nonbank, general-purpose cards—such as American Express, Discover, and Diners Club cards—presently account for more than one-fourth of all general-purpose dollar outlays. Although credit cards remain the principal type of electronic payment in the United States in terms of the number and share of transactions, the use of debit cards is growing at a much faster rate. In fact, debit cards are the most rapidly growing payment type in the United States.

A second major category of electronic payment methods is funds transfer systems. Unlike credit and debit cards, which place a payment instrument in the hands of the user, funds transfer systems are entirely instruction driven. ACH payments are the second-fastest growing payment type in the United States, growing at a 16 percent annual rate in recent years. Like debit cards, how-ever, ACH's share of overall transactions remains relatively small, and are currently at 5 percent.

The U.S. payment system is becoming more electronically capable. As previously shown, use of all major types of e-payments is trending upward and, as we will see later on, several new electronic payment systems are beginning to emerge. As we look ahead, there are several reasons to believe that this trend toward use of electronic payment systems will continue. First, the underlying demand for e-commerce activity will provide continued pressure for new and more efficient payment solutions. Second, there are many benefits associated with electronic payment methods, such as reduced costs, faster settlement, improved efficiency, and the like. Third, as demographics shift toward the young-adult group that came of age in the high-tech 1990s, the average household may be more comfortable with electronic payments of all types.

➤ Infrastructure/Security

The backbone for retail electronic payment systems in the United States consists of the credit card, check clearing, ACH, ATM/POS, and Internet infrastructures. To focus more closely on Internet-related payment technologies, let us take a moment to survey the latest Internet-related terminology. We begin by breaking the Internet economy down into four layers.

Layer One. The *Internet infrastructure layer* includes companies with products and services that help create an IP-based network infrastructure—a prerequisite for electronic commerce. The categories here are:

- Internet backbone providers (e.g., Qwest, MCI Worldcom)
- Internet service providers (e.g., Mindspring, AOL, Earthlink)
- Networking hardware and software companies (e.g., Cisco, Lucent, 3Com)
- PC and server manufacturers (e.g., Dell, Compaq, Hewlett-Packard)
- Security vendors (e.g., Axent, Checkpoint, Network Associates)
- Fiber optics makers (e.g., Corning)
- Line acceleration hardware manufacturers (e.g., Ciena, Tellabs, Pairgain)

Layer Two. The *Internet applications layer* includes products and services that build on Layer One infrastructure and make it technologically feasible to perform business activities online. The categories here are:

- Internet consultants (e.g., USWeb/CKS, Scient)
- Internet commerce applications (e.g., Netscape, Microsoft, Sun, IBM)
- Multimedia applications (e.g., RealNetworks, Macromedia)
- Web development software (e.g., Adobe, NetObjects, Allaire, Vignette)
- Search engine software (e.g., Inktomi, Verity)
- Online training (e.g., Sylvan Prometric, Assymetrix)
- Web-enabled databases (e.g., Oracle, IBM DB2, Microsoft SQL Server; only Internet/intranet-related revenues are counted)

Layer Three. The *Internet intermediary layer* increases the efficiency of electronic markets by facilitating the meeting and interaction of buyers and sellers over the Internet. Products and services in this layer act as catalysts in the process through which investments in the infrastructure and applications layers are transformed into business transactions. These categories include:

- Market makers in vertical industries (e.g., Plasticnet.com, VerticalNet, PCOrder)

- Online travel agents (e.g., TravelWeb.com, 1Travel.com)

- Online brokerages (e.g., E*Trade, Schwab.com, DLJDirect)

- Content aggregators (e.g., Cnet, ZDnet, Broadcast.com)

- Portals/content providers (e.g., Yahoo!, Excite)

- Internet ad brokers (e.g., DoubleClick, 24/7 Media)

- Online advertising (e.g., Yahoo!, ESPNSportszone)

Layer Four. The *Internet commerce layer* involves the sales of products and services to consumers or businesses over the Internet. The categories in this layer include:

- E-tailers (e.g., Amazon.com, eToys.com)

- B2B commerce enablers (e.g., Aribia, Commerce One)

- Manufacturers selling online (e.g., Cisco, Dell, IBM)

- Fee/subscription-based companies (e.g., thestreet.com, WSJ.com)

- Airlines selling online tickets

- Online entertainment and professional services

Because it is an open network, information is subject to predators at almost any point along its journey over the Internet. That being said, software has been developed that can make the Internet both secure and reliable, most notably encryption, digital signatures, and secure socket layer (SSL) and secure electronic transaction (SET) protocols. SSL is a security technology that encrypts the information purchase details, helping to ensure that information will not be accessible to anyone during the e-transaction. SET is the financial industry's effort to develop a standard, universal way of conducting electronic commerce that will offer consumers and merchants an unprecedented level of security and assurance. SET will provide the same high levels of security as users of SSL enjoy today, with the added benefit of digital signature certificates to help authenticate the identities of all parties involved in the transaction.

▮ CURRENT AND FUTURE REGULATORY FRAMEWORK

Currently, the Federal Reserve serves as both a regulator and a provider of certain payment system services; as such, it is in competition with private payment service providers. The Federal Reserve is the largest single provider of priced payment services (e.g., check clearing, ACH services, and wire funds transfer services) in the nation. The Monetary Control Act of 1980 (MCA) required the Federal Reserve to price, on a basis comparable with private business firms, all the payment services it offered at the time the law was enacted and any other services it developed after that date. The Federal Reserve's payment system missions are a complex and challenging part of its responsibilities. The Federal Reserve's responsibilities under its legislative mandates fall into four general areas:

- Supervising and regulating bank holding companies and certain banking institutions to ensure the safety and soundness of the nation's banking and financial system and to protect the credit rights of consumers

- Maintaining the stability of the financial system and containing systemic risk that may arise in financial markets

- Conducting the nation's monetary policy by influencing the money and credit conditions in the economy in pursuit of full employment and stable prices

- Providing certain financial services to the U.S. government, to the public, to financial institutions, and to foreign official institutions

There is considerable discussion about what role the Federal Reserve (and its infrastructure) should play, if any, in the retail payment system of the future. There is no easy answer to this question; however, it is clear that the private sector has been the primary driving force behind the current (and most likely the future) evolution of emerging payment technologies. These commercial providers have the creativity and financial resources to envision and design a wide variety of retail payment methods. However, given the immense challenges involved in gaining widespread acceptance of any new payment method and the Federal Reserve's current role in the U.S. payment industry, it seems likely that a collaborative effort between the government and the private sector might be required. Nevertheless, government policy on new forms of payment appears to have been to adopt a "wait-and-see" attitude. In fact, many retail payment system participants have suggested that the Federal Reserve should make greater efforts to collaborate with industry to assess the need for standards for electronic payments and processing (e.g., for privacy, security, liability, and authorization of transactions).

■ DIGITAL CURRENCY

The rapid growth of consumer transactions over the Internet has created fertile ground for future consumer payment methods. Although the Internet has provided consumers with the opportunity to connect easily all over the world, the current dominant methods for payment are still from the offline world: cash, credit cards, and personal checks. These offline methods present consumers with several limitations and inefficiencies, including a slow payment process, reliance on an alternative delivery system, and a complex tracking process. To understand what the future of digital currency will bring, we need to look at consumer-to-consumer (C2C) transactions. This is what we believe will drive advances in digital currency in the future.

➤ C2C Transactions on the Internet

At a broad level, consumer transactions can be classified into buy and sell transactions and money exchange. Buy and sell transactions include auction sites and exchanges where consumers come together, typically, to buy and sell personal items. The most popular place for these transactions is auction sites such as eBay, Onsale, Ubid, and Amazon. Since 1997, eBay has seen its customer base grow from 750,000 users to 10 million in 1999. What is more, total consumer auction sales are predicted to grow from $1.4 billion in 1998 to $19 billion in 2003.

Exchange services function like an online version of the newspaper classified advertisement. For example, consumers can post their used cars for sale at sites like Autotrader.com or their houses at Owners.com. Consumers enter these sites, enter their search criteria, and then contact the owner of the goods directly to conduct the transaction. Exchange of money via the Internet means a transaction in which consumers only send each other money, without a physical good being transferred. The reasons for such transfers include loaning money, paying off bets, or sending cash gift certificates. Instead of performing these transactions in person or by mail, consumers want to do it via the Internet because it is easier and more efficient.

So far, the evolution of C2C transactions on the Internet has only enhanced traditional payment methods like cash, check, and credit card. The chokepoint for these transactions is determining how consumers can actually exchange payment in real time via the Internet. As C2C transactions flourish, these limitations will drive continued migration both to card-based systems and to pure electronic solutions.

➤ The Business Models

It appears that all the businesses discussed in the C2C transactions space have begun to utilize traditional marketing strategies to understand consumer behaviors, to provide products and services consumers actually want. The "build it and they will come" mentality is what led to the demise of Digicash and Cybercash, as they tried to capture too large a market space.

Flooz.com is an excellent example of a company that focuses on a particular consumer need related to C2C transactions. However, this site is actually a hybrid of a true C2C payment option, because Flooz prefers its currency to be redeemed with retailers. Its business model is shown in Figure 8.4. Flooz.com has positioned its online currency as a gift certificate because this is something consumers are familiar with in the offline world.

The rapid growth in auction sites has also created an identifiable need for a new consumer payment process. The main problem is that once the auction is complete, the exchange of funds is time-intensive and sometimes risky (increasing counter party risk). The traditional method of payment for Internet transactions was to have the seller wait for the buyer to send cash, personal check, or money order via the mail and then ship the product to the buyer. These methods are ineffective because of the anonymity between consumers and the need to have real-time settlement.

This key insight led to the creation of Yahoo! DirectPay, PayPal.com, and Billpoint, all of which are focused on capturing the value of providing alternative C2C payment options in auctions and other C2C buy

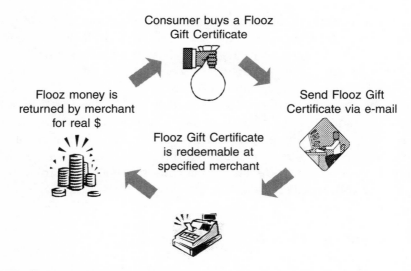

Figure 8.4   Flooz business model.

and sell transactions. The model for Yahoo! DirectPay and PayPal.com is fairly similar. These businesses have created an easy-to-use application that allows consumers, instantly and securely, to pay anyone with an e-mail address, from an existing credit card or bank account.

eBay and Wells Fargo launched the Billpoint initiative to make online payments faster and easier. This system essentially allows the seller to receive a credit card payment. Once the transaction is over, the buyer enters his or her credit card information and in real time the payment is routed to the seller's checking account through Billpoint. Evidence that these payment options are fulfilling a need is growing rapidly. For example, since PayPal.com began its service in October 1999 on eBay, more than 350,000 users have signed up, resulting in more than 10,000 new users each day. Yahoo! DirectPay, PayPal.com, and eMoneyMail are also general-purpose payment methods that address consumers' desire to exchange money without exchanging goods or services. The question of whether there is a viable and sustainable need is still unknown.

The greatest opportunity for digital currency might be through mobile commerce (m-commerce). M-commerce, the next logical step for consumers, turns cellular telephones or PDAs into devices for handling any number of purchases or transactions. The PayPal.com service, together with Pixo, is the leader in using this technology to transform a smart phone into a mobile money terminal, making C2C payment more convenient than ever before.

■ The Future of C2C

The future of digital currency will be evolutionary, rather than revolutionary. Therefore, in focusing on C2C transaction payment methods, we have identified evolving currencies in a closed system. If we look beyond their immediate use, it is easy to see how a PayPal.com, Flooz.com, or eMoneyMail might develop into the future digital currency on an open system.

The classic "chicken-and-egg" problem is one of the main reasons there has not been a successful digital currency. As a result, C2C transaction payment options focus their efforts on consumer adoption. Widespread consumer adoption will require that businesses accept a digital currency as a form of payment, and businesses will reciprocate because of the large consumer demand. The question remains, however, as to which of the options will become the standard, because it is unlikely that there will be more than one sustainable form of digital currency. It will be the business model that has the vision, global reach, and richness that will become the digital currency of the future.

■ ELECTRONIC BILL PRESENTMENT AND PAYMENT

Electronic bill presentment and payment (EBPP) has quickly become one of the true paradoxes of the Internet, because, as e-commerce has evolved, the EBPP system has failed to keep up. Despite the promises that EBPP would become the next value transfer "killer app," freeing consumers and businesses from the pain and costs of paying bills via traditional paper methods, currently less than 1 percent of eligible bills are paid online. This lack of quick adoption might be surprising given the inherent convenience and efficiency that EBPP promises businesses and consumers. Annually, business-to-consumer (B2C) paper-based systems collectively spend $36 billion to process the approximately 19 billion billing transactions in the United States alone.

It is little wonder that corporate CEOs are salivating at the prospect of online billing, given the inherent potential for cost savings. The underlying economic analysis suggests that, on average, it costs a company around $1.25 per round trip via the traditional billing method, versus $.35 via EBPP. Factor in the savings for the consumer, and the potential value creation approaches $25 billion annually in hard and soft costs for business and consumers.

Figure 8.5 suggests only a portion of the significant potential and future opportunity within EBPP. Although the B2C market represents a tremendous opportunity, it is only the first wave in EBPP value transfer. The potential opportunities also include the B2B and business/consumer-to-government (B/C2G) sectors. However, these markets are still extremely fragmented and very much in their infancy. The B2C market is the initial battleground where the development of standards, technology, and appropriate user interfaces is taking place. The convergence of Old World process and New World technologies is creating a rather acrimonious battleground as various participants seek to become the owner of a portion of the EBPP network.

Despite EBPP's enormous opportunity, adoption has been slow for this enabling technology, because of:

- Lack of common billing standards
- Consumer concerns over security
- Technological limitations
- Low customer acceptance (perceptions of convenience and value)
- Outdated business legacy systems
- Slow movement by the traditional banking industry

Though limitations certainly exist, the most critical factor is determining who controls the direct contact with the customer. The entities that can overcome extensive network externalities within the infrastructure—path dependencies for the customer—will win the battle.

➤ The Competition

The current competitive landscape is confusing and complex, because of established relationships and the motivations of various industry participants. Instead of becoming clearer and simpler, it is becoming increasingly complex, resulting in more chokepoints. Many of the re-

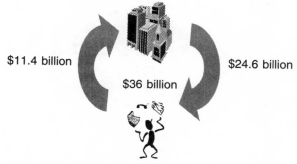

THE POTENTIAL FOR SAVINGS:

Number of U.S. reoccurring billings	$19.7 billion
Biller's cost per bill	1.25
Biller's current cost	24.625
Biller's EBPP billing cost	0.35
Biller's new cost per bill	6.895
Biller's potential savings	17.730
Billed postage saved	0.32
Billed party savings	6.304
TOTAL PARTY SAVINGS	24.034

Figure 8.5   Potential of the B2C marketplace.

lationships are forced and tenuous. The key players fall primarily within the following categories.

Customer Content Providers: Banks, Brokerage Houses, ISPs, Portals

The customer content provider's (CCP's) primary motivation is to attach to the "stickiness" of the customer mindshare. It is at this point of contact that consumers interact with EBPP services, as presented via bill processing consolidators. Of these providers, the banks have the most to gain and to lose; thus, they are wary of this new technology. The ISPs (AOL) and portals (Yahoo!) see this as an opportunity to disintermediate the banks and capture their customer relationships by becoming the primary point of contact for EBPP and other financial transactions. E*Trade recently added an online bank through which it will offer EBPP for consumers along with other traditional banking products, seeking to further attach to this stickiness. Additionally, financial software providers, such as Intuit, are aggressively investing in this enabling technology.

Bill Processing Consolidators: CheckFree, Transpoint, Spectrum

Bill aggregators such as CheckFree provide the "processing system" for EBPP. Companies like CheckFree act as intermediaries between company billers and CCPs. Thus, their primary motivation is to consolidate providers and billers into one network. By seeking strong first-mover advantage, consolidators hope to establish their processing systems as the dominant infrastructure. Bank consortiums, such as Transpoint (Citibank, First Data, Microsoft) and Spectrum (Wells Fargo, Oracle), are emerging to drive the development of an infrastructure and related enabling technologies. All parties are seeking to become the main contact point for the customer. Consolidators earn a small transaction fee for each bill processed at a CCP's sites.

Back Office Enablers: EDS, First Data

Back office gateways can be considered the backbone of EBPP. They provide the databases and infrastructure to process and store payments for the bill providers. They also perform a similar function for credit card (VISA, MasterCard) networks.

Payment Gateway Enablers: Billing Software, Presentment Software, Security

Payment gateway enablers are perhaps the wild card in the EBPP process, and extremely important because they provide the billing and presentment technologies that enable EBPP. While providing critical software and enabling technologies, they also seek to be a disintermediating force with the customer content providers. The key players are Microsoft (which owns 23 percent of CheckFree), XML technology bill presentment companies such as BlueGill Technologies, and a host of others, including Quicken, Oracle, and Just in Time Solutions.

Billers: Utilities, Mortgages, Credit Cards

Billers desire the cost-efficiencies of online billing, but want to maintain direct relationships with their customers. There is, consequently, a struggle with the banking institutions regarding who represents the consumer. Although utilities and mortgage companies have begun to adopt EBPP, credit card originators have ignored EBPP in favor of direct payment networks, seeking a more direct interaction with the customer. The potential efficiency and cost savings for billers is significant.

EBPP

Although the macroeconomic potential is significant, the impact of EBPP on individual firms will ultimately help drive widespread acceptance of EBPP. For example, Peco Energy is a small gas and electric utility with 2 million customers, serving the greater Philadelphia area. Peco sends out 80,000 paper billings daily, totaling 24 million billings annually. The company estimates that on average it costs $1.38 round-trip to process a billing, amounting to more than $33.7 million in annual billing expenses.

Peco recently implemented EBPP capabilities, utilizing the CheckFree backbone. Customers can now log onto their Citibank or Yahoo site and see their bills presented in XML format online, courtesy of BlueGill Technologies. Once a customer initiates a payment, it is processed via Oracle billing software and routed through the CheckFree clearing house. The funds are transferred from the consumer's bank account to Peco's bank account in real time. The consumer can also eventually download the payment and bill information into a personal financial software package, such as Quicken, creating a permanent record.

By utilizing EBPP, the company has cut the round-trip cost from $1.38 to approximately 35 cents per billing. If all billings were made and paid online, Peco could realize recurring savings of almost $26 million annually. Yet cost reductions, though real, are not the only driving force behind Peco's adoption of EBPP. EBPP also offers the opportunity to interact directly with the customer, which can potentially deepen and broaden the customer relationship.

➤ Business Models

Two business models are emerging within the EBPP space: the direct model, under which a biller delivers bills to consumers through an internal Web site or through a dedicated site managed by a service bureau, and the aggregator model. The aggregator model allows consumers to pay (potentially) the majority of their bills from a single site. Currently, there are two variations of the aggregator model: digital aggregators and pulp-and-digital aggregators. The primary difference between the two is that digital aggregators work directly with billers to aggregate bills delivered digitally. Pulp-and-digital aggregators offer complete service known as *scan and pay*. They have developed character recognition technologies that allow paper bills to be scanned quickly and accurately into digital format, thereby permitting all bills to be delivered digitally.

The primary rationale for the direct model is that it allows billers to maintain control over their customer relationships. The major disadvantage is that it is often biller-specific and forces customers to go to multiple sites to pay their bills, thus limiting consumer convenience and willingness to adopt. Billers that use the direct model attempt to maintain the direct customer relationship and the opportunities for customer interaction, data mining, and cross selling. Large firms, such as American Express, do not want "infomediaries" between them and the customer. Thus, the appeal for this type of biller-centric model appears to be limited to large, scalable entities with strong brands and incentives to maintain direct contact.

The emerging model in the industry appears to be the digital aggregator model advocated by CheckFree. Under this model, CheckFree is essentially the aggregating infomediary for online bills. The service is powered by CheckFree, but it is transparent to the customer, enabling banks, portals, and other sites to brand a payment site as their own. CheckFree in essence provides the operating system and coordinates the infrastructure to make all this happen. At present, CheckFree has 3 million customers processing 12 million bills a month. It provides services for more than 130 portals (Quicken, Yahoo!, Excite, and AOL), as well as having signed up more than 110 banks and 4 brokerage houses. At present, CheckFree has signed up 89 billers, including AT&T, MCI, various utilities, and cable companies. Clearly, CheckFree is regarded as the current leader in this industry and has been very aggressive in seeking first-mover advantage in this market space. With such a limited consumer base and limited payment options, though, this space is virtually wide open for those willing to make the necessary customer and infrastructure investments.

CheckFree has recently made some key acquisitions. It acquired BlueGill Technologies, which provides the technology to convert bits in billers' computers into an XML-based presentation format. This is a more efficient and effective alternative to the pulp-and-digital scan-and-pay method. In addition, CheckFree acquired Transpoint for $1 billion in February 2000. Transpoint was an online billing joint venture formed by Microsoft, First Data, and Citibank. With this acquisition, CheckFree eliminated a prime competitor and, more importantly, gained access to an online billing processor system, a banking partner, and key technology developed by Microsoft.

However, both banks and sellers are wary of the third-party intermediary, because they view CheckFree as a potential threat to their customer relationships. This concern is understandable because, as customers interact with CheckFree, banks and others are at risk of being disintermediated. Having consumers at your Web site provides the opportunity to cross sell and market services and products, whether you are a bank or a cable company. A remedy to this situation is now evolving in terms of "thick" versus "thin" presentations, which offer more consumer-centric billing capabilities.

With *thick presentation*, the consumer is provided with one-stop shopping and access at the bill payment site, including reviewing billing and payment history, making inquiries, receiving advertising, and paying bills. The primary contact for the consumer is through the portal or site where he or she interfaces with EBPP. Clearly, billers are very reluctant to adopt this type of presentation, as they are disintermediated from direct contact with the consumer.

Thin presentation, in contrast, allows only a few services to be initiated at the interface site. Bills can still be paid, but if customers want the detail behind the transaction, billing history, or a copy of the invoice, or to interact with a service representative, they are automatically directed by the third-party provider to the biller's site. Thin presentation is quickly becoming the accepted and desired standard, especially among billers that want all customer interaction to be with them. The thin model dramatically decreases the disintermediation potential for billers.

➤ The Future of EBPP

EBPP's vast potential for enhancing customer convenience, reducing consumer and business costs, and enhancing the reach and richness of interaction with the consumer is clear for both traditional and emerging industry participants. Nevertheless, EBPP will continue to develop slowly, because of the various network externalities and path dependencies mentioned earlier.

Though adoption will appear slow and tedious at times, EBPP will come to fruition. The following items identify some of the potential outcomes and the future of EBPP:

1. Consumer-centric (thin presentation) versus biller-centric models (direct) will become the standard demanded by customers. This will spur a dramatic increase in network usage.

2. Control of customer content and attachment of customer stickiness will ultimately define this battle. Ownership of the customer interface will provide competitive advantage and new opportunities, at least in the short term.

3. Banking institutions have the most to lose in terms of further commoditization of their product. They will, however, become the focal point and driving force behind EBPP and the expansion of its network. Nontraditional bill processors, such as portals and brokerages, will attempt to claim their share as well.

4. Significant market opportunities will develop for commerce services providers (CSPs) and software providers to create new and efficient means of online payment systems. The emergence of the B2C and B/C2G markets will require new solutions in terms of data consolidation, extraction, bill presentment, and security.

5. Consolidation of credit card statements will become the next battleground given their predominance in the B2C marketplace. This will pit card aggregators against credit card processors. Customer convenience and desire for one-stop shopping will be a driving force.

6. EBPP will allow the development of a whole new industry to take care of bill presentation, expense accumulation, and storage so that consumers can track detailed expenses. Microtracking of expenses could lead to enhanced "buyer's remorse," as consumers will now be able to consolidate expenses at a microlevel.

7. Public institutions such as the postal service will lose mail revenue as a result of EBPP. Potential impacts include the closure of facilities to conserve costs, increased postage rates, and the loss of direct and support postal jobs within communities. Societally, this will affect rural and poor communities the most,

in terms of lower convenience and higher costs for traditional postage.

■ E-CREDIT

It is quite clear and has been well documented that the prospects for e-commerce are enormous. According to Forrester Research, the B2B e-commerce market will hit $2.7 trillion by 2004, of which 53 percent will flow through e-marketplaces. Behind the scenes are a variety of companies and technologies, called *enablers*, competing to provide the infrastructure for e-commerce in both the B2C and B2B spaces. One enabler category that has gone largely unnoticed is the credit and financing aspect of e-commerce, which is another hot spot in the payment space.

This category presents enormous opportunity because current credit and financing capabilities are plagued with inefficiencies, since they are not designed for the Net economy. Whether a manufacturer, an e-commerce site, a business-to-business exchange, or a financial institution, managing credit and financing is essential to success. The stakeholders can be categorized simply as merchants, financial institutions, and customers.

➤ Why the Credit Process Is Broken

One of the problems with the current credit market is matching appropriate creditors and debtors efficiently, because there is no systematic mechanism to connect credit seekers with a specific profile with lenders that have a corresponding risk appetite. Moreover, even when merchants and lenders are connected, there is no efficient way to collect and analyze information to make credit decisions.

As a result, from the merchant's perspective, there are several negatives, including slow turnaround time for credit decisions, low approval rates (which decreases sales), high operating and information access costs, inefficient management of credit risk exposure, inconsistent credit decisions, and unsatisfied customers. The current credit model also adversely affects financial institutions, in ways that include limited market reach, high origination costs, and high processing costs to manually access information and make credit decisions; it is also cumbersome to optimize credit policy portfolios.

➤ Financial Products and Markets

Within the credit markets there are an endless number of financial products. The sourcing, analysis, and delivery of many of these products could be greatly improved. Table 8.1 highlights a few of the major products for the B2B and B2C markets.

➤ Leading Participants in the Credit and Financing Space

One of the leading players in the credit and financing space is eCredit. This online credit enabler has developed a proprietary global financial network (GFN) system to automate the information collection, decision-making, and matching processes. In creating this system, eCredit partners with various B2B and B2C information sources and financial institutions.

Once it signs up a merchant to the GFN system, eCredit customfits the network to match the merchant's parameters and guidelines. When a merchant needs a financial partner for a transaction, the GFN system links directly into the merchant's Web site. It then instantaneously collects data from information sources and scores the credit based on the custom-designed parameters. Once a score is assigned, the GFN system matches the score with financial partners' credit criteria, producing various financing options for the customer.

The eCredit GFN system currently provides both B2C and B2B

Table 8.1 Financial products and markets.

B2B	B2C
• Trade credit	• Credit cards
• Equipment leasing	• Installment loans
• Auto fleet leasing	• Mortgages
• Insurance	• Computer leasing
• Commercial loans	• Auto leasing
• Working capital	• Home equity loans

e-commerce sites with credit and financing capabilities. The types of financing it offers now include trade credit, equipment leasing, auto leasing, small commercial loans, computer leasing, and installment finance loans. It has signed more than 40 merchants and 10 financial institutions into the GFN system. It plans to expand its merchant and financial partner base, along with expanding the financial product offerings to include mortgages, insurance, home equity loans, and larger commercial loans.

The value propositions for merchants and financial partners are significant. For merchants, eCredit improves credit decision turnaround time from days to seconds. In addition, it increases approval rates, which increases sales and customer satisfaction. It also lowers operating and information access costs and provides a more efficient management of credit risk exposure by making decisions more standardized and consistent.

Financial institutions also benefit from the GFN system by increasing transaction volume through greater market penetration. Furthermore, it lowers origination costs and credit processing costs. Lastly, it allows financial partners to better manage their portfolios with more consistent credit policies.

---

eCredit

B2C Web-site Transactions

Gateway Computers uses eCredit as its credit and financing enabler for both B2C and B2B e-commerce. As with each merchant, eCredit worked with Gateway to custom-fit eCredit's GFN system to the specific risk parameters and guidelines for the firm.

Although all the information gathering, credit scoring, and lender matching is done through eCredit's system, the process is seamless and invisible to the customer, whose only interface is with Gateway's e-commerce site. In less than a minute, eCredit delivers a list of up to five financial institutions that are willing to approve the computer financing transaction. eCredit receives a transaction fee from Gateway and an origination fee from the accepted financial institution.

(continued)

The results for Gateway have been remarkable. At the time this book was written, the use of eCredit had increased its online approval rates from 40 percent to 95 percent, which obviously increased overall sales. Moreover, by outsourcing the data collection and credit scoring, Gateway also reduced its processing costs.

B2B Hub Transactions

Plasticnet.com is a B2B marketplace that aggregates buyers and sellers within the plastics industry. However, it lacks the credit and financing infrastructure to support e-commerce transactions, which is especially needed now that it is connecting fragmented buyers and sellers that might be conducting business for the first time.

As a solution to this problem, Plasticnet outsourced the function of scoring and analyzing trade credit terms for sellers to eCredit. After setting up Plasticnet's specified parameters, eCredit's GFN system was directly linked to Plasticnet's site. Therefore, within seconds of a plastic sale, eCredit can provide Plasticnet's buyers and sellers with real-time trade credit decisions. As a result, Plasticnet provides an end-to-end e-commerce solution to its buyers and sellers, which makes the customer experience much easier and more efficient.

➤ Online Credit and Financing Trends

The online credit market is still largely underserved and the competitive landscape has just begun to form. The first movers in this market are online intermediaries, primarily companies like eCredit. The competitive advantage for online intermediaries are first-mover advantage, superior technology, and critical mass of merchants and financial partners.

However, given the inefficiencies in the Old Economy model and the large market potential, traditional banks and financial institutions will undoubtedly enter this space. The difficulties that this group must overcome are being late to the game, notoriously slow and conservative, and lacking technological expertise. However, if they can overcome these obstacles, they will be formidable competitors because they have deep pockets, valuable domain expertise, strong brand names, and offline relationships with borrowers. Some of the potential participants could be GE Capital, Bank of America, and Wells Fargo. According to eCredit, many financial partners have been slow to join the network because they are attempting to figure out how to do it themselves.

Another potential entrant is the merchant. Merchants could develop or purchase technology to form a captive financing source. For example, a B2B exchange may form in-house financing capabilities, creating a captive finance program to complement its end-to-end solution and to expand revenue streams. FOB.com, a B2B reverse aggregator in the chemicals, plastic, paper and food verticals, is considering forming FOBCredit. There are many challenges to creating in-house financing capabilities, because it is beyond the expertise of many of these startup B2B hubs, which must first execute in their core business. However, if these companies can gain critical mass and eventually obtain a good credit rating, they might be able to pull it off because they control access to customers.

➤ Challenges and Issues with Online Credit

Without a doubt, there are many challenges and issues with online credit and financing. Because some basic transactions are well suited to the online model, more complex transactions may never be adopted. At a certain level, credit decisions are more of an art than a science. If a lender is attempting to assess a company's credit-worthiness for an equipment leasing transaction, sometimes there is much more to the decision than a D&B or the residual value of the equipment. Many times a human element must be factored into the decision equation as well. Do the lenders believe that the company's management includes good operators? Do they think the industry will remain strong? In general, the more sophisticated the financial product or structure, the less helpful an automated system will be.

An additional problem with online credit is determining end customers' needs if they are not financially savvy enough to figure it out themselves. This is less of an issue in the B2C market, but some B2B borrowers do not know what they need. For example, if a company has net operating losses, should it use a capital or operating lease for the purchase of new equipment? Based on its cash flow needs, what terms should it use—or should the term match the MACRS life of equipment? Many of these more complex transactions might be difficult to automate completely.

Another issue, which affects both B2C and B2B markets, is how financial partners can know if the data is valid and its integrity uncompromised. How does Fleet Leasing know that the data eCredit supplies is accurate? This bears on the issue of maintaining the quality of financial institutions' portfolios. Because online credit is just forming, it is difficult to measure the quality of the decisions. Companies like eCredit need to be able to track and measure the effectiveness of their decisions.

Although there are several issues and challenges regarding online credit and financing, there is certainly a need to improve the Old-Economy credit process to fit the needs of the Internet Economy. As the new process evolves, it will improve e-commerce through improved efficiencies in information gathering, credit decision making, and matching of borrowers and lenders.

■ NEW-AGE BARTER

Barter economics is another growth area in the payment space. The concept of barter predates paper currency by millennia. However, barter has begun to grow tremendously in the New Economy, because of the ability of the Internet to bring together a variety of different products and services without a complicated exchange of cash or use of credit.

The concept of barter delivers a clear value that can easily be captured on the Internet: the ability to exchange services or products of equal value without monetary transfer. Barter exchanges can be between businesses, as with BarterTrust or BigVine; or between consumers with swap groups, such as Swaprat. In 1998, it was estimated that commercial barter amounted to more than $10 billion from 500,000 companies linked to more than 1,500 barter networks around the world. Nevertheless, the fundamental issue of resolving inadequacy in value exchanged (where coming up with an exact match for two items is the issue) has created a market for a more finely divisible form of exchange value—paper currency. For online barter to succeed, a large number of available products at finely grained denominations must be available to mediate the gaps between parties. Consequently, for barter to become truly ubiquitous, it must achieve a large number of subscribers, as eBay did with auctions, and create a dominant currency standard.

➤ Barter as Corporate Cash Flow Management

Corporate barter works in a variety of different ways. The primary approach is for the intermediary to create online currency when a company has excess capacity or excess product inventory and lists that product/service as a value. By exchanging a product for a needed service or secondary product, a dollar-for-dollar exchange is created. This method gives the company greater return than liquidation at a discount. For example, a hotel chain might have excess rooms or chairs in its inventory, which it can unload and receive direct credit for from a barter agency. A second transaction could then allow the company to receive much-needed tableware in return. Because anything and everything can be bartered, the number of potential combinations for an aggregator of exchange services is huge. Yet, for the intermediaries, the main issue is how precisely to accommodate the differences in value between two parties without resorting to cash.

Effective bartering practices require, first of all, that the company select a barter service. Each service can charge monthly maintenance fees, transaction fees, and membership fees. These fees generally range from free to $100. The key to the service is its network; Bartertrust.com has bought several local networks and further consolidation among the online players is expected. The second issue with barter is effective cash management. The eventual goal is to unload all nonperforming assets with a barter exchange and receive products or services that can contribute immediately to corporate efficiency.

➤ New Currencies

Consumer barter services are also very promising because of their lack of cash distribution needs, but the key to consumer barter is remaining local with a large amount of reach. Even though a global marketplace for consumer exchange is possible (a variation on the eBay model), a large number of localized barter groups dominate the barter exchange model. Each day new "currencies" are created, called *community currencies*, which are used by locals to trade goods and services. "Ithaca hours" and "Berkeley Bread" are two examples. There are at present 50 such currencies in the United States, a number that is expected to grow as local online communities develop into marketplaces. Swaprat and Swap.com have also created online consumer exchange forums.

➤ Barter Taxes

In theory, there should be no tax advantages to bartering. However, all received assets must be disclosed to the IRS. Therefore, although some items can be deducted, just as cash transactions are, no special treatment of barter items exists. One must be careful to emphasize that the online barter model does not result in taxes only because income received is based on the net value received, which in turn is based on the disclosed exchange value.

➤ State-to-State (S2S)

One of the interesting possible applications of online barter is for states or countries to exchange vast amount of products/services or debt obligations online. It is very possible that a country like the United States could enter into an exchange with a country like Peru and exchange products for debt obligations online. Although traditional barter methods do currently exist, the exchanges are limited by their personal nature. Consequently, multicountry swap agreements, in real time and with the aid of an online aggregator and mediator, could improve liquidity in various products/services that today are wasted. Within the United States, a state barter system could possibly distribute excess state assets, such as road funds or electrical power, to other states with greater liquidity.

What is the unlocked value that venture capitalists and entrepreneurs hope will become the model for the New Economy? In the Old Economy, the real value of barter lay in turning nonperforming assets into something of value without any discount. The New Economy value might just be the creation of a new trading standard. As barter models converge more and more toward financial services, traditional forms of payment will give way to a distributed exchange system. If the liquidity and critical mass achieved significant levels, barter exchange could reduce (and in many instances eliminate altogether) the need for cash methods.

■ MICROPAYMENTS

Micropayments are the final area discussed in this chapter. Micropayments fundamentally create a new billing model, under which the individual items downloaded can be billed for separately and individually. With micropayment methods, consumers can download a song or a chapter of a book and be billed as little as 50 cents or a dollar, with that small amount being charged to their ISP or phone bill. However, there are several limitations to the widespread adoption of micropayments, due to the network externalities that currently underlie the use of traditional methods.

What is more, security issues with micropayments are primarily centered on the premise that a small charge would not require extensive use of encryption technology or other means of fraud prevention. The widespread use of micropayments is a potential breeding ground for fraud that today is not apparent. The lack of an authoritative infrastructure standard, coupled with strong network externalities, has limited micropayments from becoming a dominant means of value transfer.

➤ Micropayment Providers

Various companies have come up with different models for delivering and charging for digital content. Qpass will sell content from publishers, such as the Wall Street Journal Interactive, on a short-term or a per-article basis. Cybergold will let users purchase digital content such as MP3 songs, software, and video files using micropayments attached to the user's monthly credit card bill. Cybergold even allows reverse payments, with credits going to users' accounts based on click-throughs of ads on the Web site.

iPIN has been delivering micropayment services and utilizing the ISP bill as the payment medium. iPIN uses a system whereby an 8 to 15 percent fee is added to a transaction that has gone through its hub. The "paid content" market, including adult materials, will swell from $400 million in 2000 to more than $1.4 billion in 2003, according to Jupiter. Forrester Research claims that entertainment and music alone will account for $1 billion by 2003. The key for iPIN is to penetrate the market and unshackle the path dependencies that currently prevent micropayment methods from being widely used. Instead of using the ISP as the medium, eCHARGE lets consumers add purchases to their phone bills. eCHARGE is even interested in a prepaid service resembling a credit card account, which lets people shop freely until the amount in the account reaches a critical "over-credit" limit. This strategy is the centerpiece of 1ClickCharge's model, whereby a user adds a balance to his or her account from a credit card; this system allows one-click purchases over the Internet.

➤ M-Commerce Participants

Micropayments made over a mobile phone involve a multipurpose payment system that can handle payments anywhere a mobile phone or PDA can operate. This system is being developed with the wireless application protocol (WAP) as its primary standard. WAP allows cell phones to tap into the Internet from any wireless network: GSM, CDMA, or TDMA. WAP-enabled devices are then empowered, via third-party software vendors such as Portal Software, to link the mobile phone and a vendor of services to the mobile phone's service provider or ISP.

A clear catalyst for adoption of mobile phone payment will be GPRS (General Packet Radio Service). This technology, which is packet-based and not circuit-switched, will provide increased transmission speeds from the current 9.6 Kbps to more than 100 Kbps, and will be coupled with the use of the global phone or G3 (third-generation) phone to allow global Internet and telephone coverage. Billing, therefore, could be created on a per-packet or per-download basis. Certain online services could come along with their specific "price tags" for downloads to a mobile phone, allowing a "pay for each drink" model to develop. With the adoption of a new revenue model, telecommunications operators will need to realize that m-commerce services such as ticketing and e-commerce will be far more important than traditional voice ones. Data services will dominate; expected benefits include far greater customer loyalty and retention, reduced churn, and increased revenue streams.

The m-commerce operators will need to provide a comprehensive billing package for a large variety of services. Payment systems will have to be adaptable to a variety of appliances and be flexible enough to allow a variety of charges, from cents-per-mouse-click to hundreds of dollars for an item. The problem with large purchases will still be credit management, which today is controlled by a few large firms (TRW, Equifax). These companies currently sell their services to the credit card companies. An m-commerce operator will need to find a credit management tool so that it can diversify its credit risk exposure, yet be able to instantly load charges and create bills for its customers.

➤ Micropayment Evolution

Micropayment models are not static in nature. Fundamentally, they will provide a means of transferring value for incremental items. Micropayments will cross over Geoff Moore's technology-adoption "chasm" because a large number of extreme Web surfers are early adopters by nature. The 900 telephone number is considered the first successful micropayment method, but more online models will develop to feed the demand for quick and instant payment for performance.

What will create a ubiquitous micropayment space? Certainly, technology will have to evolve to allow for things like a clear identification of when a person is at the office, using a corporate ISP, and when that person is at home. Technology infrastructure is thus the first micropayment enabler. The merchants that are willing to provide content over a micropayment system for a large number of users are the second fundamental enabler for micropayments. Beyond path dependencies, external factors (externalities) have to be in place for the platform to be adopted. Content providers must have viral growth of their product through micropayments; this is the last enabler. When consumers are willing to spread use of downloaded products to other consumers via word-of-mouth or word-of-mouse, the micropayment model will be ensured as a key part of online success.

The Future of E-Payment

The future of e-payment services is certainly going to include a global evolution. This progression toward a global model for value exchange will begin with the utilization of niche value.

The large number of players in spaces such as electronic bill payment, credit, digital currency, and barter will force a strong demand for a metamediary to consolidate platforms, deliver consumers to the proper payment source, and consolidate services. Consolidation will first take the form of regional aggregation of services. Each global region (such as North America, Europe, or the Pacific Rim) will begin to form a consortium that will control services based on that region's spe-

(continued)

---

cific externalities. Externalities will provide the basis for a more efficient means of transferring value, because of regional standards.

A primary externality that will drive toward regional consolidation is banking standards. Banks will change to a cybermethod of payment only when all the local banks decide on one as well. Once regional banks decide on a transaction model that benefits the local consumer, a regional externality will be created that will be hard to break.

Because of infrastructure investments, telecommunications payment models are regional externalities. The development of the wireless model around certain regions will drive the development of wireless online payment models. Consequently, telecommunications will create externalities that are also difficult to dislodge.

Externalities will also be formed around regional government standards, such as European and North American (NAFTA) taxation standards. Governments will provide for online payment methods if such methods fit within their taxation and revenue systems.

The most powerful externality is the one based on prosperity imbalances. People will embrace e-payments based on their own ability to assess the technological (time) and prosperity (money) rewards. Externalities will be built around the value generated by the payment models to the specific consumer's perceived rewards for adopting an e-payment system.

Although the gaps inherent in the payment paradox are lessening, they will always remain. E-payment systems are primarily evolutionary, not revolutionary. However, because of the rapid growth of Internet commerce, we see the online payment system progressing—rapidly too, but always lagging behind. However, the today's current wide gap will certainly become narrower. Advances in payment systems will actually be an enabler of future online commerce

The second effect of consolidation will be the emergence of a global powerhouse that bridges all these externalities and creates a common global standard. This particular effect has

(continued)

already been seen in the telecommunications industry. The 3G phone is an attempt by the telecom industry to create a global phone that unifies all the regional standards and externalities. This phone promises to deliver broadband wireless services tot the entire community via a single dominant platform: maximum reach and richness. Much of the same can be said about the final phase of the e-payment model.

Beyond a global consolidator, there can be a unification of reach to the consumer: broad market adoption and richness. The combination of both reach and richness will cement e-payments models as solid, "normal" methods of transferring and delivering value. Only when this occurs will traditional forms be viewed as outdated and the convergence to online models be complete.

■ REFERENCES

Anders, George. "eBay, Wells Team Up on Web Payments." *Wall Street Journal*, March 1, 2000.

Andrews, Whit. "Microsoft Bets $15M on Maker of Micropayment Technology." *Internet World* (March 15, 1999).

Appleby, Scott, and Richard Shane. "Electronic Payment Systems." Robertson Stephens efinance research paper (January 28, 2000).

Barua, Anitesh. *Measuring the Internet Economy: An Exploratory Study.* Center for Research in Electronic Commerce, University of Texas, Austin (June 1999).

Bogestam, Kent. "Paying Your Way in the Mobile World." *Telecom International Edition* (January 2000).

Collett, Stacy. "New Online Payment Options Emerging." *Computer World* (January 31, 2000).

Cone, Edward. "OpenSite Adds to Dynamic Market." *Interactive Week* (February 2, 2000).

"ConSyGen Announces New Mobile Commerce Solution for Consumer to Business." *PR Newswire* (March 2, 2000).

Cox, Beth. "YourAccounts.com Develops EBPP Solution for FedEx." *InternetNews.com* (December 17, 1999).

Craig, Ben. "Resisting Electronic Payment Systems: Burning Down the

House?" *Economic Commentary* (Federal Reserve Bank of Cleveland, July 1999).

Crede, Andreas. "Electronic Commerce and the Banking Industry: The Requirement and Opportunities for New Payment Systems Using the Internet." *Journal of Computer-Mediated Communication* 1 (no. 3, December 1995).

Davis, Jeffrey. "Spare Change Agents." *Business 2.0* (October 1999).

Deloitte Research. "The New Economics of Transactions." 1999.

Duvall, Mel. "Start-Up Outsourcer Offers One-Touch Service." *Interactive Week* (January 26, 2000).

"EBPP." *e-business Magazine* (Winter 1999).

ecommerce.gov. "The Emerging Digital Economy II." June 1999.

Effross, W. A. "Remarks on the Report of the Consumer Electronic Payments Task Force." *Current Developments in Monetary and Financial Law.* 569–73. 1999.

Flynn, Laurie. "Bland Ambition." *Context Magazine* (March 20).

Forrest, Edward. "Practice Management Forum: To Barter or Not to Barter: That Is the Question." *Accounting Today* (September 27–October 10, 1999).

Fulford, Benjamin. "I Got It @ 7-Eleven." *Forbes Magazine* (April 3, 2000).

General Accounting Office. *Payments, Clearance, and Settlement: A Guide to the Systems, Risks, and Issues.* GGD-97-73 (June 17, 1997).

Giesen, Lauri. "Online Shopping : How Will Consumers Pay?" *Financial Services Online* (October 1999).

Good, Barbara. "Will Electronic Money Be Adopted in the United States?" Federal Reserve Bank of Cleveland (April 1998).

Hafner, Katie. "Will that Be Cash or Cell Phone?" *New York Times*, March 2, 2000.

Hagen, Paul, with Harley Manning. "Person-to-Person Payments Will Prevail." *Forrester Report* (March 2000).

Hamilton, Anita. "Personal Time/Your Technology in Brief." *Time Magazine*, March 6, 2000.

Hamilton, Kevin. "Cashing In." *Context Magazine* (Winter 1999).

Homer, Steve. "Focus: Too Soon to Bank on Cybercash." *The Independent* (London), October 20, 1999.

Humphrey, David, and Lawrence Pulley. "Unleashing Electronic Payments." *Banking Strategies, BAI Online* (November/December 1998).

Inman, Phillip. "Smart Cards Are Still Not Clever Enough." *The Guardian* (London), December 1999.

Kawamoto, Dawn. "New Standards Could Help Development of Micropayments." *CNET News.com* (November 30, 1999).

Kroll, Karen. "Barter Sheds Its Shady Image to Become a Cash-Saving Tool for Small Companies." *BusinessWeek* (October 7, 1999).

Lee Ting Ting. "Going Cashless." *Berhad New Straits Times* (Malaysia), March 1, 2000.

McCarthy, F. T. "E-Cash 2.0: Digital Currencies Are Sprouting All over the Internet. But Virtual Money Does Not Yet Pose a Serious Threat to the Real Thing." *The Economist* (February 2000).

"Mobile Money: Pixo and PayPal.com Team to Send Money Via Wireless Phones." *Business Wire* (February 22, 2000).

O'Mahony, Donal, Michael Peirce, and Hitesh Tewari. *Electronic Payment Systems*. Artech House, 1997.

Ouren, John, and Marc Singer. "Current Research: Electronic Bill Payment and Presentment." *McKinsey Quarterly* (Winter 1998).

Owlstrategy. "Getting Paid Online." February 2000.

Rivlin Committee. "The Federal Reserve in the Payments Mechanism." January 1998.

Sheehan, K. P. "Electronic Cash." *FDIC Banking Review* 11 (no. 2, Summer 1998): 1–8.

Smetannikov, Max. "Metered Billing Future Comes One Step Closer." *Interactive Week* (January 28, 2000).

Thompson, Maryann. "My How We've Grown." *The Industry Standard* (April 26, 1999).

United States Department of Commerce. "The Emerging Digital Economy." April 1998.

Vartanian, Thomas, Robert Ledig, and Lynn Bruneau. *21st Century Money, Banking, & Commerce*. Fried, Frank, Harris, Shriver & Jacobson, 1998.

Wang, Nelson. "Firms Debut Micropayment Plans." *Internet World* (March 19, 1999).

Weiner, S. E. "Electronic Payments in the U.S. Economy: An Overview." *Economic Review* (Federal Reserve Bank of Kansas City) (fourth quarter 1999): 1–12.

Weisul, Kimberly. "E-Payments That Really Work." *Interactive Week* (March 20, 2000).

Chapter

The Music
Controversy

Application or Company?

■ INTRODUCTION

The recorded music industry fears the Internet. In fact, major industry players are focused on resisting this new medium and its related technologies because they feel it is a threat to their retail business opportunities. The public witnessed the industry's resistance, as well as the complexity of the issues involved, most clearly in the MP3.com controversy. Only recently has the industry started to leverage the power of the Internet to create a potentially bigger, more consumer-centric future.

As technology develops to the point where consumers can access the Internet from anywhere, the way music is delivered from artist to consumer will fundamentally change. Currently, the consumer buys a physical product, but the development of broadband, wireless, and Internet technologies will shift this process toward the "hyper-availability" of music, where the consumer has access to any music he or she wants at any time from any place. At this point, "music" need no longer be a product that people must buy. Instead, it will denote a service, providing access to any song by any artist, on demand. Technological development and market need will overshadow the recording industry's attempts to maintain the status quo.

This chapter focuses on how technology—not just the Internet, but also hardware like satellite car radios and wireless Internet access—will change the way music will be made available to consumers, and the role music companies will have in shaping the future marketplace.

■ THE EXISTING VALUE PROPOSITION

The process of how music reaches the consumer seems simple enough, but it is fraught with inefficiency. The industry has predominantly operated on a "push" strategy: the labels prequalify the music that will be offered for sale to the buying public and communication is one-way, with few feedback mechanisms to improve either the product or the distribution process. The result is a poor value proposition that constricts the market and its potential for growth. Let us review these inefficiencies in more detail from the point at which music is chosen by the labels.

➤ A&R Filtering and "Push"

By choosing which artists to sign and promote, the record companies filter through the vast offerings of new music to pick the ones they think will be enjoyed by the most customers. This function is called A&R, short for "artists and repertoire." It is a valuable service because there is a plethora of artists to choose from and a typical consumer does not have time to sift through all of them.

When listening to a radio or watching a video channel, the consumer has no choice in what songs are played. In effect, the current music industry employs a "push" strategy, where airplay is controlled by the record labels and the media programmers make decisions on song rotations. Once the music is promoted through these channels, the public signals its acceptance or rejection of those songs through its listening trends and album purchases. Filtering is a valuable service that creates a manageable set of bands and songs from which to choose, but it may inadvertently limit purchases in general. Access and introduction to the music of lesser-known artists could increase music sales as consumers expand their loyalties beyond their favorite, familiar bands and try new, previously unheard music to enhance their overall music experiences and collections.

➤ Product-to-Brand: The Missing Link

Broadcast music suffers from a weak product-to-brand link that limits a consumer's ability to buy what he or she likes. Songs are not instantly associated with their artists, and artists are not always directly associated with their latest work. Without this ready connection, a purchase is difficult and even inconvenient for the music consumer. For instance, because songs are played in batches on the radio, with minimal attribution of each song to a particular artist, the consumer is often left wondering, "Who sang what?"

➤ Lack of Customization and Bundled Buying

The retail experience itself is an unfriendly one in which blind purchasing is the rule, as consumers are unable to listen to a full album before buying it, nor return it after opening it postpurchase. This often leads to dissatisfaction from listeners who enjoy a select few "hit" tracks on an album and are disappointed by the remaining filler. Retail listening kiosks exist, but are few in number and are an inconvenient way of judging a whole album.

The bundled nature of full albums does not allow any flexibility in customizing the music purchase. Singles, though available, are limited to the top artists and are generally not promoted by the industry because they are unprofitable. Although the fixed costs of a single are similar to those of full CDs, revenue is smaller on a per-unit basis, and demand is difficult to forecast. For the consumer, singles are also relatively expensive, and inconveniently packaged in separate physical units. Customers prefer instead to buy a collection of hit singles rather than a full album. In fact, many of the best-selling albums in recent years have been movie soundtracks or compilations. The net result is that consumers are encouraged to take a cautious spending stance, typically paying only for albums from artists who have established track records or a series of hits, and experimenting with new-artist purchases only selectively.

➤ Communication Breakdown

It is astonishing how poorly music is marketed. The labels fail to create a strong connection with their customers, and there is very little communication or exchange of information between artist and consumer. Record labels and artists do not readily know who is buying their music nor how to contact them; it is a product-based transaction that does not result in any sort of learning relationship. Targeting techniques are thus rendered useless, and the artist's "brand" is the sole marketing tool relied on to reestablish the consumer relationship each time a new album is released. An indication of how weak communication is came from a survey by the Recording Industry Association of America (RIAA), which determined that seven out of ten people did not know when their favorite artist had released a new album. Until just one or two years ago, these inefficiencies characterized the music-buying experience.

■ DIGITAL MUSIC IS CHANGING EVERYTHING

Some of the numerous technological and social changes over the past few years have the potential of changing the music industry forever. The most significant lever behind these changes is also the least surprising: The Internet's growth has made the worldwide distribution of musical content possible. With 100 million online listeners in 1999, the effect of network economies has grown even stronger, as users have found new ways to access the music they want via Web sites (both legal and pirate), to chat with fellow fans online, and to enjoy ad-free Webcasts. Feeding the growth of Internet use is the development of several new technologies designed to deliver musical content to the consumer.

➤ Digital File Compression: I Want My "MP3"

The development of the MP3 file format allowed computer users to send and download complete songs of near-perfect digital quality and in less time than ever before. Music is no longer tied to a physical CD or cassette, and can be stored in relatively small data files on PC hard drives. As an indication of the popularity of such downloads, Napster.com enjoyed in excess of 1 million users per day by early 2000.

Although the compression technology of MP3 and other file formats has made easy downloads a reality, the delivery of music over the Internet remains constrained by a lack of sufficient bandwidth. Today, it takes about 15 minutes to download a single song using a standard narrowband modem. A study from Forrester Research concluded that 76 percent of Internet users would wait no longer than 30 minutes to download an album. Consequently, the rollout of high-speed access is key to the development and mass acceptance of downloadable music. Jupiter forecasts that the number of households with DSL or cable access will jump to 11.7 million in 2002, from 2.4 million in 1999. Thus, nearly 20 percent of home Internet access will be broadband by 2002.

Beyond the limits of download speed, the adoption of MP3s has slowed as the format has come under fire from the record labels for lack of copy protection. Right now, anyone can distribute or receive a digitized copy of a pirated song for free. Although this unfettered access is the primary reason that digital music has proliferated on the Internet, it has also opened the door to several high-profile copyright lawsuits, as the recording industry tries to protect its revenue stream.

➤ Streaming Media

Instead of storing music, streaming audio has enabled quick and efficient access to music without the download wait, so consumers can "sample" music online without any purchase commitment. Streaming has also resulted in the proliferation of Web–radio broadcasts, providing online competition to traditional radio formats that employ advertising.

A significant consequence of the streaming technologies is the ephemeral, one-time experience given to the consumer. This appears to be much safer for artists and record labels, both of which worry about giving away their intellectual property. It also paves the way for the promotion of new albums and faster adoption of a new musical creation. As a result, streaming audio is positioned to lead the next wave of on-demand music delivery over the Web.

➤ Recordable CDs

The recordable optical drive is an increasingly popular way of storing digital music, offering the ability to "burn" a compact disc of digital files and then play the stored music on conventional CD hardware. A technological bridge between prerecorded CDs and digital files, CD-writers are expected to be used by 19.4 million people by 2003 (up from just 2.7 million users in 1998). This technology is also used commercially to create customized, track-specific CDs for consumers on sites like Musicmaker.com. Indeed, after largely retreating from the unprofitable singles business over the last 10 years, record labels may be forced to re-embrace this model of distribution, now that consumers have the technology to buy only the songs they really want.

➤ MP3 Players

No longer are consumers tied to the computer to listen to digital music. Though still in their developmental infancy, portable MP3 players offer significant benefits when compared to the traditional portable CD player. More importantly, MP3 players such as the Diamond Rio offer the ability to customize the selection of tracks to be downloaded, eliminating the need for bulky CD carrying cases. These players are also significantly more durable, because they lack moving parts and can be shaken (in activities such as jogging) without skipping.

➤ Wireless Access

Wireless devices will be a major means of transmitting music broadcasts in the future, freeing listeners from the inconvenient constraints of portable CD and even MP3 players. Cellular telephones and personal digital assistants (PDAs) are the most obvious channels of wireless distribution in the short term. "Anytime, anywhere" e-commerce will soon be realized, with the wireless devices used as receivers for streaming customized audio. We may eventually use wireless devices to listen to our favorite songs, and buy music and related merchandise, all remotely and on demand. In fact, pioneers like Sanyo Electric, Hitachi, and Fujitsu have all recently announced progress in the development of technology standards for delivery of secure music to mobile phones.

It is clear that digital music has far greater potential than simply downloading and storing MP3 files on a desktop hard drive. The technological developments of the last few years have empowered the listener to customize music and access it on demand without regard to place, time, or activity. Technology has liberated the digital music enthusiast from the PC and will move the enjoyment of personalized music from the laptop to the palmtop and beyond.

■ A NEW VALUE PROPOSITION: PULL VERSUS PUSH

As we compare the buying experience of the near past with that of the present and immediate future, we realize that the new technology of the last few years has created a radically new consumer for the recorded music industry. Broadly, the music value proposition is increasingly a pull-driven strategy of consumer choice, as opposed to the push marketing tactics of labels. Technology has transformed music buyers from passive ones with little control over the final product to more powerful, active buyers who will increasingly control what they listen to and purchase. This shift should make music more accessible, targeted, convenient, and (ultimately) more profitable.

➤ The Option Value of Music

When consumers purchase a CD for $15, part of what they are paying for is the option to play that music whenever they want. The CD has value because the consumer controls the music to some extent. But the consumer still has to carry a physical storage unit (the CD) or is constrained in that extra recording steps are required (such as burning a custom-mixed CD) to get truly personalized music. This is inconvenient; we suggest that if this option value of music can be created through some other, more convenient distribution method, then consumers will gravitate to that method, be it a product or a service.

➤ Freedom of Choice: A&R "Push" versus Self-Selection

The consumer's purchase begins with the introduction of new music through a test medium such as radio. Sites such as MP3.com, Riffage.com, and Farmclub.com showcase hundreds, if not thousands, of artists who do not have major record label contracts. Consequently, the consumer has access to a much broader spectrum of artists than the choices offered—normally pushed—by the labels and radio stations. In theory, such access to more artists will allow consumers to incrementally increase their consumption of music by listening to new performers. However, such sites lack an adequate filtering mechanism, limiting them to the small number of devoted music listeners who are willing to sift through much chaff to find the wheat.

➤ Product-to-Brand Linkage: Streaming Samples and Webcasting

Once the consumer has gained access to a band and its music, online audio streaming provides a tool to sample new music quickly and efficiently without committing hard dollars. In addition, the creation of streaming Webstations provides a listening experience that has several advantages for the consumer: the ability to see the artist's name and the track title as the song is played, the ability to offer targeted content for personalized listening, and no advertising. Consumers can click on appropriate links and listen to portions of new tunes at CDNow, Amazon, or streaming Webstations, then purchase the CD only if the music is to their liking. This "try before you buy" strategy ultimately lowers the inhibition to buy, enhances consumer satisfaction, and propagates future spending on an artist whose music has been sampled online.

➤ Customization and Unbundled Buying through MP3s

Of course, once a consumer hears an artist and targets that music for purchase, the sale can be transacted over the Web; online buying of CDs was one of the initial Internet sales tools. Yet the online music retailer model still focuses on the selection and purchase of CDs—physical storage repositories of bundles of music. Although this is the widespread model today, it is not likely to satisfy the ultimate consumer demands for music: accessibility and personalization. MP3's enabling of these two benefits best demonstrates that the dynamic of the music industry has shifted from a "push" model to a demand-driven "pull" model.

MP3 compression technology enables quick access to music on any number of listening devices. No physical storage device (such as CD) is directly necessary, and the music is, in a sense, "untethered." Furthermore, because each song can be a separate file, consumers can create personalized compilations that include tracks from not just one, but several, artists. Popular "hit" singles could be played without the "B" sides that often make a regular album disappointing. MP3 files create added value through more listening and purchasing variety: different artists, songs, and musical styles for true flexibility. This customization is especially attractive because a music purchase often makes a statement about the buyer's self-image. As such, it is bound to become more relevant as the ability to tailor product to individual grows. Importantly, all of this can be done digitally at limited variable cost per user, thus laying the groundwork for profitable, consumer-driven business models once legal issues and other execution difficulties are resolved.

The plethora of existing music Web sites that offer MP3 or similar file downloads is testament to the fact that downloads are fast gaining acceptance as another type of music distribution. Although recent estimates place 1999 music download revenues at less than $0.5 million, 49 percent of music site visitors listen to music clips and another 12 percent download songs for personal use. Moreover, given the popularity of pirated MP3s, it is likely that these research numbers are considerably understated. For the month of December 1999, MP3.com attracted 2.2 million visitors to MTV.com's 2.1 million; this is significant because MP3 is download-focused, as opposed to content-centric sites like MTV.com.

The practice of downloading is certainly growing among online users, but the question remains as to whether consumers are willing to search through thousands of songs to find the hits. Rather, we propose that the sheer volume of downloads available in the not-so-distant future will still require marketing to gain the attention of the online consumer. In other words, a gathering and filtering mechanism (such as the role the record labels currently fulfill) will still be required to help consumers narrow their listening choices to a manageable number.

➤ Breaking the Communications Barrier

The rise of artist-specific Web sites, such as BeastieBoys.com, provides an incredible tool to open the long-dormant communication channels between artist/label and dedicated fans. Rather than relying on sporadic, blind transactions such as the purchase of a CD or concert ticket, artists can establish relationships with fans on a consistent basis through personalized Web sites. These sites deliver the latest news, releases, and available merchandise directly to the consumers most likely to be interested in such information. In turn, the consumers can sign up for e-mail listservs and share demographic information that can be invaluable to the labels' direct marketing efforts. Perhaps most importantly, these sites let fans "interact" with their favorite artists anytime they want, thus fulfilling the emotional "celebrity idolatry" need.

■ TECHNOLOGICAL CONTROL THROUGH REGULATION

These developments in technology will change the music industry. However, regulation and legal battles are restricting the tremendous growth potential of technology. The music industry responded to the radical technological advances of the past few years with initial uncertainty, followed by aggressive defense. At stake is the fundamental issue of control—control over distribution of musical content traditionally held by major record labels and the associated retail system. The widespread acceptance of MP3 technology has created an environment in which the piracy of individual songs is easy and quite rampant. But it is the same technology that enables the compelling benefits of music accessibility and customization. The labels' efforts to control the profit stream may well impede the attainment of the consumer's ultimate music experience. Still, recent announcements of some labels' plans to sell digital music online, under cautious conditions, are encouraging.

The Recording Industry Association of America launched the Secure Digital Music Initiative (SDMI) in early 1999, in an effort to develop an industry-wide compliant standard for delivering digital music. The crux of these initial efforts lay in creating specifications for portable devices to deliver music in a secure (i.e., encrypted) format that eventually protects the artist and label from ungoverned distribution of the content. Encryption is expected to make piracy more difficult, as successive generations of players are programmed not to play music not encrypted with the latest digital "watermark." In this manner, the SDMI hopes to create an environment that protects the revenue stream flowing back to the label and the artist each time a sale of copyrighted music is made.

The recording industry's defensive stance is obvious from the various lawsuits initiated over the past year or two. These include RIAA suits against hardware innovators, pirate online intermediaries, and legitimate music Web sites:

- *Diamond Multimedia:* In response to the launch of a new portable MP3 player, the Rio, the RIAA attempted to secure (but was denied) an injunction in late 1998 against the Rio's distribution. The industry's failure to stop the Rio opened the door for the proliferation of MP3 and forced the record labels to adapt.

- *Napster:* In December 1999, the RIAA sued the "electronic bazaar for music piracy."[1] Napster.com made software available for MP3 collectors to share their files with one another across the Internet. RIAA claims that 90 percent of such files infringe on copyrights.

- *MP3.com:* Perhaps the most notorious suit to date, but surprisingly the one having the least to do with MP3 technology itself. The RIAA and the unsigned-artist Web site MP3.com have sued and countersued one another over a new service feature launched in January 2000. Called "Beam-it," the service allows consumers to instantaneously upload previously purchased CDs onto the site for accessibility from anywhere. The RIAA's case for copyright infringement centers not on the service itself, but rather on the fact that MP3.com took the unusual step of making data copies of more than 40,000 CDs on its servers to speed the consumer upload process.

These suits and the SDMI's standardization initiatives have created higher legal costs for the recording industry, overall resistance to new technology, and a delay in the availability of downloads from popular, major-label artists. Although the RIAA is acting to protect its own interests, these do not directly relate to the best interests of the music-buying public, who would benefit from new technological advances and vast download catalogs. In late 2000, the international music industry giant BMG went so far as to announce a partnership with Napster, reflecting the recognition on the part of some industry players of the emerging necessity to conquer the online music space, as well as Napster's recognition of its need to work with existing industry entities to build itself a constructive, profitable future.

■ COMPETITIVE LANDSCAPE

The advent of digital music technology has attracted many competitors to the Internet. At this time, it is unclear which will succeed and which will not—few are currently profitable and significant consolidations loom on the horizon. Following is a summary and critique of the various Internet music models in existence today (see Figure 9.1).

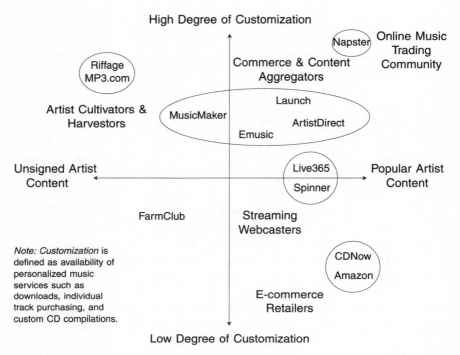

Figure 9.1   Competitive landscape roadmap.

➤ Artist Cultivators and Harvesters

Sites like MP3.com, Riffage.com, FarmClub.com, and garageband.com have created a distribution and promotional outlet for artists who do not have recording contracts. Visitors can listen to the music for free (sometimes download, sometimes only streaming). If they like what they hear, they can usually buy the band's CD, as well as link to the band's Web page to get more information. This addresses the issue of A&R blocking consumers' access to the vast majority of unsigned musical acts and allows the consumer to test music before buying. However, when left to one's own devices, the selection of artists is overwhelming. The filtering service provided by the labels' A&R people becomes valuable when a consumer is forced to find a new, likable band among the tens of thousands of artists at a site like MP3.com.

Unfortunately, the revenue model of these sites does not appear to be extremely robust, particularly among those without major label affiliations. The Web site typically receives income from advertising and takes a cut of each CD sold (usually around 50 percent of the sale). For instance, most of MP3.com's revenues are generated from advertising; the volume of CD purchases is not sufficiently large, comprising only 7 percent of revenue in 1999. Because most of the songs are available for free downloading anyway (for trial purposes), many visitors are unwilling to actually purchase the CD. In addition, these sites typically offer nonexclusive agreements with their artists that can be terminated at any time. As a result, there is no upside; the acts that do break away from the pack can get snapped up by a major record label, at which point the Web site's revenue stream from that artist stops.

Alternatively, the major labels are directly funding some sites to identify artists who already have a national fan base online, thus leading to lower-risk investments if these artists are signed to contracts. In these cases, the site serves both dedicated music enthusiasts looking for hip, relatively unknown music, and the major labels seeking the next "big" artist. FarmClub, backed primarily by the Universal Music Group, offers unsigned musicians the ability to digitally submit their recordings to the site and a chance to perform on an affiliated offline TV show. To date, FarmClub has signed few artists to major contracts, and the label has come under significant bad publicity for extorting onerous terms from the bands it chooses to spotlight. Although the Web has created new avenues for unknown artists to be discovered, the power of the major labels is still very real and plays a major role in determining a band's success.

➤ Commerce and Content Aggregators

Among the pioneers of the Internet, music Web sites (including ArtistDirect.com, MTV.com, and Launch.com) quickly morphed from simple news or e-commerce sites to commerce and content "aggregators" that sought to create a one-stop community for every music fan's needs. The music consumer often has an emotional bond with the artist, and the ability of the Web to provide more artist-specific information and content only strengthens that relationship. Music fans can find news and information on their favorite bands, post their thoughts in chat rooms, watch full-length videos, and listen to music at the click of a button. This deeper connection between the artist and consumer is expected to stimulate the demand for more music and associated content. ArtistDirect is a Web site that manages fan e-mail lists for many major-label artists. It keeps the consumer better informed about new albums, tours, and merchandise offerings to induce more spending than might normally occur.

The revenue model is based on advertising and promotional fees, as well as merchandising revenues. Consolidation and alliances have been rampant as each site attempts to build scale by offering more content to reach a broader audience. Importantly, these sites have the support of the industry, with four of the Big Five invested in ArtistDirect and Viacom backing MTV.com. In fact, many of the big record labels are investing in a wide variety of Web sites to spread their bets and, they hope, end up owning one of the winners that will remain following the inevitable shakeout.

➤ Retail Sites

Retail music sales were one of the first e-commerce applications of the Web. Today, one can choose from a seemingly unlimited selection of CDs from sites such as Amazon or CDNow, usually for a lower price than in retail stores. There is also the option of listening to some of the tracks via streaming before buying. This represents an improvement over traditional retail outlets, which typically do not allow the consumer to try before buying. CDNow, positioning itself as the original online music specialist, also gives the consumer access to considerable news and information about the bands, though it remains an e-commerce venture at its core.

The new value proposition is more apparent at Musicmaker.com, where the consumer can make a customized CD of individual songs of his or her choice. The CD is more expensive than a typical one, and the selection of artists and songs is small, with very few new popular acts available. CDNow also offers a customizable disc, but the selection is even more limited.

Broadly, the music e-commerce business model is still unproven. CDNow, though well known as an online retail outlet, might not have survived through the year 2000 were it not for its purchase by the German media conglomerate Bertelsmann. Amazon.com has quickly become the number-one online music retailer, but has done so by selling physical CDs, not digital downloads, and its divisional profitability remains disguised. Net, online music retailing provides major consumer benefits of convenience, but existing sites will need to work with the labels to fully embrace downloading individual tracks as the way to provide consumer choice.

➤ Streaming Webcasters

Webcasters like Launch.com, Live365.com, and Spinner.com allow the consumer to listen to music broadcasts over the Internet. The content varies from actual radio broadcasts, to computer-generated playlists of popular music (e.g., Spinner), to playlists selected and uploaded by other users (e.g., Live365). Even more exciting from the viewpoint of the listener is Launch.com's "LaunchCast," which uses consumers' real-time song ratings to determine personal preferences, then customizes a Webcast in real time. Given the restrictions of the 1998 Digital Millennium Copyright Act (DMCA), which limits the content that can be Webcast (specific to playing music by the same artist or from the same album, as well as user customization), this is a big step toward realization of our vision of the music industry of the future.

The revenue model among Webcasters is primarily based on advertising. Like other advertising-driven music sites, the long-term sustainability of Live365 and others is uncertain. However, Webcasts might be able to command a subscription fee once they can provide the customer with a fully customizable means of listening to music in an on-demand format.

➤ Fan Sites

With news, video, and audio content, merchandise, chat rooms, and ticket sales, fan sites provide a greater emotional tie between artist and consumer. Typically funded by popular artists' labels, fan sites are usually not designed to be profitable on their own, but serve as an additional marketing channel for the artist. With the addition of new content such as studio outtakes and live pay-per-view concerts, such sites can help drive incremental revenues for both the artist and the label.

➤ Online Music Trading Communities

Napster was not designed to be a pirate site, but it has evolved into a major target for the RIAA's antipiracy efforts, because of the Napster network's free access to the music collections of its collective members. It is likely that the lawsuit from the RIAA will force Napster to install limitations on the exchange of pirated files within its network. In addition, SDMI initiatives will make it more difficult to transfer pirated digital music to portable players. However, a significant amount of musical content is still free "shareware," including certain bands' live content (such as the Grateful Dead) and music by artists who want to promote themselves. Nonetheless, it is unclear how this business model can be profitable. Napster is a free network; once pirated copies of popular music are no longer available, the amount of traffic on the home site is expected to drop dramatically.

All of these business models begin to address some of the unmet needs of the consumer. However, there is much uncertainty as these companies battle for market share. We predict significant consolidations in the near future, as those sites that best meet consumers' needs remain standing on the stage and those that do not are left without a ticket.

■ THE FUTURE OF DIGITAL MUSIC

In this chapter, we have examined the traditional music industry and its flaws in addressing customer needs. We discussed some of the technological developments that have improved the value proposition for the customer and described the current online music landscape. Meanwhile, the process of improvement has been slowed and shaped by the record labels' attempts to maintain the status quo of controlled, bundled access to music.

How will these developments in the industry change the way music travels from the artist to the consumer? We envision three major phases that the industry will go through over the course of the next ten years.

➤ The BEAT Framework

Our predictions for the future can best be summed up by the acronym BEAT, outlined in Table 9.1.

Table 9.1 The BEAT framework.

	Phase I The Download Era (2000–2004)	Phase II The Digitalization Era (2005–2009)	Phase III The Hyperavailability Era (2010 and beyond)
B Benefit to the consumer	• Higher customization of music bundles • Enhanced interaction with artists through their Web sites	• Personalization of radio Webcasting • Convenience of storage solutions	• Choice between smart push (personalized) or instantaneous pull of anything; Full option value • Technology has disappeared
E Economic viability	• Affordability of music improves with growing offer of customizable downloads • Winning music Internet business models are emerging; success of major-backed sites	• Major labels control distribution; stores start adapting their offers (custom CDs) • Labels begin to feel the pinch from consumers who "pull" their own content from the radio via new technology and do not buy CDs	• Music shifts from product to service on a subscription basis; streaming subscriptions become the main source of revenues for labels • Radios lose some brand equity as speechless broadcast becomes more prevalent

Table 9.1 (continued).

	Phase I The Download Era (2000–2004)	Phase II The Digitalization Era (2005–2009)	Phase III The Hyperavailability Era (2010 and beyond)
A Availability and accessibility	• Availability of music increases with the Big Five offering their catalogs online • Access is still largely tied to the computer	• Possibility to capture any music in a digital format from the net-radios • Consumer must wait or program a device to wait until the desired music is on the air; not instantly accessible	• Hyperavailability through immediate accessibility (at home or anywhere)
T Technology	• No significant break-through • Standard battle continues with encryption capabilities	• Radio broadcast digitally through the Web • Standards are fully compatible with each other, low piracy • Intelligent buffers retrieve songs from radio broad-casts	• Broadband wireless access for constant instantaneous delivery • New generation of receiv-ing devices (end of the storage era)

B: Benefit to the Consumer

- *Personalization*: Is the music targeted specifically to the consumer's individual musical taste? Is it targeted to fit the consumer's mood? A consumer's mood affects what songs he or she wants to hear at that moment. As technology becomes "smarter," it can select music that is personalized to the consumer's immediate needs.

- *Customization*. How flexible is the delivery channel of music? Can the consumer pick and choose which songs to receive?

- *Interaction*. To what extent can the consumer interact with the artist? This includes any means of maintaining communication, such as official/fan-created Web sites and e-mail lists.

- *Convenience*. How easy is it for the consumer to find, receive, and listen to the music he or she is seeking?

E: Economic Viability

- *Affordability*. Is it affordable to the average consumer?

- *Business model*. How do the industry participants make money? Is the model sustainable? What, if anything, is changing?

A: Availability and Accessibility of Music

- *Variety*. Is there variety of content? This includes the availability of music from a wide array of artists, both old (established brands) and new (unbranded).

- *Access*. How does the consumer access the music? How convenient and portable is it? Is it truly on-demand?

T: Technology

- *Requirements*. What technologies are being implemented?

- *Status*. Is that technology available now?

- *Potential*. If not, can we speculate that it is likely to become available in the foreseeable future?

➤ Phase I: The Download Era

In the "download era" phase, we believe the music industry will continue to evolve as it has been for the past year. The consumer will have an increasing opportunity to access music online. Slowly but surely, mainstream consumers will adopt the Internet as a distribution point for music information, content, and sales. The Big Five labels will still control and "push" distribution, but they will begin offering their music catalogs online (in encrypted files to prevent piracy) and offer singles for sale instead of complete albums. However, the consumer's selection will still be incomplete. Most consumers will primarily buy CDs, to capture the option value of owning the music they desire. Piracy will continue to be an issue for the labels, though it will be reduced by the advent of copy-protected sound files. Technology will move quickly, but the consumer will still be tied to the PC to capture digital music.

The forces behind the BEAT framework during this phase are *availability and accessibility*. Consumers will adopt new technology when music labels provide their musical content online. Jupiter Communications suggested that this will largely be accomplished by 2002. Currently, the biggest roadblock for digital music is the scarcity of big-name acts available for download. Recent announcements by Sony and BMG indicate an increased willingness to make their content available online. As the labels become more comfortable offering their content online, with copyright protection, more consumers will experiment with downloading.

Four years may seem like an eternity in this age of monthly Internet revolutions, but our hypothesis is that the general public is slow to adopt very new technologies that change the way one experiences media. In addition, widespread (and inexpensive) broadband availability, which is a necessary element of our predictions, is several years off. It takes time for people to invest in new hardware and to adapt their behavior to the changing environment. More importantly, the music industry has a considerable investment in the CD format, and will not jeopardize this revenue stream overnight. Therefore, just as was the case with the VCR or the compact disc, it will be a few years before digital music downloading becomes a primary method of accessing music. Naturally, the companies providing this new technology will try to speed the process through marketing, but it will take time for people's existing music hardware (stereos, portable CD players) to become obsolete and actually force them to look at the new technology in the marketplace.

B: Benefit to the Consumer

The primary benefit to consumers is that there is a new place to purchase music: the Internet.

Personalization. The interactivity of the Internet allows more personalization of content. One feature, currently in development on sites like Riffage.com, recommends new bands based on a user's personal download patterns. This is similar to Amazon.com's customer recommendations indicating what similar customers have purchased.

The industry will still focus on "push" marketing, as consumer adoption of the Internet is not widespread. CDs will still be the dominant music product purchased and radio and MTV will still be the labels' primary means of promoting music to the masses.

Customization. Consumers will have greater control over the product delivered to them. As the big labels experiment with musical catalogs online, there will be a trend toward offering singles for sale rather than full albums. Some sites have begun testing the waters for the singles market. Emusic.com, for example, offers downloadable singles for sale. However, this does not apply to all albums, and in some instances only the entire album is available for download. All of the Big Five record labels have announced plans to sell singles online beginning in the summer of 2000.

Interaction. The consumer will have the opportunity to interact more with the artists as Internet music marketing becomes savvier. ArtistDirect.com allows users to search for fan-related material on approximately 100,000 bands. Such a site might direct you to both official and fan-created sites for your favorite band. Once you arrive at, for example, Backstreetboys.com, you can sign up for the e-mail listserv, watch "Millennium TV" (an exclusive streaming video of the band on tour), and e-mail questions to the band members. These sites create a year-round connection between fans and bands.

Convenience. It is already relatively easy to locate CDs for purchase using CDNow and Amazon. However, there is much greater potential. Broadcast radio will still suffer from the weak product-to-brand link. The growing minority of people who listen to Webcast sites, such as Spinner.com, can finally see which song is being played, its artist, and the album from which it came. This is required of Webcasters by the Digital Millennium Copyright Act. There is typically a link that allows the listener to click through to buy the album from one of the afore-mentioned commerce sites. Oddly enough, this DMCA requirement paves the way for consumers to "pull" music on demand by choosing Webcasts based on what is currently playing. This is currently discouraged by the DMCA, but, as we discuss in relation to Phase II, such technology will eventually shift control of music distribution from the record labels to the consumer.

E: Economic Viability

Affordability. Music will become more affordable. CDs will still be the primary means of owning music, but new pricing structures will develop for digital music. Singles will be available for purchase and download, though this product has to provide an adequate rate of return to the record labels. Sites like EMusic.com currently charge $0.99 per single, which may be too low for singles to become economically viable. Sony plans to debut its downloadable songs at $2.49, which is less consumer-friendly but probably more financially viable.

As digital downloads of complete albums grow in popularity, prices will begin to drop, reflecting cheaper production processes. This will affect the revenue streams of the CD manufacturers, distributors, retail outlets, and possibly others.

Business models. We will begin to see winning and losing business models online. Sites that create more value for the consumer will generate more traffic and revenue. Once the record labels offer their catalogs online, people will be more eager to download digital music. We already see sites that are funded by the Big Five (such as ArtistDirect, GetMusic, Launch, and CDNow). Such partnerships give these sites a competitive advantage, and they will be the first to benefit from the online availability of the most popular artists' catalogs. However, large losses may still prevent survival, as they risk running out of cash—as CDNow recently reminded the industry. Meanwhile, unsigned-artist sites like MP3.com will suffer from a lack of big-name acts, and will be forced to partner with the Big Five if they want to drive traffic.

Online winners will also be more proactive in their strategies, as opposed to focusing on defending their turf. Established industry participants who focus on their core marketing will achieve the greatest success. The Internet will increasingly be used as a marketing tool for labels and artists. Importantly, labels will need to collect data on customers, not only to better understand them, but also to diversify revenue streams as they sell information to concert promoters and merchandisers.

The labels will also find that they can leverage the brand equity of their artists by selling albums and merchandise through fan Web sites. This may require giving a greater percentage of each sale to the artist— something the labels have so far been unwilling to do. It will also require them to compete with their retail partners. If the labels do not take advantage of this relationship-building opportunity through "official" fan sites, it is likely that other entrepreneurs will do so on unofficial ones.

A: Availability and Accessibility of Music

Variety. Once the Big Five offer their catalogs online, the variety of content will appeal to the consumer. Currently there is a dearth of big-name artists available for (legal) download, but eventually download variety will be better than one could find at a retail store. Niche markets will begin to develop stronger online distribution channels, and major artists will be well represented. Without the high overhead associated with distributing a single track to the public, labels will create alternative revenue sources by offering new "online-only" tracks for sale.

Access. Access to digital music will continue to be tied to the computer. Digital music players and CD burners/writers will make digital music portable. Wireless and satellite music distribution will be in the early stages. Sites like MyMP3.com and MyPlay.com offer the ability to upload your music collection and access it from any Internet terminal, setting the stage for hyperavailability. Once the music you own is accessible from anywhere, the need to have a physical CD becomes obsolete.

T: Technology

Requirements. Technological requirements will be largely unchanged in this stage. Storage devices will remain the focus, as music will be available on demand and but must be captured through downloading. Driven by SDMI, digital music formats will contain some encryption to prevent piracy. It will take time before SDMI makes an impact; in February of 2000, it was announced that proposals for standards would still be accepted as late as June 2000.

The SDMI requirements for portable music devices will reduce piracy, as one will need the right encryption to download a song and make it portable. However, the sheer inconvenience of this copy protection will be a nuisance for the consumer, as demonstrated by new, nonuser-friendly technologies such as the Sony Music Clip. This will only highlight the need for more efficient music delivery to the consumer. Bandwidth will advance to speed up downloading, but there will still be room for improvement. Cellular and satellite technology will continue to develop, but will not play a significant role in the digital music experience during this stage.

➤ **Phase II: The Digitalization Era**

This era of the evolution of the music industry builds on the digitalization of music:

- Transformation of the delivery of content. Radio stations get fully digital through the Internet and start leveraging new technologies by delivering commercial-free, personalized content. Some business models will experiment with "digital jukeboxes" that will play songs on demand for a fee or with advertising.

- New ways of capturing music. Consumers will be able to store more music of better quality at nearly no cost. Storage space will be cheaper, as high-capacity recordable DVDs and large memory cards will allow music fans to carry their own music wherever they want. Products that serve as intelligent buffer will be able to capture audio streams based on a consumer's interests and tastes and will carry the industry into the next phase.

The driving force within the BEAT framework will be *technology*. As was the case with the radio, the compact disc, and MTV, the recording industry will come to embrace the Internet and new technology because they will establish themselves as a viable source of profit. Consumers will adopt the technological developments in digital music and will discover new ways to use the technology. The revolution in digital music is about to begin.

B: Benefit to the Consumer

Personalization. Radio broadcasting will be delivered digitally through high-bandwidth access to the Internet. Therefore, each individual can be offered a personalized selection of music, just as Launch.com's "LaunchCast" is attempting to do now. Some radio Webcasters are already experimenting with personalized radio, like the startup called NextAudio (to be launched in mid-2000).

Customization. Digital downloads accelerate. The major labels will finally have embraced the opportunities of digital delivery. Customers will now be able to create their own albums by picking the songs they want from various artists, including the most popular ones. It will also become easier to capture music in digital format from radio Webcasters.

Interaction. Music fans will access more information on their favorite stars through the Web and be immediately alerted when a new song or album is released. The music industry will work with artists to effectively market their "brands" online.

Convenience. Consumers will now get the music they want from any number of sites in a compressed file that plays on all their hardware and software devices. Download times and streaming technologies will sufficiently improve to allow adoption by a mass market.

E: Economic Viability

Revenue streams will still be very similar to the traditional music structure. Labels will control distribution and digital downloads. However, a number of technological developments will loosen the labels' control. Although some of the areas of the market pie will be in flux, the pie itself will be growing. Customization of content delivery will stimulate purchases and Web sites will act as retail stores, selling individual downloads from many labels. Physical stores will develop custom CDs burned on in-store kiosks. Webcasters will flourish in this phase, becoming a preferred marketing channel of the record labels because of increased consumer usage and the ability to earn incremental revenues from click-throughs.

The labels will *not* benefit (from a revenue standpoint) from consumers' ability to digitally capture content from Webcasts and regular radio broadcasts. The big winners from this activity will be the hardware makers: they earn revenues from selling devices that enable consumers to capture content efficiently.

A: Availability and Accessibility of Music

Variety. Now that the record labels offer their content online, variety will be broad and deep; a blend of music by established and unknown artists will be readily available.

Access. The increase in bandwidth and growth in wireless and satellite transmission will increase the number of points at which the consumer can access music. One will be able to receive digital music not only from the computer and portable devices, but also via mobile telephones, in automobiles, and at any other Internet connection.

Consumers will have the capability to capture streaming broadcasts. Jim Griffin envisioned an "intelligent buffer" that can capture Webcasted music specifically requested by the consumer, even when the consumer is not present. This increases the consumer's power over the content and allows him or her to maintain a large library of digital music that is accessible at any time. Presumably, these buffers would also connect to the Internet and be connected from all the points previously mentioned.

T: Technology

There are three important breakthroughs in technology in this phase:

- *Full digital delivery of content.* Analog is dead, streaming is king. Songs are sent via radio with artist and name information. The powerful software of database management allows the content pushed to the consumer to be the result of a selection "learned" from that consumer's personal tastes.
- *The standards have become fully compatible with each other.* Encryption has developed through the use of digital watermarks. Piracy still exists, but has become less relevant and common because of better music availability. Major industry participants therefore become less technology-wary.
- *Intelligent buffers.* All players have the possibility to store the music (they might even store singles from your car radio while

you are driving), and recorders are designed to interpret the information (name of the song and style of music) to store automatically without the DJ chatter between songs. Consumers now have the technology to reduce their reliance on physical products such as CDs. Those products lack customization ability and are inefficient to transport, but they are still widely available to those who do not have the new buffer storage technology. These consumers will instead be able to go to kiosks in record stores (or on Web sites) and record custom CDs.

➤ Transition from Phase II to Phase III—Legislation Changes

With intelligent buffers, availability is on the verge of the ultimate breakthrough: on-demand music. These buffers operate on a principle similar to the TiVo®, which digitally captures television programs that you specify onto a hard drive while you are watching or while you are away from home. Consumers will be able to record digitally from the streamed content that personalized Web radios provide.

A consumer could, for example, select a list of songs and have the "audio-TiVo®" scan the radio to find them and record them when they are on the air. In this sense consumers will be able to acquire the option value they are looking for—they can store any song they want when a radio Webcasts it. Said entertainment lawyer Ken Hertz, "Such a device could simulate a giant jukebox in the sky ... And, there's nothing illegal about buffering legal music."[2] Storage improvements now allow easy transfer to any other medium—other Internet connection points worldwide, even an old-fashioned compact disc—for play on demand.

Record companies will be threatened because of the intelligent buffers that automatically (and presumably legally—recording songs from the radio is still legal) store music for personal use. This will create a major threat to the profit stream from sales of physical CDs. Basically, the idea is that consumers will want to pull their music on demand. This will bring the transition to its next phase, the consumer nirvana of hyperavailability. At this point, music has become fully available but not instantly accessible.

Consumers' demands will dictate the direction of the music industry as technology causes it to lose control over the distribution of its product. The recording industry will fight the change, but the listening public will speak through action. A fundamental change in broadcast/ Webcast legislation will be required.

Currently, the statutory license sold to Webcasters per the 1998 Digital Millennium Copyright Act limits what they may play. It states that advance song or artist playlists may not be published, except to give "teasers" of upcoming artists. It also requires Webcasters to "cooperate to defeat scanning" (see www.riaa.com). Devices such as the intelligent buffer will undermine the record industry's attempts to protect its content.

The DMCA will have to change if the record producers want to keep control of their musical content and maintain ties to the consumer.

> Phase III: The Hyperavailability Era

The labels will realize that they need to radically adapt their business models. With the objective of recreating a relationship with the customer, music will shift from being a *product* to being a *service*. Technology in this phase will enable hyperavailability. Consumers pay a subscription to access a certain number of songs on demand anywhere, or choose to receive targeted advertising in exchange for free listening. Piracy will be eliminated because the motive to store music will be made obsolete by music's instantaneous availability.

B: Benefit to the Consumer

Personalization and customization. Hyperavailability provides the ultimate in both these dimensions. Finally, customization meets the consumer's expectations. Some pioneering technological devices push personalization a step further and deliver music you really wish for depending on your current mood.

Interaction. Artist and consumer interaction is heightened as consumers subscribe to the on-demand catalogs of individual bands and receive value-added items such as outtakes, studio jams, and lost "B" sides. No longer will listeners wonder if their favorite artist has released new material; as the artist develops fresh content, it is immediately added to the subscription service to encourage renewals.

Convenience. Conventional hardware technology will wane in importance. Consumers have the ultimate in convenient, go-anywhere listening experience. At this level of accessibility, we expect all ages of music fans to enjoy the new way of experiencing music, not just the young, early adopters.

E: Economic Viability

Revenues shift from product to service models. During the previous phase, consumers gave a significant amount of their entertainment budget to hardware manufacturers and retailers by buying equipment to search for content on the radio, TV, and Web. The music labels are now ready to take their piece of the profit pie by launching on-demand subscription services supported by the strength of their musical catalogs.

New music creation is as important as ever. Fresh content is critical to luring consumers to buy into subscription models. In the case of cable TV services, consumers resubscribe only because they know there will be something different on next month. Because fresh content is so important, the labels must continue to find fresh talent and invest capital to market new music from existing bands and fresh new faces.

Hyperavailability of content fundamentally alters all music revenue streams. The major labels accept that the wave of the future lies in streaming subscriptions, not stored downloads. They license recordings for streamed subscriptions to make the bulk of their digital profits. Various pricing strategies will probably appear, with different levels for different types of access; flat fees for unlimited access or tiered-pricing structures based on the number of songs accessed during a month. Consumers might even be able to have music on demand free if they endure advertising preceding their requests. Most music fans may be willing to get bundled monthly subscriptions that provide music access from any device (home stereo, car radio, portable player) for a set amount of time. Revenues from subscriptions could be supplemented with click-through commissions from streaming audio sites.

Not only will the labels tap new revenue streams, but they will also continue to be necessary from the consumer's perspective—there will still be a need for a filter for all the music that is now immediately accessible. For the artists, labels will continue to provide capital, promotional expertise, and A&R at various levels.

Traditional, push-driven radio stations and music television channels still provide marketing. However, they may lose some of their brand equity as consumers begin to demand personalized, speechless radio and TV content. Retail stores may no longer make money from CDs or even customized downloads, but can offer value-added merchandise such as well-detailed, ornamental boxed sets that include access to an artist-specific subscription service for a period of time. Alternatively, they might focus on selling artist-related merchandise to those who idolize celebrity musicians.

A globally bigger pie. Table 9.2 shows the significant market potential of the music subscription model.

We can conclude that once the market predominantly shifts toward monthly service subscriptions, this business could easily surpass the current U.S. market of $14 billion. Moreover, under the subscription model, we can legitimately presume that the margins will be much higher (compared to CDs), given the minimal variable costs associated with each subscriber.

Although some music futurists project a shift toward totally free content, this is probably not a plausible scenario, for several reasons:

- The labels' revenues will become highly uncertain in a context where the roles of marketing and distribution are still impor-

Table 9.2 Market potential of music subscription model.

	2004	2010
U.S. population	280	300
Penetration rate of the Internet	55%	79%
Current projected size of the music industry (under the current "product sales" business model)	$18,400	$21,000
Market Potential		
Percent of subscribers that can subscribe (having broadband access)	20%	80%
Potential subscriber base (in millions)	30.8	180
Average monthly subscription fee	$10	$10
Market size for streaming services (in millions)	$3.969	$21.6

Source: All figures for 2004 are from Jupiter Communications. Figures for 2010 are the authors' projections.

tant. The reason they get into this business—the huge upside if an album sells well—disappears if content is free. The music will not market itself. As expert Marc Schiller noted, "[M]usic needs to be marketed. There's just no question that the Internet doesn't handle the marketing for you ... . [C]ertainly new opportunities are presented by the Internet. But ... music will not suddenly sprout like a seed and turn into a beautiful flower just because it's on the Internet. It needs to be watered and properly positioned."[3]

- The revenues lost from content will have to be drawn from derivative products (t-shirts, tours, concert tickets). These revenues will never be sufficient, however, because those products are either too inexpensive, with small profit margins (t-shirts), or they are already extant and expensive (it is unlikely that concert ticket prices can be raised much more before alienating the buying public).

A: Availability and Accessibility of Music

Hyperavailability has arrived. All content has already been available on the Internet since Phase II. The real revolution in Phase III is about accessibility. Consumers can now subscribe to the "jazz channel" or "Metallica 24/7" and get an entire catalog of targeted music accessible on demand from any device that receives streamed information (wireless personal stereos and car radios, wired home stereos and PCs). CDs become obsolete, as the need to store music has disappeared. You simply have services that let you select what you want to hear and when you want to hear it. Consumers have the ultimate option value on music because they can access the music they want, at any moment, without any storage constraints.

T: Technology

Thanks to the progress in broadband and wireless communications, fast Internet access has become ubiquitous. Listening appliances go well beyond the scope of today's Rios or Walkmans; many appliances can play music. Therefore, storage devices like CDs increasingly become obsolete: There is no need to store artistic content because consumers have a total option value on music, through a means other than ownership.

Obviously, the music industry is rapidly changing, but more consumer-centric developments are in store: intelligent buffers, music on demand, and hyperavailability. As wireless technologies and bandwidth improve, it is reasonable to expect that streaming Webcasts will grow in number and improve in quality. When it becomes feasible to capture digital Webcasts and store them for later use, the label industry will have lost some of its control over the distribution of music. Given the value of building a relationship with the end user, the labels would demonstrate an astonishing lack of vision if they did not adapt and develop a means of providing music as a value-added, on-demand service to keep their customers.

This general evolution is expanding the size of the music business in general. The listener experience will be much more enjoyable when the music has been selected to personal tastes without commercials. The "push" methodology of music has constrained its growth; as a consequence of the shift to demand-driven "pull," consumer willingness to spend time listening to music and to pay for it will increase. Fans will know of new releases from their favorite artists earlier, and the diffusion process will accelerate as the selection of hits escapes the hands of the radio stations and labels. Most listeners will become music-savvy in their favorite genres, and this higher degree of involvement will stimulate the creation process tremendously and fuel the entire industry.

This way of thinking must not be limited to the music industry. Once connectivity is ubiquitous, it opens the door for entertainment in all its forms to be hyperavailable. Television programming on demand is not far off, nor are movies on demand. Bandwidth limitations currently exist, but such was the case for music as recently as five years ago. New compression formats will develop, and bandwidth will improve with broadband. Content will be ours for the taking ... and no, the revolution will not be downloaded!

■ NOTES

1. Don Clark, "Recording Industry Group Sues Napster, Alleging Copyright Infringement on Net," *Wall Street Journal*, December 7, 1999.

2. "Hype and Hope," *Business 2.0* (November 1999).

3. Bruce Haring, "Who's Wiring Hollywood?," *NARIP News* (July/August 1999).

■ REFERENCES

"Allow 5 to 10 Seconds for Delivery." *Webnoize* (January 27, 2000).

"AOL Time Warner: The Day After." *Wall Street Journal* (graphic), January 12, 2000.

Avalon, Moses. *Confessions of a Record Producer*. San Francisco: Miller Freeman Books, 1998.

"BMG Planning Digital Sales for Summer." *Webnoize* (April 6, 2000).

"Car Jammin'." *Webnoize* (February 10, 2000).

"CDNow Accountant Doubtful Company Can Survive." *Webnoize* (March 29, 2000).

Clark, Don. "Recording Industry Group Sues Napster, Alleging Copyright Infringement on Net." *Wall Street Journal*, December 7, 1999.

Cooley, Benjamin. Interview (February 3, 2000).

"DaimlerChrysler to Invest $100M in Sirius Satellite Radio." *Webnoize* (February 1, 2000).

"Digital Distribution Wars." Forrester Research, Inc. (April 1999).

"Digital Downloads Accelerate." Forrester Research, Inc. (January 2000).

Goth Itoi, Nikki. "Hard Day's Night. The Music Industry Is Struggling to Adapt to the Internet." *Red Herring* (January 1999).

Gove, Alex. "The Music Industry Needs to Offer More than Clever Business Models." *Red Herring* (October 1999).

Griffin, Jim. "How Will the Internet Age?" *Business 2.0* (December 1999).

———. "Learn from the Libraries." *Business 2.0* (February 2000).

———. "That's Right, The Women Are Smarter." *Business 2.0* (January 2000).

Haring, Bruce. "Who's Wiring Hollywood?" *NARIP News* (July/August 1999).

Hellweg, Eric. "MP3.com: Now What?" *Business 2.0* (November 1999).

———. "Musical Discord." *Business 2.0* (September 1999).

———. "The Sound of Money. The Multibillion Dollar Music Industry Has Big Ideas About How to Distribute Songs Online. One Problem: A Maverick Technology May Sink Its Plans." *Business 2.0* (September 1998).

Hill, Logan. "Net Music Show Cast Call." *Wired News* (March 2000).

———. "Rockers Meet CEOs in New York." *Wired News* (March 2000).

"Hot Web Sites." *Entertainment Weekly*, January 7, 2000, 79.

"Hype and Hope." *Business 2.0* (November 1999).

Jones, Christopher. "Making It Big with MP3." *Wired News* (February 1999).

"Kagan Panelists Discuss Online Business Models." *Webnoize* (March 30, 1999).

"Major Labels in Licensing Dispute with MTV Interactive." *Webnoize* (February 16, 2000).

Mcelfresh, Suzanne, and Stark, Paul. "Music by Modem: The Twin Tone Record Label Goes Completely Digital to Reduce Operating Costs by Two Thirds." *Business 2.0* (September 1998).

Mitchell, Dan. "Booksellers Take on Music Retailers." *Red Herring* (February 1998).

Music Business International, Inc. (MBI). *Unwired World: Music Delivery and the Mobile Industry.* February 2000.

"Music: Competitive Landscape." Jupiter Analyst Report (January 2000): 9–10.

"Music: Online Landscape," vol. 2. Jupiter Analyst Report (October 1999).

"Music: Retail & Digital Distribution Projections," vol. 1. Jupiter Analyst Report (July 1999).

"Napster Hints at Business Strategy." *Webnoize* (March 20, 2000).

Nielsen/Netratings. "Netratings for the week ended 12/12/1999." *Entertainment Weekly*, January 7, 2000.

"NTT, Matsushita to Deliver Music to Mobile Phones." *Webnoize* (February 1, 2000).

Oakes, Chris. "MP3 Revolution: Rhetoric or Real?" *Wired News* (February, 2000).

———. "Pundits Ask: Who Owns Music?" *Wired News* (February 2000).

———. " 'Save Our Napster,' say Students." *Wired News* (February 2000).

Passman, Donald S. *All You Need to Know About the Music Business.* New York: Simon & Schuster, 1997.

"Promotional Value of MP3.com Questioned." *Webnoize* (March 17, 1999).

Raik-Allen, Georgie. "Players Line Up for Battle over Online Music Industry." *Red Herring* (February 1999).

"Riffage.com Letting Bandemonium Loose on Web." *Webnoize* (February 7, 2000).

Robischon, Noah. "Free for All." *Entertainment Weekly* (March 31, 2000): 72–73.

Rose, Bill, and Larry Rosin. "The Buying Power of 'Streamies,' " *Arbitron/Edison Media Research*, February 24, 2000.

"Seattle SDMI Meeting Brings Effort Closer to Phase II Proposals." *Webnoize* (January 31, 2000).

Simons, David. "MP3 Battle Is the Same Old Song." *Red Herring* (April 1999).

"SDMI Invites Phase II Tech Proposals." *Webnoize* (February 28, 2000).

"Sony Music to Sell Downloads Later This Month." *Webnoize* (April 7, 2000).

"Universal Music Says Digital Rollout in Spring." *Webnoize* (March 6, 2000).

"Virtual Music Rocks." *Forrester Report*, 1999.

White, Erin. " 'Chatting' a Singer Up the Pop Charts." *Wall Street Journal*, October 5, 1999.

Chapter 10

The Battle for the Last Mile

■ INTRODUCTION

In a 1999 meeting, Jim Flash of Accel Partners, a leading Silicon Valley venture capital firm, told us, "Bandwidth is the oil of the information age." As consumer demand for faster e-mail, Internet access, and data transfer, as well as more robust content and interactivity, escalates around the globe, broadband will play an increasingly important role in how such content and services are delivered. The technology is still in its infancy, and many questions still remain unanswered regarding the evolution of the broadband market.

There are currently a number of broadband access platforms, which can be loosely grouped into three categories: terrestrial, which includes cable and DSL (Digital Subscriber Line); wireless; and satellite platforms. However, DSL and cable are the only platforms immediately available for wide-scale rollout to households in the United States. Wireless and satellite platforms are in the developmental stage, although their impact on future global broadband provision is estimated to be very significant. From a global perspective, it is important to note that broadband will be provided by platforms from all three segments, as infrastructure conditions and limitations will vary considerably from one country to the next.

This chapter focuses specifically on the cable and DSL buildout within the U.S. residential market, a movement commonly referred to in the communications industry as the "battle for the last mile." This topic is particularly relevant for three reasons:

1. The United States currently serves as the cornerstone of the Internet/technology economy and will continue to do so in the foreseeable future. Therefore, much of the development in the broadband market will occur in the near term within the United States.

2. The residential market is the largest potential broadband market in the United States and wider residential adoption is crucial to the viability of broadband access and content providers.

3. Cable and DSL are the only two platforms currently capable of providing broadband on a national scale. From a residential consumer perspective, cable and DSL will constitute the majority of broadband access options for at least the next 8 to 10 years.

■ OVERVIEW OF THE BROADBAND MARKET

Technically defined, *broadband* is telecommunication that provides multiple channels of data over a single communications medium, typically using some form of frequency or wave division multiplexing. In layman's terms, broadband provides a convenient, always-on service that is more than 100 times faster than current dial-up modems. To put this speed differential into perspective, downloading 60 seconds of video data over a standard dial-up connection requires approximately 20 minutes, whereas a cable broadband platform may require only 9 seconds. Unquestionably, the availability of such a high-speed service creates value for end users and, similarly, an exciting value-creation opportunity for broadband access providers. Consequently, the telecommunications, hardware, software, Internet, and media industries are strategically positioning themselves within the broadband delivery chain to capitalize on this new high-speed connection to the customer.

From 1995 to 1999, the total number of online users rose from 9 million to 45 million, an annual growth rate of 51 percent.[1] However, top-line growth in online subscribers is expected to slow considerably over the next few years, totaling 68 million by 2003—an annual growth rate of only 11 percent. Despite this slowing growth trend, broadband adoption as a percentage of online households is forecasted to accelerate significantly over this same time period. According to Forrester Research, nearly 2 million U.S. households were using broadband services by the end of 1999, constituting just 6 percent of all online households.[2] However, by 2004, broadband will reach an estimated 16.6 million households, or 24 percent of total online households—an annual growth rate of 53 percent.[3]

Early broadband adopters, or *broadbanders*, can be described as the most progressive of online users. Recognizing the benefit of faster access over standard dial-up modems and willing to pay considerably more for this luxury, they actively sought out broadband access. Slightly more than half of current broadband subscribers signed up for broadband because the Web was too slow at dial-up speeds. Fifty-eight percent of broadband consumers ranked the "always-on" nature of their broadband connection as the primary reason for switching from their dial-up connections.[4] Despite this segment's passionate attitude toward broadband, it is too small a market to return a profit based on the massive investments made by broadband providers.

To achieve a critical mass of broadband usage in the United States, providers will have to attract a wider audience. The next largest group of consumers, dubbed "smart dial-ups" by Forrester Research, represents an opportunity for broadband providers to grow their avid user base. Accounting for 54 percent of home users, smart dial-up consumers typically have slightly less household income, education, and computer experience than broadbanders, but still significantly more than the average online user. This group represents a prime opportunity for broadband providers to attain the necessary critical mass of usage.

The third group of online users is classified as *clueless dial-up* and represents 40 percent of home Internet users. These consumers are neither optimistic about the technology nor frequent interacters with it. They are satisfied with dial-up connection speeds and mostly, as the name suggests, are not even aware if broadband is available in their area. Attracting these consumers to broadband services will prove to be an arduous task for broadband providers.

Broadband providers' best opportunity for growth is to cross the chasm between smart dial-ups and broadbanders. To do so, broadband providers must make adjustments across every dimension of their business, to drive consumer awareness and adoption. Innovative marketing programs are among these adjustments and will be discussed at length in the section on DSL and cable marketing.

■ CABLE AND DSL, OR CABLE VERSUS DSL?

It is estimated that by 2004, cable and DSL together will control more than 90 percent of broadband delivery into the home.[5] Together, these two new technologies represent the next threshold in data speed. The conduits for broadband also represent the most developed infrastructures. To understand the inherent strengths and weaknesses of both cable and DSL in terms of broadband provision, a debate over their respective technological merits and weaknesses is not enough. However, an investigation of the respective infrastructures and potential consumer penetration targets will shed further light.

➤ Technology and Penetration

Cable and DSL technologies are both terrestrial, modem-based platforms utilizing existing cable and telephone lines, respectively. Cable modem technology has both strengths and weaknesses. Cable broadband is delivered over standard coaxial cable using a viable modem, providing markedly faster speeds than DSL. However, the speed of the line is affected by the fact that cable is a shared-line technology. The shared line has two important negative characteristics: (1) During peak broadband usage in a neighborhood, users will experience a significant amount of speed decay in their connections, and (2) shared, always-on lines are more susceptible to security breaches.

DSL technology delivers broadband services over existing copper telephone lines, commonly known as POTS (plain old telephone service) lines, by utilizing a pair of modems, one located in the residence and the other at the provider central office (CO). There are currently a multitude of DSL types in various stages, but the residential market will be offered ADSL (asymmetric digital subscriber line) and a slower version of ADSL called *G.Lite*. G.Lite does not require a POTS splitter to be installed at the subscriber site. It allows data and POTS voice service on the same line, thereby creating a cost-effective delivery standard for the residential market. For the purposes of this chapter, all references to DSL concern these two kinds of service.

POTS lines are dedicated between the local telephone company central office and the user's residence, making them significantly more secure for over-line data transmission than cable transmissions. This has proven to be an extremely attractive characteristic for small business owners, dubbed *SOHOs* (small office/home office). Small business penetration will be significant with DSL and will play an integral role in enabling DSL providers to attain profitability. The dedicated-line characteristic will be helpful in understanding the technological tradeoffs between DSL and cable technology. It is an appealing security feature, although the speed at which the data travels will be slower than with cable. Both technologies are still significantly faster than a dial-up connection. Speed and clarity of DSL data transmission are affected not only by distance from the central office, but also by the following two facts:

1. The average telephone line is split many times between the central office and the home.
2. The quality of copper lines (before being split) may be suspect.

Copper lines were not designed to transport bandwidth-intensive transmissions and may not be able to maintain seamless connections. Looking to the future evolution of the DSL broadband market, questions remain as to whether technological improvements will enable these lines to support the robust content demanded by consumers.

Additional problems have resulted from DSL providers installing fiber optic cable to upgrade old networks, because DSL and fiber optic technologies are not currently compatible. Although fiber optic cable is easier to maintain and has been critical in allowing phone companies to handle vast amounts of new data, fax, and cell phone transmissions, its incompatibility with DSL has created difficulties.

Cable and DSL penetration into homes do not overlap in the United States today, but they will in the next few years. In the short term, however, consumers will regard broadband as simply an increase in data speed, not necessarily a decision between cable or DSL service. To understand cable penetration in the United States, three dimensions must be analyzed: (1) cable's potential penetration, (2) the percentage of cable lines that have been enabled for two-way data transfer, and (3) current and projected consumer usage of cable as a broadband provider. According to ZDNet, 63 million households were using standard cable services by the end of 1999, constituting about 63 percent of U.S.

households. For the purposes of the cable-versus-DSL debate, however, cable penetration is measured by *houses-passed*. As this term implies, not every home in the United States subscribes to cable services, but because a terrestrial cable line runs by 68 percent of total households[6] and can therefore easily be installed in a household, both current cable users and nonusers within this networked area are considered *passed*. Of these lines, cable companies on average have upgraded more than 50 percent for two-way communication.[7] In terms of current consumer penetration, cable has established an early-mover advantage over DSL. Cable's installed base is roughly five times as large as that for DSL, totaling 1.6 million subscribers versus just 300,000 for DSL.[8] It is important to note, however, that DSL passes a larger number of U.S. households.

Based on technology and penetration, cable broadband providers have an early lead. Although cable multiple system operators (MSOs) have converged on the DOCSIS (data over cable service interface specifications) standard, the continued evolution of multiple DSL technologies leaves DSL standards less defined among local carriers. This technical uncertainty significantly undermines the advance of DSL in the broadband market. The reactive behaviors of these carriers result from fear that fast deployment of DSL will hurt profitable dial-up businesses. As a consequence, carriers tend to price DSL services higher to avoid cannibalization of dial-up service. This strengthens cable's advantage through lower pricing.

DSL is faced with uncertainty with regard to video delivery. The best ADSL lines (6Mbps) can support only one high-quality video channel at a time, and their ability to switch between multiple channels is unclear. Given cable's technical superiority, cable MSOs can benefit from bundling video services rather than merely data and voice services. Yet DSL has some advantage because of its dedicated lines, which appeal more to SOHOs and MSEs; this gives DSL a leg up on cable in the commercial segments.

➤ Fiber Optics

Fiber optic cable is unquestionably a better, more robust means (*pipe*) for delivering broadband than either cable or DSL. It provides much faster speeds both upstream and downstream (thus enabling greater interactivity) and in many cases is more easily repaired. Despite this fact, fiber optic cable will not be a major delivery vehicle of broadband to U.S. homes, because building the infrastructure would require far more time and money than broadband providers can afford. Jim Hayes highlighted this point in his *Fiber Optics Technicians Handbook:* "[T]oday, telephone and cable television companies can justify installing fiber links to remote sites serving tens to a few hundreds of customers. However, terminal equipment remains too expensive to justify installing fibers all the way to homes."[9] Fiber will, however, continue to be the major data and voice delivery vehicle for telecommunications backbones.

■ THE ECONOMICS OF BROADBAND

Profit in the broadband market will draw from access-based revenues comprised of monthly provision fees for both data and telephony; and nonaccess-based revenues from installation, specific content, transactions (e-commerce), and advertising. Currently, AOL generates one-quarter of its revenues from nonaccess-based revenues, which is approximately $1.4 billion per year. Nonaccess-based revenues will likely be generated through partnerships and strategic alliances with content providers and portals. (These alliances are discussed later in this chapter.)

Several components will drive the cost portion of the profitability analysis. Certainly the capital expenditures are substantial, and cable and DSL providers will have to amortize and depreciate these costs accordingly. Further cost components will relate to the technological limitations of cable and DSL respectively. The key external cost/revenue driver is substantial scale economies in urban locations versus rural locations (i.e., population densities, and high-income versus low-income areas).

For both cable and DSL companies, access revenues can be itemized as data, voice, or service. Primarily in an effort to bundle as many services as possible over their respective lines, both cable and DSL companies must integrate provision of voice and data. Cable companies will enter into the voice market via data provision, whereas DSL companies will enter into data and long-distance provision via their local exchange positions. Based on the premise that data provision will become increasingly important and voice provision will only be further commoditized, this chapter focuses primarily on data provision profitability. Voice provision, though a source of revenue and profits for both cable and DSL broadband providers, will not scale up in the near future as prominently as will data.

It is difficult to gauge whether the significant expenditures made by cable and DSL companies will ever pay off. The primary issue for cable is the upgrading of legacy systems to facilitate two-way capabilities, which are important for data and essential for voice. Capital expenditures for DSL are characterized by two types of network upgrades: distance degeneration and improvements to central offices.

These expenditures are offset by customer addition economics, due to the shared nature of the cable terrestrial line. McKinsey & Company estimated that over the next five years, the costs associated with adding a customer will fall from $725 to $325 for cable companies and from $1,400 to $500 for DSL companies.

The primary driver for this discrepancy is that cable builds from a shared network, whereas DSL has one dedicated copper line per residence. Despite the cost differences, broadband services will likely be priced comparably to households over the long run. Revenue models for both cable and DSL companies rely on increasing numbers of subscribers. The access-base, per-subscriber revenues for DSL versus cable are not substantially different, but the incremental revenue is a direct result of the shared-line-versus-dedicated-line tradeoff.

In contrast, nonaccess-based revenues vary substantially between DSL and cable. The primary driver for this discrepancy lies again in the technological distinctiveness of DSL and cable. DSL will appeal to small business, because of DSL's dedicated line and enhanced privacy. Cable, however, will have a predominantly residential appeal, based on video capabilities. The residential focus will also yield increased e-commerce and advertising revenues.

McKinsey & Company forecasted that cable and DSL will both break even comfortably in the next four to five years. The key components will be volume of subscribers and nonaccess-based revenues. Strategic partnerships and alliances, combined with aggressive co-marketing efforts, will help to ensure this financially appealing outcome.

➤ A Microeconomic Theory for Broadband

Broadband economics can be further explained by an economic theory for monopolistic competition: *imperfect imitability.* According to this theory, a new industry with high sunk costs and high uncertainty of postinvestment profitability would discourage new entrepreneurs. This is because new entrants are unsure whether they can imitate the success formulas of the established firms and operate as profitably thereafter to pay off initial capital investments. Faced with such high risks, they tend not to enter. The incumbents can therefore capture the profits forgone by the otherwise possible new entrants and enjoy a high level of monopolistic power and profitability. As such, those who survive at the end are rewarded with the remaining economic values in the industry.

The broadband industry fits this theory. The huge up-front capital expenditures can be seen as sunk costs: once broadband infrastructures are built, they have almost no alternative uses; hence the irreversibility of the investments. In contrast, the future profitability of broadband products and services is highly uncertain, given the rapid changes in market dynamics and technology developments. Based on these insights, we can better understand why, when faced with such future uncertainty, cable and DSL providers are pouring billions of dollars into the infrastructure buildout. These capital expenditures raise the sunk costs, and risks, for new entrants. As more entrants are scared off or driven out of the game, incumbents will remain to reap the future values. Interestingly, there has been so much interest in the broadband buildout—and so much money available to fund it—that many companies are investing substantial sums in these efforts. The quandary arises from the substantial long-term commitments required to become a broadband player, and the significant asset specificity of the infrastructure. There will surely be a shakeout over the next few years as the market works out the complex relationship between bandwidth supply and demand.

■ MARKETING AND STRATEGIC ALLIANCES

Although consumers will continue to adopt broadband, current penetration rates are still relatively low, and it will take extensive marketing to grow the customer base. As the rollout matures, it seems likely that individual markets will become saturated with broadband providers and consumers will have a variety of broadband access options. Consequently, retention of customers in a particular market will depend on segmentation and effective relationship marketing.

Broadband providers expect to establish a larger customer base through the conversion of the attractive, smart dial-up demographic. Remember, these smart dial-ups constitute the largest online segment and are most likely to upgrade their access service. The fact that the smart dial-up consumers currently access the Internet via their telephone lines may or may not imply that they will seek broadband from the same source. This depends on whether consumers are comfortable with the phone line because it already provides them with the Internet connection, or prefer a different source because they are not likely to believe that a telephone line can be a broadband source.

The conversion process is not simple. Two significant hurdles must be overcome to attain critical mass: broadband awareness and trial. Educating the 40 percent of Internet households who are not aware of broadband availability will require resourceful marketing efforts. However, even before a consumer can be converted through advertising, he or she must have had a tangible experience with broadband service, because the benefits (i.e., increased data speed) of using broadband cannot easily be conceptualized. Therefore, some consumer demonstrations must become widely available to expand customer awareness. SBC Communications, a major DSL provider, has partnered with Best Buy, Staples, and CompUSA to co-market its broadband services through in-store demonstration kiosks. Another example of these co-marketing demo efforts is the recent alliance between NorthPoint Communications and Radio Shack. Radio Shack will demonstrate, merchandise, and sell NorthPoint DSL service in all 2,200 Radio Shack stores.[10]

A more expensive path to increased consumer trials will be through free or leased broadband provision. Broadband providers will attempt to convert consumers through hardware manufacturers, like Netpliance. A third trial-generating scenario uses one of broadband providers' most valuable assets: their satisfied customers (*broadbanders*). Similar to a successful marketing program instituted by AOL, a broadband provider will compensate satisfied customers for recommending its services to friends, neighbors, and family. As the infrastructure for broadband service becomes more pervasive, retail stores will be able to offer self-installation kits. Consumers will be able to purchase "broadband in a box," much like a today's purchases of wireless phones.

Assuming that awareness and trial opportunities can be created for consumers, adoption will be the final hurdle for broadband providers in the near term. Primarily, adoption rates will be stimulated through decreases in access fees. Consumer demand is highly elastic and providers will likely have to lower prices to gain market share.

The second phase for broadband providers' marketing will be more crucial, as it pertains directly to long-term survival. As the market matures and redundant broadband service is provided, the competition to attract and retain the customer will become fierce. Forrester Research reported that although 90 percent of current broadband users are satisfied with their connection and 85 percent would recommend the service they use, most users are not particularly loyal. Once alternative access options become available, only 39 percent of this group plans to continue their current service.[11]

As broadband competition increases, effective market segmentation and targeting will become more important. For instance, segmentation can be seen in online usage patterns across age groups. The results of a 1999 Jupiter online survey are particularly revealing. Respondents under the age of 35 were primarily concerned with price, speed, and connectivity speed. Conversely, respondents over the age of 50 were concerned primarily with service and the ease of establishing a connection. The survey report went on to demonstrate differences between genders on broadband usage patterns. Men were significantly more interested in speedy video and audio service, whereas women appreciated the always-on nature of the broadband connection.[12]

■ FROM SPEED TO VALUE

The implications of widely available bandwidth for digital content, applications, and services for the residential and commercial markets are enormous. So enormous, in fact, that both sides of the supply/demand equation are recognizing that collaborative efforts are required to fully realize all of the possibilities. Our goal in the latter half of this chapter is to provide an understanding of the potential for broadband digital data transfer to transform our personal and professional lives.

Figure 10.1 illustrates the larger dynamics of the broadband content and services market. This figure reflects both the key dependencies between broadband suppliers (*pipes*) and the demand drivers (*content*) that drive up bandwidth usage. Note that the most vital dependency in this model, situated squarely between content providers and bandwidth suppliers, is the consumer. For the time being, we will not distinguish between a residential and a commercial consumer. The most important thing to note about the consumer at this point is that money is the engine of this dynamic market. Without the continual cultivation of consumers' money, bandwidth expansion will slow or

Figure 10.1   Broadband hedging.

cease entirely. Although bandwidth supply may exceed demand in the near term (as noted earlier in this chapter), this will not be the long-term situation. Consumers' dollars determine where the equilibrium between supply and demand is reached.

> ## Interdependencies between Pipe and Content

In light of recent high-profile and even higher-dollar marriages between ISPs and cable companies (*pipes*) and media delivery concerns (*content*), we must now add another component to the model: linkages between the supply-side and demand-driver participants.

By presenting this new component of our broadband market model, we intend to emphasize two points:

1.   These marriages (whether purchases, mergers, partnerships, or otherwise) represent expensive hedging strategies by parties on both sides of the consumer, primarily because no one presently knows the answer to a very important question; namely, "Where is the money that will drive the broadband market's growth? Is it in digital information transfer or in sales of new digital products and services?"

2.   *Pipes* and *content* are both recognizing that their fates are intertwined, because both are dependent upon each other for mutual success. This type of large-scale dependency is a classic example of "co-opetition": an opportunity for multiple disparate corporate entities to advance their own success through consideration of another company's good fortune.[13]

In the words of Joe Hawayek, chief operating officer of ClearBand, Inc., "Partnerships will be the catalyst that will validate the broadband space." These partnerships and alliances are forming and reshaping the boundaries between competitors on a daily basis. On the following pages, we highlight three examples of content merging with the delivery function: the AOL–Time Warner merger, the Excite and @Home union, and the Disney/ABC acquisition.

➤ Systemic Innovation

In a *Harvard Business Review* article, David J. Teece and Henry W. Chesborough propose that one needs to understand the type of innovation necessary for the product space. *Autonomous* innovation requires less centralization, whereas *systemic* innovation requires more coordination across product development groups. Furthermore, *codified* information and standards make it easier for independent entities to communicate and innovate. *Tacit* information or knowledge is more related to product systems and systemic innovation.

The broadband buildout in the United States is an example of a systemic innovation that spans many different development groups. It will require a high degree of coordination. "When innovation is systemic, independent companies will not usually be able to coordinate themselves to knit those innovations together. Scale, integration, and market leadership may be required to establish and advance standards in an industry."[14]

This scale in innovation is very important. The "companies that develop their own capabilities can outperform those that rely too heavily on coordination through markets and alliances to build their businesses."[15] Do the capabilities exist, or must they be created? If they exist, outsourcing through alliances becomes more attractive. If they have to be created, doing so in-house is a more strategically sound path.

Considerable information sharing in data formats, billing systems, and wiring topologies will ultimately result in a roadmap for the industry. With mergers like AOL and Time Warner, these companies can help define the emerging technologies and killer applications through their scale and efficient coordination. The following case study reflects the state of the AOL/Time Warner merger at the time this book was written.

Case Study: AOL–Time Warner Merger

Premise This $165 billion merger combines Time Warner's (TW) vast array of media, entertainment, and news brands, as well as its broadband delivery systems, with America Online's (AOL) extensive Internet franchises, large cyberspace community, infrastructure, and e-commerce capabilities. This deal is predicated on a vision of broadening AOL's strong brand and content with TW's media assets and 20 million cable customers.

Breakdown TW will provide an important broadband distribution platform for AOL's interactive services and drive subscriber growth through cross-marketing with Time Warner's brands. The combined brand offerings will include AOL, *Time*, CNN, CompuServe, Warner Brothers, Netscape, *Sports Illustrated*, *People*, HBO, ICQ, AOL Instant Messenger, AOL MovieFone, TBS, TNT, Cartoon Network, Digital City, Warner Music Group, Spinner, Winamp, *Fortune*, AOL.com, *Entertainment Weekly*, and Looney Tunes.

Cost AOL will certainly become significantly larger, combining its 12,100 employees with TW's 70,000. This underscores the challenge of integrating a traditional media company with a fast-moving, resilient upstart like AOL. Additionally, AOL has managed to achieve its huge lead online because of its intense focus on becoming the leader. Now it must deal with movies, TV networks, cable systems, magazines, and books.

Execution The key for AOL–TW is to be able to capture and retain new and current subscriber bases with a differentiated array of online services. With this customer focus, the company hopes to "deliver media, communications, retailing, financial services, health care, education and travel services by attacking everything from newspapers, TV, and radio stations to phone companies, banks, brokerage firms, auto dealerships, travel agencies, the local photo shop and the corner bar."

Bottom line AOL hopes to infuse its current services with TW's brands and content to become the dominant online services provider. TW's distribution will further its lead by sign-

(continued)

ing up millions of new customers for broadband access, before it is forced to unlock its doors in the name of open access. By then, AOL will be positioned to capitalize on its lead, as the marketplace becomes increasingly more confusing for the consumer.

Although some observers have debated the AOL decision to own access to traditional content, the merger presents some compelling advantages. AOL–TW is advancing in a space that depends on a series of interdependent innovations or, in the words of Henry Chesborough, "systemic innovations." In this case, partnering companies will not be able to coordinate effectively enough to deliver a desired integrated product. Chesborough argues that "key development activities that depend on one another must be conducted in-house to capture the rewards of R&D investments. Without directed coordination, the necessary complementary innovations required to leverage a new technology may not evolve."[16]

With AOL–TW, both companies are focused on the consumer and are able to increase consumer usage of their services. By continuing to attract customers through these brands, AOL will have the opportunity to create customized, "sticky" applications that will be a key factor in maintaining and growing its various streams of revenue. As a result of increased coordination and a better-aligned team, it will be able to develop products such as AOL TV more quickly. Also, in a space where change is constant, AOL–TW will have an advantage in its ability to react quickly to even the slightest shifts in consumer preferences and to develop the leading solutions in this new medium.

■ CULTIVATING DEMAND: A MORE ROBUST BROADBAND MARKET MODEL

Bandwidth suppliers and content providers could be thought of as a man with a carrot and stick, leading the rabbit of consumer demand along. This model emphasizes that both pipes and content must work together to manage the cultivation and expansion of consumer demand. Pipes and content are both dependent on the rabbit's progress down the path if both are to realize the riches on the horizon. We describe the careful leading of the bunny for the mutual gain of everyone as *managing stick length*, which means:

- If content and products develop ahead of consumer expectations (*the stick is too long*), and the benefits of these products are not made apparent to the consumer, then consumers' financial support will remain stagnant—the rabbit will not move down the path and pipes and content providers alike will fail to remain economically viable.

- If the pipes encourage giving away new content and high-bandwidth digital products (*the stick is too short*), then consumers will eat their fill and find no compelling reason to pay either for new products and services or for the increased bandwidth needed to enjoy the delivery and use of them.

We believe the major players on both sides of the consumer dependency—that is, both pipes and content—should adhere to this model of *managing the stick length* of digital offerings, to carry the consumer market along a consistent, expanding path of growing bandwidth demand and usage. In this way, both will acknowledge and strategically integrate their co-dependency on consumer expenditures as the determinant of the long-term economic feasibility of this market.

■ DRIVING DEMAND

Industry and research speculation about the future of broadband-enabled digital entertainment and commercial offerings falls into one of two camps:

- "What we've got now, but faster!"
- "Interactive, immersive, addictive."[17]

The first of these groups is characterized by:

- TV and film executives' desire to protect experience and assets in traditional broadcast content.

- Web content creators' remaining trapped at the home-page model of content design and delivery in the near term.

Some key examples of digital products in this category are:

- Streaming video and audio
- Internet-based voice telephony services
- On-demand video and applications
- Online teleconferencing
- Rich (multimedia, graphics-heavy, and deep) Web content for businesses

The near-term economic viability of digital products in this category is all but assured; 63 percent of those considering faster Internet connections want to download more video and audio.[18] An industry quote demonstrates the pervasiveness of this mindset: "[C]ontent is critical; providing access isn't enough, you have to have compelling applications and the killer apps are audio and video." Simply put, bandwidth suppliers like the possibility of pushing a great deal of traditional content at consumers in higher volumes, because it is cheap and available now. However, we wish to note that these offerings do not represent the greatest potential for consumers and businesses.

The second of these camps represents a more forward-thinking, sophisticated concept of harnessing the possibilities of widely available, inexpensive access to bandwidth in the home and office. As Peter Jacquerot, head of international marketing for interactive content forerunner ICTV, Inc., said, the new frontier of digital offerings should be "clearly more than narrowband content that runs faster; it's a range of applications that can only be delivered in a broadband environment."[19] The notion here is that bandwidth is not beholden to the content. Instead, bandwidth availability is a given, and content developers build out digital entertainment and commercial offerings directly to consumer needs and wants. Here are just a few examples of these types of digital offerings:

- Interactive television and sports coverage
- Home entertainment delivery not constrained by separate devices (i.e., DVD and CD players)

- Multiuser, remote gaming applications capable of an almost unlimited simultaneous user base

- Always-on, personalized news and information services in home and office

- ASPs; these are already present, although typically over dedicated digital traffic lines between host companies and commercial partners rather than Internet traffic backbone pipes.

The addictive component of these products and services must not be discounted. With an always-on connection, consumers will find their usage rising steadily as compared to present dial-up digital information options. Combined with sticky content, products and services will sink their hooks into consumers and require more time for increased benefit. These services will have a multiplicative rather than additive effect on consumer bandwidth usage. As one industry reporter declared, "[B]roadband has the potential to deliver an experience that hooks users for hours. But Web and TV executives' current thinking won't get them there. Instead . . . they must expand their vision, creating all-consuming, user-controlled worlds."[20]

Delivery of digital content will not be limited to PCs. Television-based (set-top cable boxes, satellite) and dedicated wireless devices present increasingly attractive opportunities for content developers and therefore for bandwidth suppliers. The most likely outcome of increased bandwidth in the near term will be a consolidation of digital delivery pipes at dedicated geographic locations. Furthermore, the increased consumption of high-bandwidth content will necessitate improvements in delivery hardware. Portable, touch-sensitive, wireless screens with Walkman™-style processors are a more viable alternative to the television in the long term, because televisions are necessarily big and heavy. In the near term, however, the enormous installed base of televisions presents such a low-fixed-cost opportunity to convert and deliver high-bandwidth content to consumers via cable modems that these seemingly archaic devices will actually increase in importance in the residential environment.

The killer apps, products, and services driving bandwidth growth will not come from traditional content providers. In the words of one researcher, "[B]reakthrough broadband experiences will be created by a handful of early start-ups."[21] The valuable skill required to develop new forms of content—anticipating consumer demand—is generally a poor match with established companies whose revenue model is based on the delivery of traditional media content. Furthermore, large, established media and content providers like Viacom, Warner Brothers, and Disney have made investments in assets that are specifically suited to traditional channels.

➤ **Smartband**

Smartband is the future of broadband. We see bundled, high-value products with individual rather than demographic-level capability as the future of broadband digital content. Smartband offerings will combine interactive elements; personalized life-maintenance, time-saving solutions; and self-regulating applications to monitor end users' requirements and applications for these products. These bundled products will offer more than entertainment and personal time-management solutions. They will represent fundamentally new ways to consume information relevant to our daily personal lives. True bundling entails more than simply compiling one bill for telephony, television, wireless voice and data services, and Internet connectivity, although this will be a reality over the next few years.

Case Study: SBC–Sterling Software Acquisition

Premise SBC announced plans to acquire Sterling Commerce, which provides Internet-enabled B2B software, for $3.9 billion in cash. SBC needs this type of acquisition to strengthen its data and Internet capabilities, which are critical to its long-term success. This transaction capability allows SBC to move up the value chain and leverage its upgraded network, as well as its partnership with the long-haul fiber network of Williams Communication Group (WCG). This deal is congruent with SBC's plan to become a national, even global, provider by expanding its geographic reach and breadth of services.

Breakdown Sterling works with a business and its suppliers to set up an e-community within which business can be conducted and transacted securely. Sterling's expertise allows

(continued)

two companies' different software systems to communicate and run their procurement processes over the Internet.

Cost In addition to the steep acquisition price, SBC has committed $6 billion (twice its original estimate) to upgrade its network and DSL-enable 80 percent of its customers by 2002.

Execution The market clearly has doubts about execution and is not currently favoring long-term strategic moves that deliver value that is not yet perfectly visible. As with many ILECs, many view the company as a slower-moving, Internet-challenged telecom company. Concern remains over SBC's ability to run fast-paced Internet operations. Robert Rosenberg of Insight Research remarked that it would be a great purchase if "SBC had to just put bodies into slots." SBC shares finished down on the announcement and it has lost a third of its market value since December of 1999.

Results SBC can add Sterling's service to its DSL, local, cellular (and soon long-distance) services, and Yellow Pages advertising. The hope is that once the e-community is established, the customer will be reluctant to switch to a competing provider for communication services. Additionally, SBC hopes to generate more traffic over WCG's network and obtain better pricing with the fiber carrier.

Bottom line Sterling has more than 45,000 customers worldwide, including 487 companies in the Fortune 500, so SBC plans to enter 30 out-of-region markets to provide a complete network of services to these large providers, as well as to SOHO users.

■ FUTURE TRENDS

The fulfillment of high-value-added bundled services will be pervasive, integrated applications and data delivered to a host of independent devices connected either by terrestrial lines or always-on wireless transfers. Smart, interconnected appliances are but one example of dedicated devices that will take and receive information over a common bandwidth. The commercial space will be less infused with separate, dedicated digital information delivery devices and less reliant on personalized products and services, but total bandwidth consumption will nevertheless grow drastically in the commercial environment because of increased reliance on digital information and the reduction of matter-based knowledge transfer.

The future will be rooted in the combination of complementary products and services presented to the consumer through the high-bandwidth backbone.

■ NOTES

1. Zia Daniell Wigder, Joe Laszlo, Robert Leathern, Jeff Makowka, and Ken Allard, "The Evolution of Access—Navigating the Changing Online Landscape," Jupiter Communications, Strategic Planning Services, 1999.

2. Patrick Callinan, James L. McQuivey, and Christine Ham, "Barriers to Broadband's Boom," *Forrester Research* (January 2000).

3. "Cable Modem and DSL: High-Speed Growth for High Speed-Access," *Yankee Group Report* (January 2000).

4. Callinan, McQuivey, and Ham, "Barriers to Broadband's Boom," *Forrester Research* (January 2000).

5. John Zahurancik, "Residential High-Speed Internet: Cable Modems, DSL, and Wireless Broadband," Strategis Group (February 15, 2000).

6. Andre Dua, Erwin Miedema, Chantal Sabajo-Tjong, Sven Smit, and Menno van Dijk, "Battle for Control of the Home: Industry Dynamics in the Broadband World," McKinsey & Company (April 9, 1999).

7. "Broadband!," *McKinsey & Company Special Report* (January 2000).

8. "Broadband," *New York Times*, January 17, 2000.

9. Jim Hayes, *Fiber Optics Technicians Handbook* (Albany, N.Y.: Delmar Publishers, 1996).

10. Greg Stone, NorthPoint Communications, Interview, March 14, 2000.

11. *Ibid.*

12. Zia Daniell Wigder, Joe Laszlo, Robert Leathern, Jeff Makowka, and Ken Allard, "The Evolution of Access—Navigating the Changing Online Landscape," Jupiter Communications, Strategic Planning Services, 1999.

13. Adam Brandenburger, M. Barry, and J. Nalebuff, "Co-opetition: 1. A Revolutionary Mindset That Redefines Competition and Cooperation; 2. The Game Theory Strategy That's Changing the Game of Business," Doubleday, 1997.

14. Henry W. Chesborough, and David J. Teece, "When Is Virtual Virtuous? Organizing for Innovation," *Harvard Business Review* (January-February 1996).

15. *Ibid.*

16. *Ibid.*

17. Mark E. Hardie, with Josh Bernoff and Tim Grimsditch, "Hooked on Broadband," *Forrester Research* (July 1999).

18. Matt Broersma, "What Will Drive Demand for Broadband?," *ZDNet News* (June 26, 1999).

19. Peter Jacquerot, ICTV, Inc. International Business Development, E-mail interview, February 24, 2000.

20. Hardie, "Hooked on Broadband," *Forrester Research* (July 1999).

21. *Ibid.*

■ REFERENCES

"Application Service Provider Leadership Study: Building, Managing, and Growing an ASP Business." International Data Corporation, 2000.

Bilotti, Richard, Gary Lieberman, and Benjamin Swinburne. "Cable Television." Morgan Stanley Dean Witter U.S. Investment Research, 1999.

Blackley, Neil, Paul Sullivan, and Jessica Reif Cohen. "Broadband Interactive Services—The Next Wave." Merrill Lynch & Company, 1999.

Brandenburger, Adam, M. Barry, and J. Nalebuff. "Co-opetition: 1. A Revolutionary Mindset That Redefines Competition and Cooperation; 2. The Game Theory Strategy That's Changing the Game of Business." 1997.

"Broadband!" *McKinsey & Company Special Report* (January 2000).

"Broadband." New York Times, January 17, 2000.

Broersma, Matt. "Behind the Broadband Spending Spree." *ZDNet News* (1999).

———. "What Will Drive Demand for Broadband?" *ZDNet News* (June 26, 1999).

———. "Why Fast Access Is So Slow Afoot." *ZDNet News* (1999).

"Cable Modem and DSL: High-Speed Growth for High Speed-Access." *Yankee Group Report* (January 2000).

Callinan, Patrick, James L. McQuivey and Christine Ham. "Barriers to Broadband's Boom." *Forrester Research* (January 2000).

Cauley, Leslie, William Boston, and Gautam Naik. "Deutsche Telekom Sets $3 Billion Cable Deal." *Wall Street Journal,* December 2000.

Chesborough, Henry W., and David J. Teece. "When Is Virtual Virtuous? Organizing for Innovation." *Harvard Business Review* (January-February 1996).

Dua, Andre, Erwin Miedema, Chantal Sabajo-Tjong, Sven Smit, and Menno van Dijk. "Battle for Control of the Home: Industry Dynamics in the Broadband World." McKinsey & Company (April 9, 1999).

"Excite@Home Furthers Reach in Mobile Industry, Works Towards Advancing Wireless Standards." Excite@Home Press Release, 2000.

"Excite Rising." *CableWorld Magazine*, News Today, 2000.

Flash, Jim (Accel Partners). Interview, 2000.

"General Introduction to Copper Access Technologies." ADSL Forum, 1998.

"Global Broadband Access Markets: xDSL, Cable Modems and the Threat from Broadband Satellite, Wireless, and All Optical Solutions." Pioneer Consulting White Paper, 1998.

Gunther, Mark. "These Guys Want It All." *Fortune* (2000).

Hardie, Mark E., with Josh Bernoff and Tim Grimsditch. "Hooked on Broadband." *Forrester Research* (July 1999).

Hayes, Jim. *Fiber Optics Technicians Handbook*. Albany, N.Y.: Delmar Publishers, 1996.

"Hughes to Invest $1.4 Billion in Broadband Satellite Network." InternetNews.com ISP News Archives, 1999.

"ICTV Selects Smashing Ideas for Broadband TV Interface Production." ICTV, Inc. Press Release, 1999.

Jacobus, Patricia. "Northpoint Makes Content Play." *CNET News* (2000).

Jacquerot, Peter (ICTV, Inc. International Business Development). E-mail interview, February 24, 2000.

Lemos, Rob. "Who Will Rule the Broadband Era?" *ZDNet News* (1999).

Lewis, Peter H. "How Not to Be a Zombie." *New York Times*, 2/17/2000, (2000).

Lopez, Maribel. "Beyond Broadband." *Forrester Research* (2000).

Nabi, Marc E., and R. Burns McKinney. "The Future Is Now for Direct Broadcast Satellite (DBS)." Morgan Stanley Dean Witter, 1999.

"Next Generation Broadband Satellite Networks—A Market and Technology Assessment Report." Pioneer Consulting White Paper, 1999.

PanAmSat. *1999 Annual Report*. 2000.

Pareketh, Michael K., Lou Kerner, Vik Mehta, Jimmy Y. Wu, Rakesh Sood, and Dan Degnan. "Internet Broadband: Raising the Speed Limit." Goldman Sachs Investment Research, 1999.

Pollock, Andrew. "After Space, Hughes Battles Time." *New York Times* (2000).

Reali, Patti. "The Worldwide 1998 Cable Modem Market: Ramping Up for Broadband Access." Dataquest Market Statistics Report, 1999.

Rohde, Laura. "McCaw Leads White-Knight Charge for Iridium." *The Industry Standard* (2000).

"The Role of OFDM and Its Variants in Broadband Wireless Access." Adaptive Broadband White Paper, 1999.

Sawhney, Mohan. "Earth, Wind and Sky: Trends in Global Communications." Northwestern University, Kellogg Graduate School of Management, 2000.

Schiesel, Seth. "Broadband Internet: How Broadly? How Soon?" *New York Times* (2000).

Shephard, Brett. "Bell Atlantic Means Business in DSL." Telechoice, Inc., 2000.

Siklos, Richard, Catherine Young, Andy Reinhardt, Peter Burrows, and Rob Hof. "Welcome to the 21st Century." *Business Week* (2000).

Simons, David. "What's the Deal?: Broadband Bugs Bunny." *The Industry Standard* (2000).

"16 Million + High Speed Homes by 2004." ISP-Planet.com, 2000.

Stewart, Bruce. "Satellite Superguide." *ZDNet News* (1999).

Stone, Greg (NorthPoint Communications). Interview, March 14, 2000.

"Telecommunication Services." Morgan Stanley Dean Witter U.S. Investment Research, 1999.

"Value Added Services Over DSL: Business Case Documentation." Cisco Systems, 1999.

Wigder, Zia Daniell, Joe Laszlo, Robert Leathern, Jeff Makowka, and Ken Allard. "The Evolution of Access—Navigating the Changing Online Landscape." Jupiter Communications, Strategic Planning Services, 1999.

Wilson, Carol. "Broadband: Get Ready for the Gale." *ZDNet News* (1999).

Zahurancik, John. "Residential High-Speed Internet: Cable Modems, DSL, and Wireless Broadband." Strategis Group (February 15, 2000).

Zerega, Blaise. "Highway to Nowhere: Without Killer Apps, There Is No Reason to Hop on Broadband." *Forbes* (2000).

Zohar, Mark, Brendan Hannigan, Justine Bruton, and Erin Roland. "The Dawn of Mobile eCommerce." *Forrester Research* (1999).

Chapter

11

Commercializing
Genomics

■ INTRODUCTION

The recorded history of humankind can be read as a timeline of technological innovation. We have used our intellect and ingenuity to
empower ourselves and enhance our quality of life. This chapter explores the processes of technological innovation as they are mani-
festing in the commercialization of genomics technologies and the
development of a genomics industry.

Our approach begins with a theoretical foundation, but we aim to
develop a pragmatic framework for the often nonobvious path from
breakthroughs to profits. We will summarize the journey of a new idea
as it becomes a commercially viable product, and we will note *what*
must happen, *when* it has to happen, and *who* should be involved, based
on our analysis.

We will examine lessons from the past to develop a roadmap of
what to expect—or at least hope for—with regard to a fundamental
new capability in medical science: the ability to sequence, record, and
analyze the entire human genome. We will examine the participants in
the current race to record this basic human instruction set, then look
forward to anticipate the commercial implications.

Finally, we will examine the ethical implications of genomics for future development. These include the role of government and the tradeoffs between intellectual property protection and putting knowledge in the public domain.

➤ Models of Technology Diffusion

Technology Transfer Model

Let us first introduce a model of technology transfer described by technology consultant Robert Carr. He defined the different market drivers affecting the handoff of technology from the research environment to commercial entities. This framework will later be used to examine the role of research institutions in a recent major scientific undertaking, the Human Genome Project (HGP).

The time technology spends on the pathway from discovery to commercial application has decreased considerably, because the highly competitive nature of many industries makes the adoption of new technologies crucial to success. As a result, the roles of research and development in the value chain have become increasingly important. Federal and university laboratories have enormous potential to contribute to technology development. There is a widespread perception that the federal laboratory system, in particular, has reaped insufficient returns from its substantial research efforts. In the past, those efforts focused primarily on one customer, the military. Consequently, federal laboratory researchers and directors gained very little experience in commercializing technologies. Over the past 20 years, however, U.S. legislation has facilitated the transfer and commercialization of federally funded technology, and federal labs are recognizing and fulfilling this need. The Department of Energy, for example, cites improving technology transfer as part of its mission statement:

> With the cutbacks in basic research funding, leveraged technology collaborations have become increasingly important to both DOE missions and to economic competitiveness. One of the four key priorities for the DOE is identified as leveraging science and technology to advance fundamental knowledge and our country's economic competitiveness with stronger partnership with the private sector.

Furthermore, universities are continually seeking new ways to fund research projects, capitalize on new technology flow, and attract talent. Robert Carr described some general mechanisms of technology transfer used by universities and federal institutions: *market-pull, technology-push,* or *modified technology-push.*

Market-pull. In a market-pull model, the primary driver of research is the commercial market. Research and development are directed by a private organization. An advantage to this method is that the marketability of the technology is studied by businesses in advance of the research, resulting in a high rate of successful commercialization. Unfortunately, a large segment of U.S. industry is unaware of resources and capabilities available from research centers and federal laboratories. These laboratories are beginning to realize the need to market themselves to raise awareness among commercial industries.

One formal mechanism facilitating a market-pull interaction between research centers and commercial companies was set in place by the federal government. Many laboratories actively pursue collective arrangements under the authority of a cooperative research and development agreement (CRADA), a result of the 1986, 1989, and 1995 Technology Transfer Acts. Since their inception, CRADAs have been effective in breaking down barriers between government research and industry. CRADAs provide both legal vehicles for cooperative R&D between laboratories and industry and opportunities for both sides to leverage their investments in the R&D project. Industrial investment since the inception of CRADAs validates the market's interest in technology. Another benefit to participating companies is that they are able to negotiate exclusive licenses for inventions created from these collaborations. An example is the agreement between Lawrence Livermore National Laboratory and Perkin-Elmer Corporation to develop advanced analytical instrumentation for DNA sequencing. Lawrence Livermore alone initiated more than 100 CRADAs from 1992 to 1994.

Technology-push. Although the market-pull model generates high return on research dollars, the mechanism is typically used to facilitate evolutionary technology developments. Very few technology breakthroughs are the result of research focused on a particular problem. Historically, most revolutionary technologies, such as nuclear energy, are a result of technology-push. Furthermore, because many technologies are discovered through laboratory serendipity, an important process lies in determining the best way to market and transfer these new discoveries.

Although technology-push is inherently more difficult than market-pull, the research institutions using it most successfully are those that initiate significant marketing efforts. The idea is first to accumulate a significant inventory of technologies, then actively market them to industry. An extremely efficient model of this approach is the Technology Licensing Office of the Massachusetts Institute of Technology, one of the most active university patenting and licensing offices in the country. M.I.T. currently has more than 1,000 issued U.S. patents in its portfolio and is adding at least 100 more each year. The core of the office is a staff of technically trained, business-oriented people. Their marketing efforts focus on industry, venture capital sources, and entrepreneurs to find the most effective way to commercialize new technologies. Royalties derived from licenses ($14.3 million in 1999 alone) support further research and are shared with inventors to provide incentives for further innovation. This formalized process allows inventors to focus on research activities while the Technology License Office aids in the complex tasks of patenting, marketing, and licensing of inventions.

There are also many examples of technology-push within private companies. A striking example of revolutionary technology pushed to various markets from within a private company is GORE-TEX®, an expanded Teflon sheet manufactured by W.L. Gore Associates. A single remarkably versatile polymer, polytetrafluoroethylene (PTFE) is the basis for Gore's inventions. PTFE was originally discovered in 1938 and is commonly known by the DuPont branded name Teflon®. Bob Gore found that stretching PTFE created a strong, porous material. The company has since developed dozens of products incorporating GORE-TEX®, including artificial veins for vascular surgery, insulation for high-performance electric cables, fabric for outerwear, dental floss, and liners for bagpipes. This serendipitous discovery resulted in a technology valuable to numerous commercial companies.

Despite the successes, technology-push is the more difficult mode of disseminating knowledge to the market. In fact, according to management guru Peter Drucker, there are seven sources of innovative opportunity, the least reliable and predictable of which is new *knowledge*. In addition to being difficult to predict, new-knowledge innovations must maintain a clear focus on strategic positioning. Losing focus on strategy and becoming enchanted with innovation can cause a company to struggle. Modified technology-push is a solution that can be employed to maintain this focus.

Modified technology-push. Modified technology-push typically occurs when an institution develops technologies for which a commercial market is known to exist. Typically, no specific industry partner or business is involved at the onset of the research, but the demand is well known. The laboratories work under the premise that if and when a new discovery is made, there will be a market for the technology somewhere. This type of research is often done in a collaborative manner among various research centers. The Human Genome Project, discussed later, is an excellent example of modified technology-push technology transfer.

The market-push/technology-pull models, and the hybrid modified technology-push model, describe the structural possibilities for organizations charged with stimulating and managing innovation. Though they lay a foundation upon which innovative activity thrives, these models view innovation as only two subprocesses: research and *everything else.*

A Value Chain for Commercialization

Vijay Jolly, in his seminal 1997 book, *Commercializing New Technologies,* laid out a conceptual framework for the processes involved in leading a technological breakthrough from the "eureka" moment to a viable commercial product. He began by making a key distinction between a *technological innovation* and *product development.* Simply put, a technology can be thought of as a new capability, whereas a new product is more aptly described as an application. This distinction is particularly noteworthy in that the framework subsequently laid out in his book is intended to describe the path of new technology.

Jolly's framework consists of five key stages: *imagining, incubating, demonstrating, promoting,* and *sustaining.* These stages are connected by four bridges that enable *passage* from one stage to the next.

Jolly's work focused on which stakeholders, VCs, potential customers, potential producers of complementary products, and manufacturers are vital to the successful marketing of a new technology. His work is not from the standpoint of "how do scientists pay their economic rents"; rather, it is a diagram of which partners, financial and otherwise, are essential in the process of making a new technology happen. Jolly clearly stated, as history has shown, that often the creator of the technology is but a link in a larger value chain of participants, each of whom is equally crucial. As he said, "Commercializing a new technology involves performing nine different activities well."

Jolly's linear model can be viewed as inclusive or representative of many earlier, traditional views of technology innovation, including those put forward by James Bright, Robert Cooper, and the National Society of Professional Engineers. However, those earlier formulations lacked the description of the requirements needed to move a technology to the next stage. These requirements are met by mobilizing a set of *stakeholders*, allies that must be behind a technology if it is to bridge the gap to the next major subprocess.

Jolly explained how different stakeholders serve specific functions as technologies are developed. In the first stage, *imagining*, the originators of technological breakthroughs need to mobilize the interest and endorsement of their colleagues to *bring them on board*. Imagining can take on different forms, including dreaming up an idea, solving a customer problem, reacting to a competitive threat, pursuing a problem deeply (the proper example for model genetic research), or even serendipity. Moving beyond the stage of imagining, like the rest of the path of technology, "is above all an exercise in resource assembly and collective enterprise."

The second major subprocess, *incubating*, involves testing the technology and defining its commercializability. The goal of this stage is to assign an expectation of value for the technology, which includes conceiving potential applications; considering nonobvious or out-of-context opportunities; and protecting the technology via patent, copyright, and the like. The incubating stage ends with the mobilization of resources to move on toward demonstrating the new technology. During incubation, innovators consider many different alternatives: early-stage exit licensing, demonstrating technology with government (or university) support, developing intercompany partnerships (in the case of corporate R&D), forging test and development agreements with license options, and using private venture capital resources. At this stage, crucial, path-dependent decisions are made concerning future equity distribution and the success or failure of a technology. The factors that drive these decisions include: technical resources for testing and evaluation, market and customer knowledge, supplies of key components and materials, and access to facilities suitable for large-scale clinical trials.

The next crucial subprocess is *demonstrating* the viability of the technology in its commercial context. This stage encompasses what is traditionally considered *product development*, and includes good design, price considerations, customer utility, and so forth. The success of product development and the bridge to the next key subprocess, promoting, involves mobilizing market constituents who will become co-stakeholders in the success of a technology. These include interest groups, opinion leaders, standards bodies, partners in delivery, distributors, manufacturers, and suppliers of complementary technologies.

Promoting adoption, *mobilizing* complementary assets for delivery, and *sustaining* each relate to business execution. In the Jolly model, *promoting* includes other typical new product marketing decisions: price, placement, and positioning. With regard to new technology, this includes adapting the product for use, making the technology invisible, and correctly positioning the technology to address the proper demand.

Mobilizing complementary assets is a combination of two ideas: anticipating network externalities and ensuring that complements have access to the necessary technology, and properly handling the *make or buy* decisions surrounding manufacture of the product. Optimal decisions are made with regard to who makes what, and who is allowed to participate in what.

Sustaining, in the Jolly model, means creating customer lock-in with the technology, adding services, and generating additional revenues through planned obsolescence. These final two key subprocesses, promoting and sustaining, and their linking bridge (mobilizing complementary market assets) also point to an additional key stakeholder who can supply exceptional managerial skill.

Both views of technology commercialization lend insights to our understanding of the field of genomics. The structural description of technology-push and market-pull dynamics helps us understand how genomics came to be and how it will be transferred from the public to the private sector. The linear, evolutionary, *value-chain* model illustrates the patterns future developments are likely to follow. However, before applying the models, it is necessary to review exactly what genomics is.

■ GENOMICS: WHAT IS IT?

Formally speaking, *genomics* is the study of all the genetic information of a species and its relationship to disease. Genomics is a relatively new discipline that is considered the future basis for targeting drug development and other applications such as genetic agricultural products. There is great excitement surrounding the field, as it is expected to cause a medical revolution in the design of drugs targeted at specific diseases.

A *genome* is the entire set of DNA in an organism. A *gene* is DNA used in arranging amino acids to form the proteins required by an organism (*gene expression*). Genes regulate human physiology and also play a key role in human health and disease pathways. Depending on the cell, some genes are active while most are passive. Some diseases arise when genes are either over- or underexpressed.

DNA is codified using four similar chemicals (called *bases* and abbreviated A, T, C, and G). The human genome has 3 billion pairs of bases that are arranged along chromosomes in an order unique to each individual. Chemical bases that vary between any two individuals are known *as single nucleotide polymorphisms* (SNPs, commonly called snips). The same genes that vary between individuals because of SNPs are known as *alleles*. Alleles may be responsible for differences in proteins produced from gene instructions. Although most of these differences have no medical significance, some SNPs may be associated with diseases, predisposition to a disease, or even predictable responses to pharmaceuticals through the modification of associated proteins.

Each SNP represents a potential genetic marker. These genetic markers can be used to create genetic linkage maps, in turn used by scientists to perform linkage analysis. A *linkage analysis* is the process of mapping genetic patterns to inherited diseases. This is done by comparing the genetic composition (*genotype*) of individuals with the disease against genotypes of individuals without the disease. Genotypes are associated with a disease through a complex, statistical comparison of genetic markers.

SNP analysis can be used to measure the association between a genotype and a disease. Through SNP analysis, scientists' understanding of the numerous genetic and environmental factors bearing on health and disease will grow enormously. One specific method of SNP analysis uses microarrays, where sample tissues are combined with thousands of genes on a glass chip. By studying the way the DNA binds to the genes, researchers can obtain vital information about which genes are active or inactive in various disease states. This accelerates diagnostic tests, pharmaceutical therapies, and prevention programs, while increasing the efficacy of pharmaceuticals and decreasing the cost of research and development.

■ APPLICATIONS OF GENOMICS: SO WHAT?

The mapped human genome and databases of both SNPs and specific identified genes are important because they will be tools. Unraveling the human DNA is not the equivalent of discovering the key to immortality. Rather, the tools produced by this research will result in a dramatic increase in the rate of scientific knowledge enhancement.

The pharmaceutical industry, university and government research efforts, and society at large will benefit from the development of genomic tools. These benefits can generally be grouped into four key categories: screening, drug narrowcasting and customization, accelerated drug development, and gene therapy and modification. *Screening* refers to the ability to exploit different genetic patterns to identify subgroups. Polymorphism analysis is already used for clinical trial selection today, and use will certainly increase—drug companies currently use millions of people in trials each year—to a cost of around $14 billion.[1] Screening tools promise to be insignificant in cost in clinical trials, and should yield results that explain a drug's efficacy in specific populations.

Also, drug companies will be able to differentiate between populations genetically, and thus will be able to "narrowcast" existing drugs and new drugs to the specific populations. For example, imagine a disease state that is caused by a certain type of cell malfunction. Several key proteins are involved in the process that is not working properly, each generated by different genes. In this example, a treatment that focuses on fixing one of these proteins would only address the population with a genetic mutation associated with that protein. The people in whom the disease was caused by an absence of one of the other proteins would not be helped. This will lead to more effective treatment and patient management, and should encourage reintroduction of existing drugs that were shelved because they were effective only 20 percent of the time; this will allow pharmaceutical companies to recoup more of the investment associated with these drugs.

A logical outgrowth of the narrowcasting notion is what is known as *pharmacogenomics*: custom-tailoring treatments for people based on their individual genetic makeup. According to Bear Stearns & Co., approximately 100,000 people die every year from adverse drug effects. As the medical community strives to reduce this figure, doctors, drug companies, and hospitals will show great interest in tailoring remedies to individuals using genetic information about individual metabolism and reaction potential.[2]

Perhaps the most frequently discussed application of genetic information is the accelerated development of new drugs. The advantage will derive from the ability to conduct large-scale, cost-effective screening and association studies to identify new genetic links to diseases. The discovery of a genetic association with a disease state is a nontrivial breakthrough—it opens up a new biological pathway that can be addressed at multiple points by different approaches. New pathways can be patented upon discovery, as they are akin to the understanding of a biological process that underpins most drugs developed through molecular biology.

Furthermore, related genomic tools, such as high-throughput screening, combinatorial chemistry, and computer-aided drug design, will provide scientists with a head start in their quests for new drugs. To understand the magnitude of this change, consider that "the global $250 billion pharmaceutical market has been built on fewer than 500 drug targets (i.e., 500 gene products)."[3] A comparison of this figure to the 250 new targets guaranteed to Bayer by genomic player Millennium Pharmaceuticals over the next 5 years illustrates a major inflection point in pharmaceutical research.

The final area of benefit will come in the form of new gene therapies and gene modifications. After detecting that a disease state is caused by a specific SNP, gene therapy will introduce an agent, or *vector* (experiments today use reprogrammed viruses), that will produce a genetic "patch" to repair the faulty or malfunctioning process. Before this can be undertaken, knowledge must be assembled outlining relationships between genes and identifying genes that serve multiple functions.

Gene modification implies finding mutations that are likely to occur before a child is created, and introducing a corrective patch in the reproductive cells of prospective parents. Although this broaches uncharted ethical territory, it is hoped that society will permit science potentially to remove some devastating hereditary diseases, such as Tay-Sachs disease or Canavan Syndrome.

Though the possibility of altering the human genome seems far off, the practice of genetic modification is not new. The modification of plant genes has been done since the days of Gregor Mendel. It follows that the largest near-term potential for gene modification is agribusiness. Scientists are already creating plants that generate their own pesticides and produce additional vitamins, all in an effort to increase both yields and nutritional value.

■ THE HUMAN GENOME PROJECT: WHAT IS IT?

The Human Genome Project (HGP) is a worldwide research effort, the goal of which is to analyze the structure of human DNA and determine the location of the estimated 100,000 human genes. In parallel with this effort, the DNA of a set of model organisms is being studied to provide the comparative information necessary to understand the functioning of the human genome. The information generated by the HGP is expected to provide the roadmap for biomedical science in the 21st century.

➤ HGP Origins

The roots of HGP can be traced to Walter Gilbert, a Harvard University biologist who first championed the idea. James Watson, co-discoverer of the structure of DNA, also was involved in the early stages. Initial support came from the Office of Biological and Environmental Research (OBER) of the Department of Energy (DOE) and its predecessor agencies, the Atomic Energy Commission and the Energy Research and Development Administration.

At a March 1986 international conference in Santa Fe, New Mexico, OBER and leading scientists assembled to determine the feasibility of implementing such a project. When participants enthusiastically endorsed the notion, OBER initiated several pilot projects. DOE's Biological and Environmental Research Advisory Committee (BERAC) was designated to provide program guidance.

An April 1987 BERAC report recommended that DOE and the nation commit to a large, multidisciplinary, scientific and technological undertaking to map and sequence the human genome. The DOE was given the lead role for this project, because of its resources and related technology development.

The turning point for coding the entire human DNA was a 1988 National Research Council (NRC) report sponsored by the Department of Energy entitled *Mapping and Sequencing the Human Genome*. The report outlined a phased approach that would begin by constructing maps of the genome. The eventual goal of sequencing human DNA was to be postponed until new technologies made it faster and cheaper.

The National Institutes of Health (NIH) also played a key role in creating the HGP. Like the DOE, it was earmarked for leadership by the 1988 NRC report. Today, NIH's National Human Genome Research Institute (NHGRI) coordinates NIH's involvement with the HGP. The NIH's involvement in the HGP includes physical mapping and the development of index linkage markers and technology. The NIH also provides support for genetic mapping based on family studies and, following NRC recommendations, researches relevant model organisms. DOE-supported genome research for the HGP focuses on human genome research and comparative mouse genomics through large-scale physical mapping, instrumentation technology development, and improvements in database capabilities.

The DOE-NIH U.S. Human Genome Project formally began on October 1, 1990. The HGP was originally structured around five-year goals for the following areas:

- Mapping and sequencing of the human genome
- Mapping and sequencing of the genomes of model organisms
- Data collection and distribution
- Ethical, legal, and social considerations
- Research training
- Technology development
- Technology transfer

The project's first tangible goal was to map the search for genetic defects that cause hereditary diseases.

➤ HGP Evolution

Rapid technological improvements have significantly altered the timeline and course of the HGP. In 1991, a discovery was made by Dr. J. Craig Venter, a biologist working within the NIH. Venter hypothesized that he had found a technological improvement that would help to identify genes quickly. Dr. Venter's process included looking for an active gene and sequencing a small portion of it. This partial sequencing then served as a tag to identify the gene.

Dr. Venter's ideas quickly became maps aiding in the rapid identification of genes. However, progress was slow in the actual sequencing of the genome. The technological problems of sequencing were partially solved in 1995, again by Dr. Venter, who had since moved from the NIH to the Institute of Genomic Research in Rockville, Maryland. Dr. Venter, using a new approach of "whole genome shotgun sequencing," published the entire DNA sequence of the microbe *Haemophilus influenzae*—the first sequence of a free-living organism. Shotgun sequencing involves chopping the entire genome into small pieces, sequencing each piece, then reassembling them in correct order.

The competing approach to shotgun sequencing, supported by NIH-funded scientists, was to start with a smaller chunk of the genome, then break it into pieces—an approach that left far fewer pieces to reassemble. A Stanford University team won a PR victory for the NIH by sequencing the genome of baker's yeast using the NIH's techniques.

Building on this momentum, six labs were assigned in April 1996 to sequence a long stretch of human DNA. The goal of this project was to have 3 to 5 percent of the human genome sequenced by 1999. The project was to complete the original HGP goal in 2005.

The race to sequence the human genome continues to accelerate. To date, the HGP claims to have 83 percent of the genome sequenced, including 65.5 percent in working draft sequence and 17.5 percent in high-quality sequence.

Currently, there are several contributors to the HGP within the United States and abroad. Within the United States, research funding from the DOE and the NIH is provided to laboratories, colleges, and universities. At any given time, the DOE Human Genome Program funds about 200 separate investigators. In addition, the DOE and NIH genome programs set aside between 3 percent and 5 percent of their respective total annual budgets for the study of the project's ethical, legal, and social issues (ELSI).

Internationally, at least 18 countries have established human genome research programs. Some of the larger programs are in Australia, Brazil, Canada, China, Denmark, European Union, France, Germany, Israel, Italy, Japan, Korea, Mexico, Netherlands, Russia, Sweden, the United Kingdom, and the United States. Some developing countries are participating through studies of molecular biology techniques for genome research and studies of organisms that are particularly interesting to their geographical regions. The Human Genome Organization helps coordinate international collaboration in HGP research.

➤ Private Sector

In 1998, the Perkin-Elmer Corporation, whose PE Biosystems subsidiary was the main supplier of high-throughput sequencing equipment used for genomic research, recruited Dr. Venter to form a new venture. Immediately after the formation of Celera, they announced their intention to sequence the entire human genome by mid-2001. Since inception, Celera has stated that it plans to make sequencing data publicly available to ensure that as many researchers as possible have access. This announcement spurred the publicly funded Human Genome Project to announce that it would have a rough draft of the genome, containing 90 percent of the human DNA sequence, by the spring of 2000. The final sequencing of the genome was to be completed by 2003, two years ahead of the original 2005 due date. On April 6, 2000, Venter announced that Celera had completed sequencing the genome and was currently working only on assembly.

Celera's revenue model differs from those of many existing genome research companies in that Celera allows free access to much of its data, only charging a subscription to customers for nonexclusive access to SNP databases and value-added analytical tools. Additionally, Celera plans to become an e-commerce portal, serving both pharmaceutical customers and the consumers that Celera hopes will demand specialized diagnostic products. In fact, the company has stated its goal of becoming the "Bloomberg of the scientific community."[4] Meanwhile, Celera is still heavily engaged in protecting its intellectual property by filing for patents on many discoveries.

Before Celera was formed, numerous private competitors would not give away information. Incyte Genomics, a genomic research company formed in 1991, also had the goal of becoming the scientific equivalent of Bloomberg. Incyte's revenue model entails charging customers for a subscription to Incyte's genomic database, which contains a bioinformatics platform and computer simulation to assist customers in drug development. If this development results in any drugs, Incyte will collect royalty payments. Additionally, Incyte places genes from its databases onto microarray chips for customers' use. As of early 2000, Incyte led the industry in intellectual property protection, with more than 350 gene patents issued and more than 6,500 applied for. In fact, before Celera entered the market, much of Incyte's business model relied on intellectual property and the customer's inability to access public information, so it is unclear how they will adapt to this new strategy.

Affymetrix is one of the few companies offering a tangible product in the current genome marketplace. It currently provides the industry with the GeneChip™ system. This consists of disposable DNA probe microarrays containing gene sequences, instruments to process the arrays, and software to manage the information. Additionally, Affymetrix is engaged in research to determine specific genes of interest to customers for compilation into a database. Thus, Affymetrix obtains revenues from the sale of equipment and recurring revenue from sales of custom and standard chips.

Human Genome Sciences (HGS) takes specific gene identification a step further and actually performs drug research. Customers pay for a co-exclusive subscription to HGS's database, and then pay a licensing fee to develop the drug for commercialization. Of the drugs HGS is currently testing, two may substantially improve the effectiveness of cancer therapy by shielding tissues from toxic cancer treatments while leaving cancer cells vulnerable. HGS holds more than 100 gene and drug patents.

Drug research and creation is the business of Millennium Pharmaceuticals. Millennium uses a high-throughput screening method to increase the probability of success and reduce the time to market. Once the drugs are developed, Millennium obtains money by licensing the drugs to a company that will commercialize the product. Currently, Millennium is focusing its drug development in the areas of cancer, obesity, infectious diseases, and central nervous system diseases. It has applied for more than 500 patents and has been awarded more than 40.

Table 11.1 summarizes and compares the major private-sector participants in the genomics field.

■ ANALYSIS OF GENOMICS COMMERCIALIZATION

➤ The Technology Transfer View

Earlier we introduced models of technology transfer exemplified by publicly funded research institutions. The Human Genome Project, directed by the DOE and the NIH, is functioning within a modified technology-push framework. No company or specific group of companies is specifically funding or directing the project, as in the market-pull model. The research is not focused on making "blue sky" technology breakthroughs. Rather, it is focused on the broad market

Table 11.1   Profiles of the major genomics companies.

	Founded	What They Do	Key Person	Customers/ Partners	Revenue Model	Market Cap (4/11)
Human Genome Project	1988	Discovers genes and renders them available to public	Martin Frazier, Ph.D., Director of DOE Life Sciences	DOE, NIH	None	N/A
Celera	1998	Generates and sells genomic information from genome shotgun technique	J. Craig Venter, Ph.D., President, Chief Scientist	Tracking stock of PE Corporation (formerly Perkin-Elmer); partner with Compaq Computer Corporation	Customers pay for a subscription to their database; planning to become an e-commerce entity	$5.0 billion
Incyte	1991	LifeSeq database of human genes and gene fragments; "Bloomberg" of scientific community	Randal Scott, Ph.D., President, Director, CSO	Pharmaceutical companies	Customers pay for a subscription to their database and milestone and royalty payments	$2.5 billion

Affymetrix	1993	GeneChip™ System (microarrays for DNA analysis)	Stephen Fodor, Ph.D., Chairman & CEO	225 Units; Eli Lilly; Merck; Pfizer; others	Selling GeneChips, DNA microarrays	$2.9 billion
Human Genome Sciences	1992	R&D of protein drugs and diagnostic products; includes research on SNPs and pathways	William Haseltine, Ph.D., Chairman & CEO	Human Gene Consortium Partners; Schering-Plough; SmithKline Beecham, Takeda Chemical; Synthelabo; Merck KGaA	Customers pay for a co-exclusive subscription to their database, and milestone and royalty payments	$4.4 billion
Millennium Pharmaceuticals	1993	Applies genomics to drug development Current areas include cancer, obesity, infectious diseases, central nervous system diseases	Mark Levin, Chairman, CEO, & President	Alliance partners; Warner-Lambert; Monsant	Licensing and technology transfer	$5.8 billion

need for intimate knowledge of the human gene sequence. There is also consensus that this new knowledge will have a profound impact on the future of the health and agricultural industries worldwide.

One of the DOE's roles in this project is to build a scientific infrastructure for the private sector. "The DOE wants to get the best science out to the community," says Marvin Frazier, director of the Life Sciences Division. He compares the DOE's work on the human genome project to the building of the freeway system in the United States. Making raw genomic data publicly available is a major component of this "scientific freeway."

The Human Genome Project, however, will not lead to a single technology. The commercialization of products has occurred along the path of federal and university research. This piecemeal transfer of technology has taken the form of licenses in areas such as gene mapping, gene sequencing, instrumentation, and new ventures. An example is Hyseq, Inc., founded in 1993 by former Argonne National Laboratory researchers to commercialize a gene sequencing technology. The advantages of this technology include the ability to move rapidly, with lower operational costs, in a less bureaucratic environment, while maintaining a strong commitment to the technology. Most institutions, particularly universities, give staff members a wide range of support to locate capital and find space in a business incubator.

Vijay Jolly's model for technology commercialization is broad, as the process works differently in various industry structures. Still, the model is not broad enough to accommodate genomics as a whole. Rather, it must be applied to specific genomic applications, current and predicted. The most obvious subgroups for such application are the ability to sequence and map, the analytical tools necessary to use this information, and the ability to develop new drugs and therapies. Genomics represents a number of interdependent value chains of technology commercialization, with the first developed products becoming enabling technologies for a subsequent chain of technologies.

The wet-chemistry ability to sequence genes has existed since the 1980s, with the development of the polymerase chain reaction (PCR) and other mechanical techniques. Naturally, these breakthroughs attracted praise within the biomedical community and attracted public and private funding to support the research. Improvements in the efficiency of gene sequencing, concurrent with huge advances in computing power, gave sequencing ability a much more exalted role: the ability to map the entire human genome.

Considerable debate lingers over the accuracy of the shotgun technique promoted by Venter. We consider the early agreements with large pharmaceutical companies as the first-round beta testing of the data generated through massive mapping. The bridge yet to be fully crossed is mobilizing market constituents; several obstacles must be overcome before the technology can be promoted as a sustainable business. A component of the bridge—attracting scientific users and penetrating deeper into big pharmaceutical companies' business—depends on the analytic tools used to exploit this data.

Jolly's capability-based model can also be applied to the analytical tools used with current genetic information. Such tools do exist, and scientists tap the DOE's GenBank frequently, utilizing what is known about certain genetic strands that have already been isolated and mapped. However, a robust set of new tools will be necessary to: (1) understand if causal links exist between some rarely expressed DNA and mutations observed elsewhere; (2) establish causality between individual or groups of SNPs and observed disease states; and (3) fully understand variations in SNPs in the context of the entire genome across a broad population sample. In industry lingo, these types of tests include linkage analysis, disequilibrium studies, candidate gene studies, and whole genome scans. These tools are now imagined and incubated at most of the key private-sector participants. These analytical technologies will reach the demonstration phase as the companies begin to roll out next-generation database access offerings.

➤ A Roadmap for a Hypothetical New Drug

The most instructive application of the value chain for technology commercialization is to track the path a new therapeutic solution will take as a result of the technologies previously discussed. That is, genomic companies, in addition to developing targets, are also generating automated machines that identify genes, use PCR to make the genes copy themselves and express in proteins, and then use combinatorial chemistry and high-throughput screening to find compounds that adhere to the molecules. Early support and enthusiasm will be based on the market potential of a treatment. Incubating will involve taking the known adhering compound and linking it to a desired biological functionality. We believe that incubating will take place within several groups: genomic biotech companies (like Human Genome Sciences), university/corporate joint research efforts, big pharmaceutical companies, and a new class of speculative R&D organizations that will focus on specific diseases.

We expect these incubators to receive funding from venture capitalists, drug companies, and, to some extent, NIH and government grants. The stakeholders necessary for the demonstration stage will be suppliers of capital (big pharmaceutical companies, government, and perhaps VCs) and suppliers with trial process expertise. There are two possibilities for this stage. Either big pharmaceutical companies will invest in a drug and shepherd it through trials and internal marketing and manufacturing divisions, or stand-alone players will represent each of these specific skill sets. The traditional explanation for consolidation within the pharmaceutical industry is portfolio diversification. Blockbuster drugs are few and far between, and the cost of unsuccessful R&D is high. However, genomics will improve the success rate of drug development. An article in *Fortune* described this effect: "Drug researchers' crummy batting average seems about to change—imagine 20 DiMaggios stepping up to the plate each inning."[5] If we are to understand the implications of this improved "batting average" for the drug business, we should first review the industry's current structure.

➤ Pharmaceutical Industry—Historical Perspective

Historically speaking, the pharmaceutical industry has been dominated by several large participants with substantial financial resources at their disposal. The viability of these industry behemoths has depended in large part on each firm's success in discovering, testing, developing, marketing, and selling blockbuster drugs for mass-market consumption. Each "big pharma" has at least one blockbuster drug in its portfolio of marketable pharmaceuticals; notable examples include Prozac®, Lipitor®, and, most recently, Viagra®.

The large pharmaceutical companies are currently vertically integrated. A pharmaceutical company typically consists of five main functions: discovery, development, manufacturing, marketing, and sales. Although most pharmaceutical companies also contract independent firms for each of these functions, outsourcing is limited. Indeed, virtually all of the spending on manufacturing, marketing, and sales is done internally.

The strategy of finding blockbuster drugs has been necessitated by the expense of the efforts involved in bringing pharmaceuticals to market. The beginning of the development process, known as the discovery of new chemical entities (NCEs), is a mixture of art and science. Successful researchers capitalize on industry experience, intuition, and defined scientific procedures to identify NCEs. Naturally, the serendipitous nature of drug discovery results in the identification of only a small number of NCEs. A scientist could realistically hope to discover only one or two successful targets over a lifetime of dedicated research.

Once a target is discovered, a scientist then endures the laborious and time-consuming task of developing the NCE. This entails testing thousands of iterations of the NCE to find its most powerful form. In a single year, a researcher would produce 50 to 100 compounds at an estimated cost of $5,000 to $10,000 per variation. As with discovery, experience plays a large role in determining which variations to test.

With a limited number of targets, the goal of a pharmaceutical company is to develop a compound that provides effective treatments to the largest segments of the population. The successful development of a blockbuster drug creates large monopoly rents to be put toward future research for the next blockbuster drug. Therefore, the success of a pharmaceutical company depends on its current portfolio, number of blockbuster drugs, and list of compounds under R&D.

➤ Pharmaceutical Industry—Future Vertical Landscape

In the future, the business model focusing on the development of blockbuster drugs will no longer hold for pharmaceutical companies. Although pharmaceutical companies will certainly continue to pursue NCEs with the greatest potential to be blockbusters, revenue streams from blockbuster drugs will no longer be necessary to cover R&D costs. Instead, pharmaceutical companies will pursue the smaller revenue streams of niche NCEs to cover reduced and more efficient R&D outlays.

As the discovery process becomes more efficient over time, pharmaceutical companies will be confronted with the task of prioritizing NCEs for limited development funds. This will place a greater importance on future revenue stream projections for various NCEs.

Signs of change are already creeping into the pharmaceutical industry. In recognition of the changes in the drug development process brought about by genomic research, pharmaceutical companies have set up increasing numbers of research deals with genomics firms over the last five years. In addition, pharmaceutical companies are starting to use contract manufacturing organizations (CMOs) and contract research organizations (CROs) with greater frequency. This trend is expected to continue for the foreseeable future.

The implications of these changes are profound. The recent trend of outsourcing key segments of the value chain to niche companies threatens to deprive the large pharmaceutical companies of important revenue streams. Unless the pharmaceutical companies maintain the latest scientific tools for discovery and development in-house, upstream providers will gain supplier power and extract profits from the companies.

A key success factor for pharmaceutical companies is to develop best practices in drug discovery and development skills. This will require pharmaceutical companies to employ cutting-edge research scientists who are familiar with the latest techniques in genomic research.

At the beginning of the value chain, a few niche players will dominate the discovery phase of drug development. These companies will be the experts on analyzing genomic information for links between genes and disease. Successful firms will use computer-automated linkage analysis, combinatorial chemistry, and high-throughput screening.

The competing vendors of genetic information will be delineated by three variables: the depth of their downstream activities (do they develop drugs? Targets? Or just sell data?); their intellectual property (IP) position with regard to *which* biological pathways the industry chooses to pursue first; and tools for studying genetic material. We suspect the latter will be a key swing factor, as we anticipate conflict-of-interest issues and overlapping IP claims among key market participants.

Looking forward, we expect that sustainability will come to the firms that are able sufficiently to mobilize complementary assets in the marketplace. This may mean the development of custom analyses for large clients or exclusive agreements with big pharmaceutical companies.

Clinical development and testing of NCEs represents the next stage in the value chain. Companies operating in this segment will either be pharmaceutical and discovery-phase companies partnered to name potential drug targets, or contract research organizations contracted by discovery-phase firms identifying their own NCEs.

Manufacturing will be farmed out to CMOs, with a few pharmaceutical companies retaining manufacturing operations for compounds requiring a complex understanding of the manufacturing process.

Marketing and sales will continue to be the domain of big pharma. However, with the change in medicine from generic to customer-centric care, a primary goal of marketing and sales will be the development of brand equity. For marketing and sales to thrive, companies will need to build franchises around disease types or genetic market segments.

■ THE PUBLIC POLICY IMPERATIVE

➤ Intellectual Property Controversy

A leading topic of controversy in human genome research is the issue of intellectual property rights. A recent patent frenzy, perpetuated by a few major companies, has garnered attention well beyond the scientific community. The project started as a race to decode the entire genome sequence, but is now a contest to commercialize it. A tremendous amount of intellectual property has been created and captured because of gene research, but none has raised as much controversy as the gene patents. Two of the leading commercial entities, Celera and Incyte, are filing for an unprecedented number of U.S. patents for the sequencing of genes. Incyte already holds more than 350 gene-related patents, has 6,500 applications pending, and planned to file 15,000 in the year 2000. Celera also filed for about 6,500 patents in 2000, but would not disclose its current number of applications.

The concern is that these patents will slow, rather than speed, further research into the development of useful treatments. If these companies do not produce a product, but keep others from doing research, there is a real opportunity cost to society. Many companies that file for patents do understand the gene's potential use, and are simply making guesses about the gene's function. The patent effectively acts as a placeholder until further research can be done to fully understand the gene. In some cases, other scientists who are unaware of the filed patent are doing further research. For example, a patent issued to Human Genome Sciences gives the company control over use of a gene in commercial development of a new class of AIDS drugs—even though the company knew nothing of the gene's link to AIDS when it applied for the patent.

This controversy spurred British Prime Minister Tony Blair and U.S.

President Bill Clinton to issue a statement calling for free access to the raw data of the human genetic code. Though seemingly innocuous— all the participants intend to place raw genome data in the public domain—the statement was a strong signal that the government could strip companies of existing IP rights. This may seem outrageous, but there is historical precedent for such an action. In late 1947, researchers at Bell Labs invented the first transistor. Within two years, the Justice Department filed an antitrust suit against AT&T for giving preferential treatment to its manufacturing subsidiary, Western Electric. To avoid spinning off Western Electric, AT&T was forced to license all existing transistor patents to any interested domestic firms for free. Certainly, the genomic intellectual property issues are likely to be observed quite closely by the government to ensure that one or a few companies do not hurt the public good by attempting to hoard much of the information.

The debate may be a bit late, as the U.S. Patent and Trademark Office has already issued more than 400 human gene patents, and tens of thousands more await approval. Even before the Blair–Clinton statement was issued, the U.S. Patent Office had proposed toughening its standards by requiring applicants to demonstrate the function and usefulness of their discoveries.

The decoding of the human genome has generated a gold rush, with companies working quickly to capture downstream revenue from exclusive rights to genes. The manner in which these companies plan to utilize these rights will affect the patent debate. For example, Incyte's business plan is to sell cheap access to its patented genes and turn a profit on volume. This approach is less bothersome to those who wonder whether genes should be patented at all. Even the NIH, to date, has had no disagreement with Incyte over the terms of access to its patent portfolio.

In a statement to the U.S. House of Representatives, Celera also made clear its business objectives regarding gene patenting. It stated that one of its founding principles is to make the genome sequence freely available to researchers, when it is complete, on Celera's Internet site. Celera has filed thousands of provisional patent applications, but will later decide which genes are medically important enough to file full patent applications. Celera "will look at thousands of genes to determine which ones have the greatest relevance for human health and are most likely to be developed into commercial products by pharmaceutical companies."[6] However, other gene-hunting companies have demanded high royalties on just a few sought-after genes.

A wave of intellectual property will emerge when researchers develop innovations based on the completed gene information. The raw genetic data will be the clay that researchers sculpt into whatever novel inventions they desire. However, should the patents filed be granted, these breakthroughs will be made possible by cross-referencing the original gene patents.

➤ Ethical, Legal, and Social Issues

In addition to the IP issues of genomics, there are other considerable ethical, legal, and social issues (ELSI) to tackle. ELSI issues are far-reaching, ranging from privacy and data access to fairness. In this section we discuss the ELSI issues that must be solved before the fruits of the HGP's labor can be harvested.

One major ELSI concern is the privacy and confidentiality of decoded genetic information. To address this issue, guidelines must be established to determine the ownership and control of this data. For instance, if a married couple has genetic screening performed to eliminate hereditary diseases from their children's DNA, who will have access to this very private information? Measures will have to be put into place so that this type of information is not shared with potentially interested third parties such as employers, insurance companies, law enforcement agencies, and the military. If it is determined that this data should be shared with third parties, what guidelines will there be on use?

Thought should also be given to where the line should be drawn for gene therapy. For instance, it is commonly agreed that gene therapy is appropriate for curable, life-threatening diseases. However, how should we treat minor disabilities or physical attributes such as height and eye color? There will be a large gray area of ELSI as society figures out which cases justify gene therapy and which do not.

Along these lines, the advent of gene therapy will create a great temptation for genetic enhancement. Should aspiring parents be able to pick and choose the physical attributes of their children? If so, what are the ramifications for the human gene pool in the long run? This topic in particular has become a great source of consternation and spawned a media frenzy over the potential for creating a "superior" human race.

The cost of genetic therapy will be prohibitive for most people. This brings up the issue of fairness in genetic technologies. Who will have access to these expensive medical treatments? Who will pay for them? If cosmetic genetic enhancement is made legal, personal financial positions would create a natural self-selection process. Is this fair?

The recent completion of human genome sequencing has raised concerns from prominent scientists over the dangers of genomics research in combination with the computing power implied by Moore's Law. A prominent Sun Microsystems computer scientist, Bill Joy, spoke out about these dangers and the controls needed to keep these technologies out of the hands of irresponsible individuals. He conjectured that if curbs are not put in place, the future of mankind could be at stake.

■ CONCLUSION

Genomics will revolutionize the health care industry and dramatically improve the human condition. However, it is not a singular breakthrough; rather, genomics is a sequential evolution of related technologies. Despite considerable controversy and public feuding, the development of genomics is a collaborative effort, a modified technology-push conceived by the public sector and handed off to the private sector.

As the private sector embraces genomics, we expect profound changes in the pharmaceutical industry, including change in the vertical chain from discovery to sales and the emergence of niche players. Power will shift upstream to drug discovery and development. Furthermore, downstream marketing organizations will adopt consumer-focused strategies.

The shakeout of the vertical chain will depend on the resolution of the intellectual property controversy. The litmus test for the solidification of intellectual property positions will not be market capitalization or economic equality, but rather the structure criteria that allow the fastest diffusion of new drugs into the marketplace.

Beyond the intellectual property debate, genomics presents myriad societal questions that require resolution, to ensure that the potential of this promising area of science is realized without endangering the future of our species.

■ NOTES

1. Ethan T. Lovell and David T. Molowa, *Celera: The Genomics Bellwether.* Bear, Stearns & Co. Equity Research (May 27, 1999).
2. *Ibid.*
3. *Ibid.*
4. Celera, http://www.celera.com/home.asp (2000).
5. David Stipp, "Hatching a DNA Giant," *Fortune* 139 (no. 10, 1999).
6. J. Craig Venter, *Prepared Statement of J. Craig Venter, Ph.D. President and Chief Scientific Officer Celera Genomics, a PE Corporation, Before the Subcommittee on Energy and Environment, U.S. House of Representatives Committee on Science* (April 6, 2000).

■ REFERENCES

➤ Web Sites

Affymetrix Inc. http://www.affymetrix.com/.

BBC News. 1999. http://www.bbc.co.uk/hi/english/sci/tech/newsid_452000/452293.stm.

Celera. http://www.celera.com/home.asp. Accessed 2000.

Human Genome Project. http://www.er.doe.gov/production/ober/hug_top.html; http://www.ornl.gov/hgmis/.

Human Genome Sciences. http://www.hgsi.com/.

Incyte. http://www.incyte.com/.

Millennium Pharmaceuticals. http://www.mlnm.com/MLNM99.shtml.

M.I.T Technology Licensing Office. http://web.mit.edu/tlo/www/.

United States Department of Energy. http://www.doe.gov.

W.L. Gore & Associates and GORE-TEX® Products Home Page. http://www.gore.com.

➤ Other Materials

Affymetrix Inc. Form 10-K Report to U.S. Securities and Exchange Commission (for year ending December 31, 1998). 1998.

Begley, Sharon, et al. "Decoding the Human Body." *Newsweek* (2000).

Bishop, Jerry E., and Michael Waldhoz. *Genome: The Story of the Most As-*

tonishing Scientific Adventure of Our Time—The Attempt to Map All the Genes in the Human Body. New York: Simon & Schuster, 1990.

Carr, Robert K. "Doing Technology Transfer in Federal Laboratories." In *From Lab to Market: Commercialization of Public Sector Technology.* New York: Plenum Press, 1994.

Cave, Damien. "Killjoy." *Salon Technology* (April 10, 2000). http://www.salon.com/tech/view/2000/04/10/joy/index.html.

Conley, James G. Remarks to Master of Management Candidates of the Kellogg Graduate School of Management, Northwestern University, Evanston, Illinois. 2000.

Drucker, Peter F. *Innovation and Entrepreneurship Practice and Principles.* New York: Harper & Row, 1985.

Dyson, Freeman J. *The Sun, the Genome, and the Internet: Tools of Scientific Revolution.* New York: Oxford University Press, 1999.

Frazier, Marvin (Director of Life Sciences Division of DOE). Personal conversation, April 6, 2000.

Gibson, David V. "Inter-Organizational Technology Transfer: From Standard Technology Packages to Spin-Offs." In *Commercializing High Technology.* New York: Rowman & Littlefield, 1997.

Goldsbrough, Peter, Pete Lawyer, and Gayatri Sondhi. "The Pharmaceutical Industry into its Second Century: From Serendipity to Strategy." Boston Consulting Group, *BCG Report* (January 1999).

Gwyne, Peter. "Research Fellows: Big Pharma Wants the Rewards that Biotech Research Has to Offer." *Red Herring* (no. 77, 2000): 306.

Human Genome Sciences Inc. Form 10-K Report to U.S. Securities and Exchange Commission (for year ending December 31, 1998). 1998.

Incyte Pharmaceuticals Inc. Form 10-K Report to U.S. Securities and Exchange Commission (for year ending December 31, 1998). 1998.

Jacobs, Paul, and Peter G. Gosselin. "Experts Fret Over Effect of Gene Patents on Research." *Los Angeles Times*, February 28, 2000.

Johnstone, Bob. *We Were Burning: Japanese Entrepreneurs and the Electronic Revolution.* Boulder, Colo.: Westview Press, 1999.

Jolly, Vijay K. *Commercializing New Technologies: Getting from Mind to Market.* Boston: Harvard Business School Press, 1997.

Kassicieh, Suleiman K., and Raymond H. Radosevich. *From Lab to Market: Commercialization of Public Sector Technology.* New York: Plenum Press, 1994.

King, Ralph T. "Mapping Human Genome Will Bring Glory to Some, but Incyte Prefers Cash." *Wall Street Journal*, February 10, 2000.

Langreth, Robert. "Celera Expects to Finish Assembling Human Gene Map by End of the Year." *Wall Street Journal*, January 11, 2000.

———. "For Gene-Decoding Leader Celera, Next Challenge Is Making Money." *Wall Street Journal*, February 3, 2000.

———. "Gene-Sequencing Race Between U.S., Private Researchers Is Accelerating." *Wall Street Journal*, March 16, 1999.

Lind, Douglas D., and Christopher Leonard. *Celera Genomics Group: Human Genome Sequencing Completed Early*. Morgan Stanley Dean Witter Equity Research (April 6, 2000).

———. *Celera Genomics Group: Resuming Coverage with an Outperform Rating*. Morgan Stanley Dean Witter Equity Research (March 9, 2000).

Lovell, Ethan T., and David T. Molowa. *Celera: The Genomics Bellwether*. Bear, Stearns & Co. Equity Research (May 27, 1999).

Matthews, Jana B. "Forming Effective Partnerships to Commercialize Public Sector Technology." In *From Lab to Market: Commercialization of Public Sector Technology*. New York: Plenum Press, 1994.

Milton, Gabriel B. *The Human Genome Project*. Dorland's Directories: Medical & Healthcare Marketplace Guide 51. 1996.

Owen, David. "Patenting Human Genes." *Mill Hill Essays 1995*. National Institute for Medical Research, 1995. http://www.nimr.mrc.ac.uk/mhe95/genepat.htm.

PE Corporation. Form S-3 Report to U.S. Securities and Exchange Commission (for year ending December 31, 1999). 1999.

Philipkoski, Kristen. "Celera a Cinch in Genome Race." *Wired News* (January 11, 2000). http://www.wired.com/news/technology/0,1282,34372,00.html.

———. "Incyte Incites Concern." *Wired News*. (February 16, 2000). http://www.wired.com/news/technology/0,1282,34372,00.html.

Ridley, Matt. *Genome: The Autobiography of a Species in 23 Chapters*. New York: HarperCollins, 1999.

Roberts, Leslie. "Unlocking the Secrets of DNA to Cure Disease, Slow Aging." *U.S. News & World Report* 128 (January 2000).

Sedaitis, Judith B. *Commercializing High Technology*. New York: Rowman & Littlefield, 1997.

Stipp, David. "Hatching a DNA Giant." *Fortune* 139 (no.10, 1999).

United States Department of Energy. http://www.doe.gov. Accessed 2000.

Venter, J. Craig. *Prepared Statement of J. Craig Venter, Ph.D. President and Chief Scientific Officer Celera Genomics, a PE Corporation, Before the Subcommit-*

tee on Energy and Environment, U.S. House of Representatives Committee on Science (April 6, 2000).

Waugaman, Paul G. "Technology Transfer Management at Smaller Institutions." Technology Commercialization Group, LLC and the Southern Technology Council, 1999.

Chapter 12

Epilogue
Venturing Beyond Boundaries

Life always seems to come in opposites or silos. Good versus evil. Right versus wrong. Yin versus Yang. Us versus them. And so it is as we strive to understand the ever-changing landscape of business and technology. Old Economy versus New Economy. Offline versus online. B2B versus B2C. Wired versus wireless. Commerce versus e-commerce. Licensed versus hosted software. These dichotomies and boundaries that structure our world seem fundamental to our understanding of the world. Indeed, we all use boundaries as guideposts in our journey of learning. As we have seen in most chapters of this book, boundaries help us to make sense of the world by organizing concepts and objects into neat categories. Boundaries are the scaffolds that we use to build our mental models. If we aren't careful, however, these very scaffolds that help us learn can imprison us and prevent us from advancing our learning. We must use boundaries, but we must then lose boundaries. In this final chapter, we discuss the nature of boundaries, the role that they play in helping us learn about new business models and new technologies, the impediments that the place in our learning, and how you can break free from boundaries. By going beyond boundaries, you can reconcile paradoxes and gain deep insights into the future of value and profit in the Network Economy.

■ UNDERSTANDING BOUNDARIES

The dictionary defines a boundary as "something that defines and limits". This definition itself illustrates the paradoxical role of boundaries—they help us define a concept or an object, but, like all definitions and labels, they are limiting. We define a boundary as *a tool that we use to structure or demarcate a concept or object*. Boundaries can work in many ways. They can be *taxonomies* that we construct by classifying an object or a concept into multiple categories. For example, industries are classified into a number of categories in terms of Standard Industry Classification (SIC) codes. Boundaries can be *hierarchies* that structure a concept into several layers of sub-concepts. For example, we define the organizational structure of a firm in terms of a hierarchy of reporting relationships within the firm. Boundaries can be *demarcations* used to define the scope of a concept or object. For example, the Internet, the Intranet, and the Extranet are boundaries that delineate the scope of an organization's network infrastructure and applications. Whatever the specific type, all boundaries help us to create *schema*—a generalized plan or scheme by which we comprehend ideas or objects of knowledge.

Boundaries can be *dichotomous* or *multichotomous*. Dichotomous boundaries are binary—they classify an idea or an object into two mutually exclusive and opposite categories. For example, companies tend to view other firms as either competitors or partners. Multichotomous boundaries classify a concept into multiple categories. For example, functional areas within a firm can be classified into marketing, sales, finance, technology, operations, human resources, administration, and legal departments. Table 12.1 lists some examples of boundaries that we can use to understand the structure and operations of a business.

■ BOUNDARIES AS SENSEMAKING TOOLS

Boundaries supply meaning by allowing us to structure unfamiliar concepts into a neat set of categories. These categories become the basis of *mental models*—the theories that we carry in our heads about how the world works. By helping us to construct mental models, boundaries help us to quickly understand new concepts by applying familiar theories. Boundaries also help us to communicate efficiently by providing a common vocabulary for describing concepts to other people.

Table 12.1 Boundaries and the Nature of a Firm.

Type of boundary	Idea or object that is classified	Categories that result
Dichotomous	How the firm relates to other firms	Competitor versus collaborator
	What the firm produces	Products versus services
	How the firm sources inputs	Insourcing versus outsourcing
	How the firm goes to market	Offline channels versus online channels
	Types of assets a firm owns for e-commerce	Brick-and-mortar versus pure-play dot com
	Types of Business-to-Business exchanges	Vertical exchanges versus horizontal exchanges
Multichotomous	Vertical boundaries of the firm (hierarchy)	Organization chart with different levels in the hierarchy
	Horizontal boundaries of the firm (functions)	Departmental classification showing different functional areas of he firm
	Structural boundaries of the firm (divisions)	Strategic Business Units (SBUs) or lines of business
	Geographical boundaries of the firm (regions)	Regional organization showing different geographies that the firm operates in
	IT infrastructure and network applications	Intranet, Extranet, and Internet that define the audiences and the scope of network applications
	Business models for e-commerce	B2B, B2C, C2B, C2C

To appreciate the role of boundaries as sensemaking tools, consider the concept of Business-to-Business (B2B) e-commerce. This concept contains two boundaries that provide structure and meaning to the concept. First, Business-to-Business is a boundary that defines this concept as a category of commerce conducted between businesses (as opposed to B2C commerce and C2C commerce). Second, e-commerce is a boundary, because it distinguishes traditional land-based commerce from commerce conducted over an electronic network. These two boundaries help us to quickly make sense of an abstract and unfamiliar concept.

To see how boundaries can help us to communicate ideas more efficiently, consider the way an entrepreneur described his business. He presented his venture as a "wireless ASP in the health care vertical". Translation: His venture focuses exclusively on customers in the health care industry, as opposed to serving a wide range of industry segments; it provides applications over a wireless network, as opposed to a wired network; and it rents its software as a service over a network, as opposed to selling a software license for on-premise use by customers. As long as both parties in this conversation are familiar with these three concepts, these boundaries can be used to describe a complex business venture in very few words.

To appreciate the role of boundaries as learning tools, consider how we can use boundaries to understand the evolution of B2B e-commerce. B2B e-commerce can be classified into two dimensions: the nature of the transactions (linear chains versus nonlinear networks); and the nature of the standards or the infrastructure used to conduct these transactions (private/closed versus public/open). Crossing these two dimensions, we can create the time-honored tool of the business school professor—the 2x2 matrix (see Figure 12.1). This matrix characterizes the evolution of B2B e-commerce across four generations. The first generation was "one-to-one" Electronic Data Interchange (EDI), where businesses transacted on a point-to-point basis over a closed EDI network. The advent of the Internet and its open public infrastructure gave rise to "one to many" B2B e-commerce, as firms like Dell and Cisco began to sell their products directly to business customers over the Internet. This was still a linear transactional model, but the transactions were conducted over a public and open infrastructure. The third generation of B2B e-commerce was marked by the evolution of e-marketplaces— "network-centric" commerce conducted through independent third-parties, or more recently, through industry-sponsored consortia. Most

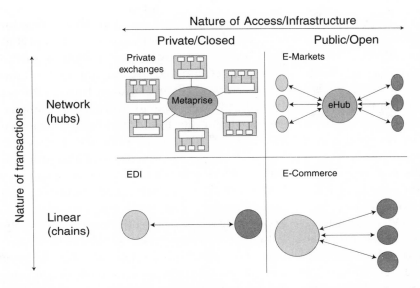

Figure 12.1 Boundaries as learning tools: understanding B2B evolution.

recently, a fourth generation of e-commerce has begun to emerge, with the creation of private networks by firms like Wal∗Mart and Hewlett-Packard to transact and collaborate with their strategic suppliers and channel partners through a common infrastructure. This simple example shows how we can understand seemingly complex business concepts very effectively by constructing boundaries to structure the concepts.

■ HOW BOUNDARIES LIMIT OUR THINKING

While boundaries are useful, the very act of creating a boundary to understand a concept can begin to limit our thinking, because it often gives rise to false dichotomies. When we classify ideas into opposites, we can become victims of duality. Duality is the idea, attributed to the French philosopher Rene Descartes, that there often exist two eternal and opposing principles that are irreducibly different—e.g., matter versus spirit, or body versus mind. Every dichotomous boundary we create gives birth to duality by emphasizing the black and white end-points of a continuum of gray. One only has to glance at a business magazine to see these "black and white" opposites in action—dot coms versus brick-and-mortar companies, Old Economy companies versus new economy companies, and so on. In fact, even the concept of e-commerce seems to suggest that "commerce" and "e-commerce" are different and distinct ways of doing business. And now, we have "m-commerce" or mobile commerce, which suggests that its immobile cousin is a different animal. History bears witness to the fact that many new technological innovations tend to be defined in dual terms by juxtaposing them against older and more familiar technologies. Hence the "horseless carriage" (the automobile), the "iron horse" (the locomotive), and the "wireless phone" (mobile phones). The past acts as a crutch that helps us understand the future. But in doing so, it limits the way we think about the new technology. After all, a crutch is not a leg!

Why do we tend to gravitate towards opposites and extremes? Very simply, because black and white are easier to understand than shades of gray. However, in focusing on the black and white extremes, we often lose sight of the fact that while the endpoints are dual, the underlying continuum is unified. Indeed, the purpose of black and white is to illuminate the nature of gray. This is the paradox of opposites. At a deeper level, opposites are often two sides of the same coin. Where we see apparent opposites or duality, there is often a deeper principle at work, unifying the opposites into a broader construct. To overcome the illusion of duality, we need to search for the unifying principle.

To find this unifying principle, we must shift our focus to the middle, and try to find the "gray" that goes beyond black and white, and allows us to see the unity in opposites. By fixating on the end-points, we cause the pendulum of our understanding to swing violently between the extremes of black and white. Upon deeper reflection, we see that the pendulum usually settles in the middle as a unifying principle emerges to unite the opposites. Figure 12.2 illustrates this idea within the domains of business and technology. For instance, the boundary between E-business and business is blurring, as the Internet becomes an integral tool for doing business. Similarly, the pendulum that swung in favor of pure-play B2B exchanges now seems to be swinging back to the other extreme, with the announcement of brick-and-mortar industry-sponsored B2B exchanges. Ultimately, it might settle in the middle through the creation of hybrid designs that combine elements of independent exchanges, with the participation of industry players. Even the manic-depressive behavior of the private equity markets and public markets originates in this wildly swinging pendulum, as venture capitalists and public market investors go from one wave to

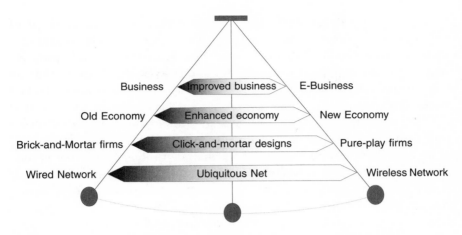

Figure 12.2   The pendulum swings, but the truth is in the middle.

another wave of ideas—B2C to B2B to infrastructure investments to optical networking. In all these cases, the truth is somewhere in the middle. All B2C companies will not die, despite the popular wisdom that now tars all consumer-focused Internet companies with the same brush. And all optical networking companies will not become billion-dollar companies, just because a few companies in this space have shown promise. The true search for value and profit has to be done at the level of the individual company and its business model, not at the level of the sector. Betting on "hot" and "cold" waves of business models is a herd mentality that has created the extreme volatility that has become endemic to the stock market. Somewhere between the extremes of boom and bust, hype and doom, lie the realities of business and value creation.

■ THE DEATH OF BOUNDARIES

There was a time when it was easy to define a business and its com-petitors in terms of industry boundaries. Firms within an industry had similar histories, similar capabilities, and competed using well-defined rules of engagement. In fact, strategy frameworks such as management thinker and author Michael Porter's structural analysis of industries presuppose the existence of an industry with clear boundaries. Indus-try boundaries serve as a frame of reference for defining competitors, rivals, and substitutes, and for creating positions of competitive advantage. In a world of well-defined boundaries, the corporate strategist's task was to understand the boundaries that defined the business landscape, and to find the hills and valleys that positioned a business most advantageously. Strategy was a game of chess played on a black and white grid.

In the Net Economy, the strategist's role is to question and redraw and redefine boundaries. Strategy is a boundaryless world is the ability to create boundaries that help managers see and use the landscape creatively, and then break these boundaries to move on to the next cycle of business innovation. In fact, nowadays, it is hard to even define an industry. Net entrepreneurs instead use the concept of "space" (as in—"we are in the partner relationship management space"). The idea of "competitive space" suggests boundaries that are blurred and constantly shifting. Firms increasingly find themselves collaborating with the most unlikely partners, and competing with unfamiliar players. Enron, an energy company, is moving into the bandwidth trading business. Microsoft is in the cable industry. Xerox competes with Hewlett-Packard as copiers and printers converge, and Hewlett-Packard competes with Kodak as imaging goes digital. No boundary is sacred in the Net economy—functional boundaries, enterprise boundaries, competitive boundaries, industry boundaries, and market boundaries are disappearing before our eyes. The death of boundaries can confuse and disorient us, if we are used to thinking in traditional terms. However, it can also lead to dramatic new opportunities for value creation. But first, we must learn to go beyond boundaries, and think out of the box.

■ HOW TO BREAK FREE

How can we use our insights about the nature of boundaries to break free from the walls that imprison our ways of thinking and doing business? What practical strategies can we use to open our minds to new ways of framing and thinking about the world? And what are some examples of the insights that these strategies can produce in the context of E-business?

While there are many ways of moving beyond boundaries, here are some practical ideas you can use to gain new insights and to find new ways to create value.

➤ Rebelling—Kill the Sacred Cows

To break free from boundaries, it often pays to start by questioning the very nature of existing boundaries. The result of this exercise is to *surface* hidden business assumptions, so you can question them and redraw boundaries. In the realm of boundaries, what you don't know *can* hurt you, because you are not even aware of the limits you have imposed on your thinking. Consider the operating system Linux that is taking the developer community by storm. Linux is developed by a loosely organized community of developers, outside the walls of any single company. It is offered free of cost to users, and no single firm owns the intellectual property. This "open source" model of software development, enabled by the Net, seems inconceivable for firms like Microsoft, who have long held that operating systems need to be developed by a single firm, and the source code is the "crown jewel" that should never be given away. The open source movement questions the very foundations of how software is designed, updated, sold, and supported. In the Net economy, sacred cows make the best eating!

➤ Reversing—Invert Your Vantage Point

Sometimes, we get so used to observing customers and markets from our point of view that we forget what the world looks like from the *customer's* point of view. If we reverse our vantage point and look "outward-in" instead of "inward-out", we can often see the world in a very different light. This is the strategy of reversing boundaries. Consider a simple example—why are markets always defined in terms of sellers and products? Why can't they be defined in terms of customers and activities? By realizing that the way customers think is very different from the way marketers sell their products, we can create entirely new markets—markets that are defined around clusters of customer activities, rather than in terms of products and services. The boundaries of these activity-centric markets, called *metamarkets*, are derived from activities that customers consider to be logically related. For instance, HomeStore.com has created a metamarket around the "home ownership experience" by facilitating the end-to-end activity sequence of searching for a home, evaluating a home, negotiating for a home, buying a home, financing a home, remodeling the home, and procuring a whole range of home-related services. By connecting home buyers and home owners to a vast range of home-related product and service providers, HomeStore.com has built a valuable franchise for itself. Other firms that are building metamarkets include C I Net in the technology arena, Edmunds.com in the automobile arena, and WeServeHomes.com in the home services arena. Think in reverse, and you may be able to leap forward!

➤ Abstracting—Look for the "And"

Whenever there is a discussion about opposites or substitutes—an "either-or" debate, you can often gain insights by thinking more broadly, and searching for a complement—an "and". As Edward De Bono, the creativity guru, advises—"look for *Po*—the idea beyond Yes and No". By reflecting on the unifying principles that may synthesize apparent dualities, you can often transcend narrow boundaries that frame many debates involving opposites. For instance, in thinking about e-Commerce, much has been said and written about who will win the battle for the customer—"pure play" dotcoms or brick-and-mortar companies. On deeper examination, this is a vacuous debate, because *customers* don't come in offline and online versions. Customers will demand multiple points of presence, and new hybrid businesses that combine offline and online businesses will eventually be the winners. Different channels provide different service outputs with differing levels of efficacy. By mixing and matching multiple channels, firms can create hybrid service outputs that are customized for specific customer segments. In this hybrid world, the Internet, the salesforce, and the channel partners all complement each other to create value for customers. There is no disintermediation or reintermediation. All that happens is that functions get reallocated across channels, in a way that allows each channel to do what it does best. Once you think in terms of reallocating functions, it becomes clear why firms that lack a multiple-channel presence are handicapped, because they cannot mix-and-match with the same degree of flexibility that multi-channel firms can. One reason the stock market has savaged the stocks of Business-to-Consumer e-commerce firms is due to the fact that they do not offer a complete solution to customers, and cannot derive synergies across multiple channels of distribution.

> **Refining—Evolve to the Next Level**

Boundaries are useful for structuring an unstructured landscape, but they need to be progressively refined as the landscape evolves and becomes more complex. By continually refining boundaries to keep pace with the evolution of the landscape, we can ensure that we continue to advance our thinking to higher levels of understanding. Consider how the refining strategy could be used to understand the ongoing evolution of B2B e-marketplaces. When e-marketplaces first burst forth on the scene in 1998, it was useful to classify these marketplaces into two simple categories—*vertical marketplaces* that focused on a specific industry (e.g., plastics, steel, chemicals), and *horizontal marketplaces* that focused on a specific business process (e.g., logistics management, credit, supplier verification). This two-dimensional framework became a popular way to understand the then-nascent world of B2B e-marketplaces. However, the world moves on, and newer business models emerge as evolutions, combinations, and mutations of earlier models. In the B2B e-marketplaces arena, the simple (and, in retrospect, simplistic) two-dimensional framework has now given way to several next-generation designs (see Figure 12.3). For instance, one category of B2B firms, including Collabria, Bidcom, and Buzzsaw, are focusing on *collaboration*, not *transactions* alone, and are creating platforms for collaborative commerce that we call *workflow marketplaces*. These workflow marketplaces combine the transactional functionality of e-marketplaces with the workflow and collaboration functionality that is needed for complex project-oriented procurement situations. Another category of entities, including Ventro, Covisint, and Exostar, is evolving beyond transactional marketplaces to create complete solutions for enabling supply chain management within specific industry domains. These solution-focused firms, who we call *metamediaries*, combine procurement platforms with a whole range of value-added services that complement the procurement transactions. In doing so, they are starting to look like vertical-horizontal hybrids. And a third category of firms is focusing purely on building liquid trading exchanges for pure commodities. These firms, including Enron Online and Altra Energy, are focusing on operational excellence and volume, and operate on low transaction fees.

These next-generation designs will probably give way to another generation of designs that will be further evolutions and mutations of

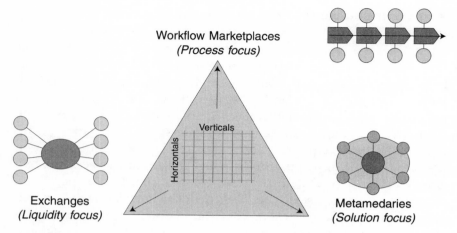

Figure 12.3 Evolving B2B e-commerce models beyond horizontals and verticals.

the second-generation e-marketplace designs. The moral—keep throwing away your old crutches, and keep acquiring new crutches that will take you to the next level in your journey of learning.

➤ Bridging—Connect the Silos

It is often difficult to eliminate boundaries in the short run, because obliterating boundaries requires changing organizations and their attitudes. A pragmatic approach in this case is to cross boundaries by making connections across boundaries, just like a bridge joins the two banks of a river without eliminating the river. Bridging can be accomplished by *spanning boundaries* by developing the ability to see across boundaries by being empathetic with people from other disciplines or backgrounds. *Cross-pollinating* knowledge and best practices across constituencies will also create bridges. General Electric (GE) employs both strategies. It recently appointed Scott McNealy, Chairman and CEO of Sun Microsystems, who has come to symbolize the New Economy, to the board of General Electric (GE), an icon of the Old Economy. By doing so, GE has laid the foundation for a human bridge between the Old Economy and the New Economy. GE's sharing of best practices in its Crotonville learning center is an attempt to cross-pollinate ideas across diverse businesses. True innovation often occurs at the grout between the tiles that separate functional areas and business units.

➤ Trespassing—Travel to Strange Knowledge Domains

One reason that we tend to not think out of the box is that we don't tend to stray outside the box much. In our day-to-day lives, we are so focused on building our expertise in our chosen domain, that we ignore most domains of knowledge that are in our peripheral vision, or beyond. After all, it is so difficult to keep up with your own field of knowledge that it seems impossible to read or learn about things that may not be directly relevant to your job. However, by slavishly sticking to our knitting, we end up closing the doors of perception to the winds of fresh ideas. The best ideas often come from unexpected directions and strange people, especially in a connected world that does not respect artificial boundaries that separate knowledge domains. To broaden your horizons, it is very important to occasionally travel to strange knowledge domains by learning things and meeting people who are well outside your traditional domains. Bill Gates, the founder of Microsoft, is famous for taking a week off every year to study a completely different field from software design. While we all cannot be Bill Gates, a very fruitful way to go beyond boundaries is to read something different, and to talk to someone strange once in a while. And it is important to do so with a mind emptied of preconceived notions and ego. If you empty your cup (your mind), it will always be full, because you will learn from every conversation. If your cup is full with ego and pre-conceived ideas, it will always be empty and devoid of ideas that can help you transcend boundaries.

■ CONCLUSION

The role that boundaries play in our lives can be summarized by the following Zen koan:

First, there is no mountain.
Then, there is a mountain.
Then, there is no mountain.

At first, any new knowledge domain is like a featureless landscape. There are no mountains, no valleys, and no rivers. As we seek to gain familiarity with the landscape, we create boundaries that help us to structure the landscape and to orient ourselves within the landscape. Boundaries are the mountains and valleys that provide definition to the landscape. However, as we become intuitively and intimately familiar with the landscape, we transcend the boundaries we had created. Again, there is no mountain. This is the process of using, then losing, boundaries. And this is the process that will lead us to new destinations in our quest for value and profit.

Diagnostic Tool for Startup Companies

Early Stage

Category & Questions	Weight (out of 100%)	None	Bad	1	2	3	4	5	6	7	8	9	10	Great	Deal Breaker	Points*
Management	———	0		1	2	3	4	5	6	7	8	9	10	→	X	☐
Does the manager/team have passion?																
Does the manager/team have a clear vision?																
History of past success																
Experience of management team																
Skill set of management team																
Degree of "owneritis"																
That certain "je ne sais quoi"/luck factor																
Perceived ability to execute																
Market Opportunity	———	0		1	2	3	4	5	6	7	8	9	10	→	X	
Market potential of idea																
Quality of pure business model																
Threat of competition																
Market position/density in space																
Originality of idea																
First-mover advantage																
Current/Potential alliance partners																

Category & Questions	Weight (out of 100%)	None	Bad									Great	Deal Breaker	Points*
		0	1	2	3	4	5	6	7	8	9	10		
Product and Service	—	0	1	2	3	4	5	6	7	8	9	10	X	☐
Demand for product														
Degree of addressing customer needs														
Technology														
Funding	—	0	1	2	3	4	5	6	7	8	9	10	X	☐
												TOTAL (out of 100%)		☐

*For points, multiply weighting by ranking in each stage.

Later Stage

Category & Questions	Weight (out of 100%)	None	Bad									Great	Deal Breaker	Points*
Management	—	0	1	2	3	4	5	6	7	8	9	10	X	☐
Does the manager/team have passion?														
Does the manager/team have a clear vision?														
Experience of management team														
Skill set of management team														
Degree of "owneritis"														
That certain "je ne sais quoi"/luck factor														
Ability to execute														
Adaptability of management team														
Success of team in meeting original goals														
Ability to attract and retain talent														

Category & Questions	Weight (out of 100%)	None 0	Bad 1	2	3	4	5	6	7	8	9	Great 10	Deal Breaker X	Points*
Market Opportunity	___	0	1	2	3	4	5	6	7	8	9	10	X	☐
Quality of pure business model														
Adaptability of business model														
Revenue-generating ability														
Profit potential														
Defensibility of business plan														
Competitive position														
Market potential of idea														
Current/Potential alliance partners														
Product and Service	___	0	1	2	3	4	5	6	7	8	9	10	X	☐
Demand for product														
Degree of addressing customer needs														
Technology														
Strength of brand														
Fulfillment & client service														
Funding	___	0	1	2	3	4	5	6	7	8	9	10	X	☐
Number and quality of other investors														
Projected use of funds (legitimate vs. zombie)														
% of company owned by VCs														
Number and quality of similar investments														

TOTAL (out of 100%) ☐

*For points, multiply weighting by ranking in each stage.

Index

337